finding
freedom

finding freedom

HARRY *and* **MEGHAN**
and the Making of a Modern Royal Family

OMID SCOBIE AND
CAROLYN DURAND

ONE PLACE. MANY STORIES

HQ
An imprint of HarperCollins*Publishers* Ltd
1 London Bridge Street
London SE1 9GF

First published in Great Britain by HQ
An imprint of HarperCollins*Publishers* Ltd 2020

First published in the United States by Dey Street an imprint of
William Morrow, a division of HarperCollins Publishers,
New York in 2020

HB ISBN 978-0-00-842410-7
TPB ISBN 978-0-00-842411-4

MIX
Paper from
responsible sources
FSC C007454

This book is produced from independently certified FSC™ paper
to ensure responsible forest management.

For more information visit: www.harpercollins.co.uk/green

Printed and bound in Great Britain by
CPI Group (UK) Ltd, Croydon CR0 4YY

Designed by Paula Russell Szafranski
Frontispiece by WPA Pool/Getty Images

Do not go where the path may lead, go instead where there is no path and leave a trail.

—Ralph Waldo Emerson

CONTENTS

finding
freedom

PROLOGUE

It was a blink-and-you'll-miss-it moment. As we watched Meghan smooth the belt of her crisp white LINE the Label coat and brush a loose lock of hair out of her eyes, she looked over at a nervous Harry and put her hand on his back, rubbing the same spot several times. He was used to being in front of the press, but this time was different. He wasn't advocating for one of his charities or urging leaders to take climate change seriously; he was sharing something personal: the news of his engagement to Meghan. Holding hands, they made their way to the throng of photographers waiting nearby.

"You've got this," she whispered to the prince as they walked out of a small gate at the side of Kensington Palace and up the long, canopied path to the Sunken Garden, whose lily-covered water in the ornamental pond and colorful pansies, tulips, and begonias made it one of Princess Diana's favorite spots on the estate she once called home.

This was the couple's big engagement photo-call, at which I

had arrived with only minutes to spare after a frantic highway dash from a long weekend break in Oxfordshire. Carolyn, ahead of me, was already in her place with the small huddle of royal correspondents who work directly with the royal households on a daily basis. As longtime members of this group, she and I receive intel as we shadow senior members of the British royal family at home and abroad.

The privilege of covering the royals so closely is that you are front and center for those landmark moments in their lives. We were on the steps of the Lindo Wing when George, Charlotte, and Louis each were born. It's easy to take for granted these moments, which will one day be part of the history books. But as Harry grinned at Meghan, who held his hand between both of hers, and the cheers of well-wishers gathered in Kensington Gardens erupted in a "hip hip hooray!," even the most hard-nosed reporters there smiled. The feeling of magic in that moment was undeniable.

Carolyn and I have closely followed the work of the Royal Family since long before Meghan joined what is known as the Firm. For years we have traveled with William, Kate, and Harry around the world. From Singapore to the Solomon Islands, Lesotho to India, the United States to New Zealand, we shared the same planes and dizzying itineraries as these young royals. I've always likened royal tours to a class field trip or camp, because you're cramped together on big buses and clamoring to get the best rooms at the hotel. There's also a sense of camaraderie, not just among the reporters, staff, and security guards but also with the royals themselves.

Take the time I lost my passport in São Paulo, Brazil. I was frantically searching my bag at the airport when I got a call from one of the palace aides. I could hear Harry's distinctive laugh in the background. They had found my passport on the floor. Not wanting to leave me high and dry in Brazil, the prince sent over one of his protection officers, passport in hand, to my terminal so I could get to Chile on time. The next time I saw Harry, however, he forwent my name, instead calling me "Passport." As we Brits say, he likes to take the mickey.

Being far from the scrutiny and pressures of home was also an opportunity for heart-to-hearts. On that same trip, Harry confessed to me at a small drinks gathering at our hotel that he really wished he were "just a normal guy" who could pack up and spend a year in Brazil pursuing his own passions. He said that he hated smartphones being constantly thrust in his face, that the thrum of professional camera shutters going off sometimes made him feel physically ill.

Carolyn and I always knew Harry dreamed of a life away from palace walls, but while traveling with the prince, particularly in the countryside, we noticed that his wish to be connected to everyday rural life was often accompanied by a sense of sadness. Although an impossibility, he wished to connect with the locals without the fuss his arrival always meant.

Then, as now, Harry deeply craves normalcy of the kind that his mother, Diana, tried to replicate for him on trips to amusement parks and McDonald's. (How funny to know that the favorite part of a Happy Meal for this child, born of unimaginable wealth and privilege, was getting the cheap plastic toy inside.)

Harry is different from his brother, William, who takes after their orderly and pragmatic granny, the Queen. He's emotional and clings to utopian ideals, yet in his way, admirably so. His desire to live outside of the Palace bubble—in everything from being a "hugger" at official engagements to insisting he serve on the front lines of war as a member of the armed forces—is a positive attribute, even if at times it causes problems for the rest of the royal family.

His wholeheartedness allowed him to start a new chapter in royal history when he fell in love with Meghan Markle.

Being a mixed-race Brit was one of the reasons that I, like a lot of the younger and more diverse demo the Duke and Duchess of

Sussex turned into royal watchers, found the American actress marrying into the House of Windsor so fascinating. Funnily enough, I met Meghan before Harry did. Back in 2015, I chatted with her for the first time at a Fashion Week event in Toronto after she did press interviews on the carpet. No one was more amazed than me when just a year later, Meg (as her close friends and now husband call her) captured the heart of the most eligible bachelor this side of the pond.

Even in the early days of their relationship, it was clear that Harry had found a woman who awakened his sense of purpose with humanitarian passions that mirrored his own drive to support those on the margins of society. The world watched in amazement as the couple's relationship rapidly developed. And Carolyn and I watched, too, as a number of tabloids went on to accuse Meghan of being a demanding and difficult social climber. Some of the British press did little to hide racial undertones in snarky commentary and headlines.

The narrative that emerged was most surprising to Meghan, who brought to her charitable interests and official engagements as the newest member of the royal family the same go-get-'em approach she's taken from the time she was an eleven-year-old writing letters of protest to national leaders, including Hillary Clinton, over a sexist soap ad. It's not unknown for her to stay up late into the night before events, doing her own research and preparing her own notes despite having a staff for just such work. "It's the only way I know how to do it," she confessed to me. That's part of what made the prince declare he'd found the "teammate" he had always been looking for.

So, it was a surreal moment to be giving Meghan a big farewell hug in one of the state rooms at Buckingham Palace in March 2020 as she wrapped her last solo royal engagement. She and Harry had made the difficult decision to step back as senior working royals in a bid to protect their family. We had only been in the opulent 1844

Room for only happy occasions, such as engagements with the Queen or media receptions. Now even the malachite candelabras illuminating portrait paintings cast a gloomy light as the newest members of the royal family were saying goodbye not just to their staff but to an entire way of life.

Carolyn and I had been with Meghan for her final engagements but it was still hard to believe that this would be the last one. Staff who had been with the couple from day one were mourning the end of what was supposed to be a happy story: two people fall in love, get married, have a baby, serve the Queen, the end. Instead, they were leaving the country. As Meghan gave me a final hug goodbye, she said, "It didn't have to be this way."

Yes, Carolyn and I witnessed the many private and public struggles Harry and Meghan went through in the first two years of their marriage. Still, this was not the ending to the book that either of us expected to write—or that the couple expected to be living.

As a rule, no member of the British royal family is officially allowed to authorize a biography. However, Carolyn and I were able to gain extensive access to those closest to the couple: friends, trusted aides, senior courtiers, and many individuals in the Sussexes' inner circle. We also accompanied Harry and Meghan on hundreds of their engagements, work trips, and tours, spanning from Ireland to Tonga, all in an effort to create an intimate and accurate portrait of a truly modern royal couple who, whether their decisions have won them praise or criticism, have always remained faithful to their own beliefs.

—Omid Scobie and Carolyn Durand, London, 2020

INTRODUCTION

With the last of their luggage arriving onto the four-acre Mille Fleurs estate in Victoria, Canada, where they would be staying for the next six weeks, Harry and Meghan breathed a collective sigh of relief. Most of their belongings had already been placed in advance of their arrival in the grand his-and-hers walk-in closets of the 11,416-square-foot mansion they had rented from an acquaintance. They were worlds away from Frogmore Cottage, their home in Windsor—but that wasn't necessarily a bad thing.

Though the smiles on their faces at public engagements had been consistent through their departure, the weeks leading up to their Air Canada flight from London's Heathrow Airport in mid-November were anything but cheerful. Having recently launched lawsuits against three British tabloids for invasion of privacy and phone-hacking allegations, the Duke and Duchess of Sussex seemed more a target of the press than ever.

For Harry especially, it was all getting to be too much. "Doesn't the Queen Deserve Better?" screamed a *Daily Mail* headline, which the prince read online. He couldn't understand why the media were so hell-bent on tearing them down. "These people are just paid trolls," he later told a friend. "Nothing but trolls . . . And it's disgusting."

Scrolling on his iPhone, he sometimes couldn't stop himself from reading the comments on the article.

H&M disgust me.
They are a disgrace to the royal family.
The world would be a better place without Harry and
Meghan in it.

The last comment had over 3,500 upvotes.

Harry instantly regretted opening the link. His stomach tied into the same knot every time he saw these sorts of comments. "It's a sick part of the society we live in today, and no one is doing anything about it," he continued. "Where's the positivity? Why is everyone so miserable and angry?"

It wasn't just the press or online trolls getting to Harry. It was also the institution of the monarchy. Barely a week went by without an aspect of their internal affairs or matters of private discussions being twisted and leaked to the press. They felt as though there were very few members of the Palace staff they could trust. Harry's relationship with his brother, William, which had been strained for a while, was only getting worse.

If there was any silver lining, it was confirmation that their decision to take some time away from the public eye and the "noise," as Meghan called it, was exactly what they needed. The outdoors and relative remoteness of the property in Vancouver Island's North Saanich neighborhood would do them good—particularly after what had been a whirlwind six months since welcoming their first child in May. The new parents had worked nonstop, all while under the relentless spotlight that defines what it means to be part of the British royal family.

Even though Harry and Meghan were surrounded by pristine nature, they were anything but serene. "The 'break' was actually far from that," said a source close to the couple. What appeared to the outside world like an idyllic getaway was actually an angst-ridden time, with Harry and Meghan spending hours mapping out various scenarios for their future. The prince had hit his boiling point over the ongoing arguments, rumors, and annoying back-and-forth with the Palace.

The year had seen a number of personal highs for the couple, of which the most significant was the birth of their son, Archie. The September issue of British *Vogue*, which Meghan guest edited, had become their fastest-selling issue ever, and the capsule clothing collection she created to raise money for the women's unemployment charity Smart Works had been an instant sellout at Marks & Spencer and other retailers. Harry recently launched Travalyst, a new global sustainable travel initiative that he hoped would change the tourism industry for good.

Harry and Meghan planned to keep working during their stay in Canada. They had a lot on their to-do list, including finishing setting up their nonprofit organization and continuing to advocate for the charities that they were royal patrons of back home. But somehow it all felt easier to do in the Canadian estate's wood-paneled study that looked out over the manicured grounds' white spruce and birch trees (even if in reality they usually wound up working in the kitchen, leaving their MacBooks to make cups of tea or coffee).

Their decision to go abroad—and stay abroad for Christmas rather than return for the traditional festivities at Sandringham, the Queen's country estate in Norfolk, with other senior members of the royal family—only reinforced the negative narrative about the couple in the UK. Newspapers were calling it a "major snub" to the Queen, even though in reality Harry had okayed his plans with his grandmother—and boss—before they left the country. The Queen, who saw Harry and Meghan regularly since they all lived on the Windsor estate, actually encouraged him to take the trip. After all, they had spent the past two Christmases at her Norfolk retreat, and other family members—including the Cambridges—had skipped festive visits here and there, too.

The Christmas decorations were not going up yet. They still had Thanksgiving to think about, and Meghan's mother, Doria, was preparing at that moment to travel from her home in LA to the estate in Victoria. Meghan and her mother, who couldn't wait to see her Archie, had been excitedly exchanging texts before the trip. Her grandson was growing fast and had gotten much taller since she last saw him in the summer. "He's in the ninetieth percentile for height," Meghan boasted to friends, before she eagerly offered to pull out her phone to show some of the many photos she had of her boy.

Though their Canadian home was temporary, Harry and Meghan had done everything they could to make sure it was baby-friendly. Sharp corners were proofed with discreet rubber pads and certain items of furniture moved out of harm's way. With the six-month-old now standing and shuffling along the edges of furniture more than crawling, they didn't want to take any risks. They also tried to paparazzi-proof the property. Additional fencing had been installed around the perimeter to prevent the long camera lenses they knew would eventually show up from interrupting their daily walks with Archie around the wooded landscape and sandy beachfronts.

Protecting Archie and maintaining his privacy was a top priority for the couple. It started when they chose not to give their son a royal title. Harry, who learned the dark side of growing up in the royal fish bowl early on in his life by watching his mother relentlessly chased by the paparazzi, and Meghan, quickly getting the same lesson, both wanted to ensure their son chose his own destiny rather than being forced into one by virtue of the family he had been born into.

Those first days at the waterfront home delivered the peace Harry and Meghan had been longing for. It was the first time in months that the couple—who started their days with yoga and making breakfast together—had felt any sense of calm. But despite the quiet that surrounded them, Harry and Meghan were in turmoil. A heavy decision weighed on them. After almost three years of regular attacks from the British press and a family they felt had not done enough to support them, things had to change. How and what that meant still needed sorting out, but they knew that they had to follow their hearts.

1

London Calling

Her first morning after landing in London in June 2016, Meghan headed straight to Selfridges. The young American actress was on a mission: shoe shopping.

In the Oxford Street department store, she roamed the thirty-five-thousand-square-foot shoe hall—the largest in the world—looking at her favorite designers, including Stella McCartney, Chloé, and Marc Jacobs, to see if she could find a pair worth the obscene price tags. Even though the hit cable drama *Suits* she starred in was now in its sixth season, Meghan was still a careful shopper. Having spent part of her childhood in a cramped converted-garage apartment in the heart of Los Angeles, the only child of divorced parents who had financial struggles, she didn't like to waste money on trends that quickly went out of style. If she was going to invest in something, she wanted it to last, like her Sergio Rossi heels. A worrier as a kid, Meghan still harbored the feeling at times that when good things came her way, they could disappear in an instant.

But if Meghan was feeling a little expansive surrounded by the high-priced stilettos and sandals on that late June morning, she could be forgiven.

She was fresh off a luxurious girls' weekend to the Greek island of Hydra—a trip she had organized to celebrate the upcoming wedding of Lindsay Roth, one of her best friends from college. As maid of honor, Meghan took her duties seriously, having arranged days filled with hiking, swimming, napping, and enjoying the local cuisine of the island, which, located two hours by boat from Athens, can be traveled only by bicycle or donkey.

The weekend was a far cry from the typical Vegas-style bachelorette party of climbing into limos and getting wasted in clubs, all while wearing what Meghan called "headbands of the phallic persuasion." Instead, the group of women found more sophisticated pleasures in the Mediterranean sun and sea, fresh Greek salads and fish, lots of wine, and one another's company.

The entire event was classic Meghan: simple yet indulgent, fun in a quiet and intimate way—and all meticulously planned. From the time she was a student, juggling school and jobs, through her years grinding out auditions for bit parts, to her becoming a successful TV star who continued to push the boundaries of her career by launching a popular lifestyle website, Meghan always had a plan. She worked hard not only crafting those plans but also seeing them through.

Her trip to London was no exception. Shoes were just the start of the itinerary she had filled completely before arriving in London. Meghan had a list of restaurants she wanted to eat in, bars that she wanted to go to, and people she wanted to meet.

It was an exciting time for the thirty-four-year-old. Her success in the competitive world of show business, which had started to open doors to opportunities of all kinds, was a product of the confidence, perseverance, and willingness to work harder than her peers that she had displayed since she was a little girl.

Meghan's self-assurance was partly due to her parents' devotion to their daughter. Her mother, Doria Ragland, and dad, Thomas—who met on the set of *General Hospital*, where he was a lighting director and she a temp in the makeup department—split up after two years of marriage. But they remained unified in the one child they shared—co-parenting Meghan without much friction, sharing custody, and celebrating holidays together.

There was no greater sign of Thomas and Doria's dedication, however, than their commitment to Meghan's education. Neither of Meghan's parents went on to attend college immediately following high school, even though Doria was in a club for gifted students at Fairfax High School in LA. After graduation, she went to work at the antiques store owned by her father, Alvin Ragland, and as a travel agent in the start of what would become a long string of jobs. Doria didn't go to college until much later in her life because her family couldn't afford for her to attend. And because of her own experience of struggling financially due to her lack of higher education, she always stressed to Meghan how important that was.

When it came to Meghan's schooling, both Thomas and Doria wanted the best of the best—starting with the Little Red School-house, a small, prestigious private elementary school that had been educating Hollywood's elite (including Johnny Depp and Scarlett Johansson) since the forties. From there, Meghan attended Immaculate Heart, an all-girls Catholic middle and high school in Los Feliz.

Keenly aware of how much her parents had sacrificed for her to attend such institutions, Meghan felt personal responsibility attached to her privilege. "Both my parents came from little, so they made a choice to give a lot . . . performing quiet acts of grace—be it a hug, a smile, or a pat on the back to show ones in need that they would be all right," she wrote in 2016 on her lifestyle blog *The Tig*. "This is what I grew up seeing, so that is what I grew up being."

Meghan was driven. Always first to raise her hand when the teacher wanted an answer or a volunteer to read out loud, she had stellar grades and attendance. Her sense of accountability extended beyond the school grounds. As a young girl coming face-to-face with a homeless man on the streets, she begged her mother, "Can we help him?" It's not unusual for children who have come across people in need to want to help, but the difference with Meghan was that she didn't forget once they had moved on. The rest of the day, and long after, she was left with a nagging question: "What can I do?"

At ten, Meghan first went abroad to Jamaica with her mother, who took her past the resorts that most visitors stick to and into the slums so she could get an education on how those less fortunate lived. At thirteen, Meghan volunteered in a soup kitchen on LA's Skid Row. "The first day I felt really scared," Meghan said. "I was young, and it was rough and raw down there, and though I was with a great volunteer group, I just felt overwhelmed."

Wrestling with whether she should return to the soup kitchen, she turned to her theology teacher at Immaculate Heart, Maria Pollia. A Catholic Worker volunteer, Maria had a lot of experience in working with people living in the margins of society—and she wanted to inspire the young, earnest student before her to do the same.

"Life is about putting others' needs above your own fears," Maria told Meghan. The young student returned to the soup kitchen.

"That has always stayed with me," Meghan said.

Meghan's willingness to help others and her drive to excel meant she often was deemed "fake" by classmates at school who felt it was impossible for anyone to be that "perfect." However, Meghan never thought she was perfect. In fact, she often felt she had more to prove. Being biracial and not always knowing where she fit in, there was a part of her that just wanted people to see she was great at whatever she did. She didn't like the idea of being seen as an underdog.

In high school, Meghan's drive continued to bloom. She joined every club, from the yearbook committee to the Genesian Players theater group. She was voted homecoming queen. A natural performer and someone who sought out praise, Meghan was coming into her own.

Gigi Perreau, who taught Meghan acting for several years, said, "She was incredibly hardworking. I was bowled over by the strong work ethic she had at such a young age." Meghan threw herself into even the smallest of roles, like when she played a secretary in a production of *Annie*.

Thomas often helped out with set design for Meghan's school plays and "came to as many of her presentations as possible," Perreau said. "You would always see his face in the audience, beaming with pride for his little girl."

He also played a critical role in Meghan's development as a feminist and, as she called herself, a "female advocate." When she was eleven years old, her class was watching a TV show when a dishwashing liquid commercial aired with the tagline "Women all over America are fighting greasy pots and pans." A boy sitting nearby shouted out, "Yeah, that's where women belong, in the kitchen!"

Thomas encouraged Meghan, who was upset over the incident, to write letters of protest over the ad. She mailed off letters to "the most powerful people I could think of," including First Lady Hillary Clinton, Nickelodeon news anchor Linda Ellerbee, and the dishwashing soap manufacturer—and they all responded. She received a letter from the White House; Nickelodeon aired an interview with Meghan; and the detergent manufacturer changed the commercial's tagline to "*People* all over America are fighting greasy pots and pans."

Meghan's interest in acting turned into a career goal in high school, but her mother—always focused on the importance of higher education—advised her to get a college degree. And she wanted her daughter to have a career path in case acting didn't fall into place for her. That wasn't an issue for Meghan, who chose not to go on any professional auditions until she graduated high school and had already secured a place at Northwestern University.

She had enrolled in the private college located in a Chicago suburb, ranked one of the top schools in the nation, when she booked her first bit part in a Tori Amos's music video of the song "1000 Oceans." Blink and you might miss Meghan's cameo as a passerby examining an enclosed glass box with the singer inside, but she earned $600 and, within weeks, auditioned for another role in a Shakira video. (She didn't get the part in the video—and in fact didn't get another acting gig until she appeared on *General Hospital* in her last year of college.)

At Northwestern, Meghan again found herself surrounded by mainly affluent students from affluent families. A work-study student, she juggled a full course load and part-time jobs to defray the cost of tuition and room and board. That was in addition to the babysitting she did to cover extra expenses, performing as a theater major, *and* volunteer work.

"I can't imagine how the days are long enough for you," said a good friend who went with Meghan to pick up her latest work-study assignments from the school office. She marveled at her friend's ability to balance the pressure and rigor of her academics with everything else.

"How do you have time to do all this stuff?" her pal asked.

By not partying like most of her normal college kids. Her friends would never run into Meg, as they called her, at a bar in the middle of the week. Friday nights, when her sorority sisters were all going out to parties, Meg was headed out to professors' houses to babysit. She rushed Kappa Kappa Gamma, eventually living in the sorority house and making some of her closest friends, including Genevieve Hillis and Lindsay. But even Meghan's Greek life was less *Animal House* and more Elle Woods. As rush and recruitment chairman, she was in charge of bringing new people into the sorority and making them feel welcome. She also raised money for charity with events like a dance marathon she participated in with her other sorority sisters. The women danced for thirty hours to benefit Team Joseph, a nonprofit working on a cure for Duchenne muscular dystrophy. "It got so tiring," Meghan admitted.

By her junior year, she had finished most of her credits, so with the help of her father's older brother Mick, she secured an internship at the US embassy in Buenos Aires. No one in the family was quite sure what Uncle Mick did, whether his communications job in Buenos Aires was actually a cover for a job in the CIA. But regardless, his connections allowed a twenty-year-old Meghan to broaden her horizons beyond the stage.

"I had always been the theater nerd at Northwestern University. I knew I wanted to do acting, but I hated the idea of being this cliché—a girl from LA who decides to be an actress," Meghan told *Marie Claire*. "I wanted more than that, and I had always loved politics, so I ended up changing my major completely, and double-majoring in theater and international relations."

Meghan took the Foreign Service Officer Test, a prerequisite for a job as a State Department officer. When she didn't pass the highly competitive test, she was extremely disappointed. She wasn't used to failing. It was a major blow to the confidence she had always tried to protect.

And so, in 2003, after graduating from Northwestern, Meg found herself back in LA. She was a struggling actress who supported herself between auditions with odd jobs, including a stint as a calligrapher. In 2004, she was hired by the Paper Source, a high-end stationery store in Beverly Hills, where she received a two-hour-long training session in calligraphy, as well as gift wrapping and bookbinding. While working there, she did the wedding invitations for the actress Paula Patton's 2005 wedding to the singer-songwriter Robin Thicke.

The first few years of her "hustling" for auditions, as she later described it, were marked with long periods without work. And when she did land parts—such as playing "hot girl" in the 2005 Ashton Kutcher romance *A Lot Like Love*—they weren't exactly Academy Award–winning material.

In 2006, she became a Briefcase Model on *Deal or No Deal*, one of twenty-six women wearing matching outfits and each holding a case with anywhere between 1¢ and $1 million. The NBC game show was not only a steady paycheck but also a hot new property. After the premiere in December 2005, its first season averaged between a whopping ten and sixteen million viewers per episode. While following seasons dipped considerably in viewers, it maintained a strong appeal, spawning a syndicated series and a host of tie-in products, such as video and board games.

"Hello, ladies!" the host, Howie Mandel, said to the perfect rows of Briefcase Models on set.

"Hi, Howie!" they replied in unison.

That was the opening drill for the thirty-four episodes Meghan appeared in in 2006 and 2007. As Briefcase Model #24, she, like the rest of her fellow models, opened up her case whenever a contestant trying to win a million dollars called out her number.

Meghan and the other women recorded up to seven episodes in a day. Shooting so many in such a tight block meant long days. Afterward most of the other models liked to go out together, sometimes not even waiting to take off their show makeup before hitting happy hour. Not Meghan. While she was friendly enough, she didn't go out with the other women. "She was popular with all the other girls," said Leyla Milani, a fellow Briefcase Model. "But as soon as we were done, she would be off to something else." Just as in college, Meghan was working when her peers were blowing off steam. She even kept busy during breaks on the set of *Deal or No Deal*. "When other girls were gossiping or chatting," Leyla said, "she would be by herself reading scripts and preparing for auditions."

After two seasons on the game show, Meghan was ready to put down her silver briefcase. Over the next three years, she kept up the auditions, booking a Tostitos commercial and small roles in a few films and TV shows, including *Horrible Bosses*, *CSI: NY*, *Knight Rider*, *Without a Trace*, and *'Til Death*. In a two-episode arc on the CW reboot of *90210* in 2008, her character, Wendy, stirred up trouble when she was caught giving oral sex to playboy student Ethan Ward in a school parking lot. Meghan was hesitant to shoot the scene, but struggling actresses can't be picky.

She never stopped pushing, even when she thought she blew her audition for the series-regular role of the gorgeous and confident paralegal Rachel Zane, in *Suits*, a new show for the USA Network. Meghan didn't cry or go home to eat a pint of ice cream. Instead, she called her agent.

"I don't think I did a good job in that room," she told him. "I need to get back in there."

"There's nothing you can do," he said. "Just focus on your next audition."

2

When Harry Met Meghan

When Meghan arrived in London, it had been five years since she moved to Toronto to star in *Suits*, and her life was worlds away from that of the struggling LA actress driving to auditions in a run-down Ford Explorer that she didn't have enough money to fix when the automatic locks stopped working (and so spent five months entering through the trunk).

While her role on the USA Network drama wouldn't have put her on the A-list in cities like LA or New York, she was very quickly adopted as a Canadian celebrity. Even as her star rose, Meghan never stopped working to expand her opportunities. After hiring the London-based PR firm Kruger Cowne to promote her interests, she began commanding cash—upward of $10,000 an appearance—to turn up at red carpets, such as the September 2014 Marchesa Voyage for ShopStyle collection launch in New York City, or as a speaker, as she was for Toronto's 2015 "Dove Self-Esteem Project" and the Women in Cable Telecommunications Signature Luncheon in Chicago that same year.

When she signed with Kruger Cowne, Meghan also linked up with APA, one of the world's largest commercial talent agencies, to develop her career as a lifestyle influencer based on *The Tig*, the blog she launched in 2014. A place to curate of all her passions (food, fashion, and travel—as well as social issues such as gender equality) filtered through an "aspirational girl-next-door vibe," the blog was named after Tignanello—the full-bodied red wine that won her heart after the first sip.

"It was my first moment of getting it—I finally understood what people meant by the body, structure, finish, legs of wine," she wrote. "*The Tig* is my nickname for me getting it. Not just wine, but everything."

The Tig wasn't the first time that Meghan had taken to the Internet to not only express herself but also to reach out to others. From 2010 to 2012, she wrote *The Working Actress*, an anonymous blog that detailed the pitfalls and triumphs of struggling to make it in Hollywood. She had always enjoyed writing in school and even thought about becoming a journalist at one point, as it was an opportunity to channel her creativity and frustration. The blog captured the heartfelt moments of joy when she booked a job and the despair and rejection actors felt each time a role was lost in an industry often driven by appearance rather than by talent. While she never publicly acknowledged authorship of the popular blog, it was one of the industry's worst-kept secrets that she was the face behind it—and she quickly became recognized for its clever advice and honest anecdotes.

Where *The Working Actress* was raw and candid, *The Tig* was polished and optimistic. Whether it was Meghan walking a rugged coastline in a perfectly belted camel coat or a "Tig Talk" with famous pals like the actress Priyanka Chopra or a recipe for "spicy broccoli and hempseed stew," the website was curated eye candy that she hoped would be "the breeding ground for ideas and excitement—for an inspired lifestyle."

The newest face in her working world was Violet von West-enholz, a PR executive from Ralph Lauren who had scheduled several events during Meghan's summer trip to London, where the actress would be one of the many celebrity brand ambassadors for the label. In addition to the fashion world, Violet was also well-known in English society. Her father, Frederick Patrick Piers Baron von Westenholz, a former Olympic skier, was one of Prince Charles's oldest and closest friends, so Violet and her siblings grew up skiing in Switzerland with Prince William and Prince Harry.

On the calendar for the actress was Wimbledon. With Ralph Lauren as the fashion sponsor in charge of the official merchandise, Violet arranged the tickets and passes. On day two of the tournament, Meghan sat in the stands to support her friend Serena Williams. Meghan first met the tennis champ at a Super Bowl party in Miami in 2010. Out of all the stars and athletes there, Meghan and Serena "hit it off immediately," as Meghan later described. Connecting over "good old-fashioned girly stuff," the women snapped photos of each other on their phones.

At Wimbledon, however, Meghan was serious while watching Serena battle it out against Amra Sadikovic. She was the first to pump her fist when her friend scored a point or stand to cheer when the tennis champ won a set. She hadn't known much about tennis before becoming friendly with Serena, but now she was a fan.

Meghan did tear herself away from the action long enough to spot British actor Dominic Cooper in the VIP bar area, where she joked about having a small crush on the *Preacher* star and deliberated whether she should talk to him. She decided not to approach this nice English gentleman. She was too busy having fun with her girlfriends.

Violet wasn't the only one setting up meetings for Meghan in London. A few months before she arrived in town, Jonathan Shalit— who has helped carve out television careers for Simon Cowell,

Mel B, and other British household names—signed Meghan to his talent agency, Roar. The hope was for Meghan to enter a new space, perhaps hosting a food-centric TV show.

Jonathan's interest in the American actress for some kind of food, travel, and culture show stemmed from *The Tig*, which was exactly the kind of future Meghan hoped would blossom out of her website.

"There is a vision, and it's a big one," Meghan said about *The Tig*, which she dreamed about spinning into a cookbook or a lifestyle brand. "The opportunities are endless."

While the actress-turned-lifestyle-guru Gwyneth Paltrow, who turned her website *Goop* into a $250 million empire, was an obvious source of inspiration in marketing herself, Meghan had another one far closer to home in Jessica Mulroney—Canada's most prominent lifestyle influencer and a very close friend.

Jessica and her husband, Ben—the eldest son of the former Canadian prime minister Brian Mulroney and the host of the entertainment show *eTalk*—were the city's hottest young power couple. She parlayed the brand-name Canadian family she married into and her sense of style into a boutique career as an influencer, stylist, and wedding planner. Her Instagram feed was filled with pictures of domestic perfection—like Jessica with her long, blown-out brown hair, her blue eyes fringed in black lashes, reading a book on the floor with her adorable twin sons, Brian and John, her lean legs crossed and on her feet a pair of sky-high black stilettos.

After the women were introduced by a local fashion publicist, Jessica not only encouraged Meghan to follow the same path but also introduced her to an exciting, fizzy social scene filled with high-profile charity events, the openings of new hotspots, fabulous restaurants, and fancy friends like Michael Bublé. Jessica and Ben were good friends with the Canadian singer-songwriter and his wife, the Argentinian-born actress-model Luisana Lopilato, whose intimate parties at their home in Vancouver were a coveted invite. When Meghan snagged a seat at his dinner table in November 2015, it provided fodder for a blog post of the singer's favorite holiday songs titled, "Tig Tunes with Michael Bublé."

By 2016, *The Tig* and her Instagram account had gained a big enough following that she felt in a position to think about opportunities outside of *Suits*. Eager for a change, she had signed to a literary agency in the United States and was in talks to release a food-focused book to capitalize on her new platform. While Meghan was in London, Jonathan, in his uniform of black vest, white shirt, striped tie, and brightly colored socks, pitched a show where she would travel the world, discovering new foods with a focus on sustainability. Think Padma Lakshmi meets Anthony Bourdain.

Jonathan wasn't the only well-known industry type Meghan networked with while in England's capital. She also met up with *Good Morning Britain* host Piers Morgan at his local pub in Kensington, the Scarsdale Tavern. "I'm in London for a week of meetings and Wimbledon," Meghan had quietly direct messaged via Twitter to Piers after she arrived in the British capital. "Would love to say hi!" They had never met before, but she was keen to know the controversial and outspoken personality behind the outrageous tweets about Donald Trump, who he became frenemies with on the NBC reality series *Celebrity Apprentice*.

Meghan showed up to the cozy, dark pub looking "every inch the Hollywood superstar," Piers described in the *Daily Mail*, "very slim, very leggy, very elegant, and impossibly glamorous. She was even wearing the obligatory big black shades beloved of LA thespians."

During their two-hour drinks, Meghan sipped dirty martinis while the two discussed gun control, her career, her childhood dreams of becoming either president of the United States or a TV journalist, and her biracial upbringing. Piers was charmed.

Just before eight o'clock, Meghan bade Piers farewell, as she had to run to her dinner date at 5 Hertford Street with Misan Harriman, whose father, Chief Hope Harriman, was one of the founding fathers of modern Nigeria. Misan—the founder of the website whatweseee.com and the director of the global network of polo games called British Polo Day—could often be found at polo matches alongside Prince William and Kate Middleton.

Misan invited Meghan to the members-only club-restaurant in Mayfair, which was said to be one of the most prestigious clubs in the world. Members who have made their way through the un- marked maroon door on Hertford Street to dine by candlelight in the private rooms with silver service included George and Amal Clooney, Mick Jagger, and Harry's cousin Princess Eugenie. While Meghan might have enjoyed sipping gin fizzes under the club's hushed lighting, what she really looked forward to was a blind date she had planned for the following evening.

It was summer, and she was newly single. Although her two- year relationship (her first serious one since her divorce three years earlier) had only recently ended, Meghan still very much believed in finding lasting love. During her visit to London, however, Meghan joked to a pal that she'd settle for "a nice English gentleman to flirt with."

Except this date was with no ordinary guy. Over lunch on July 1, Meghan revealed the mystery man's identity to her London- based agent Gina Nelthorpe-Cowne. Gina and Meghan, who first met at the 2014 One Young World Summit, had traveled to numer- ous overseas jobs together and even took a side vacation during a work trip to Malta in March 2015. So the actress felt she could confide in the agent as a friend.

"I'm going on a blind date tonight," Meghan said coyly, after finishing off her salad at the Delaunay restaurant, near London's Covent Garden.

"Who is it?" Gina asked. "Do I know him?"

Meghan leaned in excitedly and whispered, "I'm sure you know him. It's Prince Harry."

Floored by the news, Gina asked her friend in a hushed tone, "Do you know what you're letting yourself in for?"

"Well, it's going to be an experience," Meghan said, "and at least it will be a fun night."

"This could be *crazy*," Gina said, trying to impress upon the American the insane and unique culture of tabloid coverage in the UK that came with dating a royal. "You will be the most wanted woman."

Meghan wasn't thinking that far ahead of herself, particularly since the woman who had set her up with the prince said, "Let's just get you in a room together and see what happens."

Despite reports that Violet von Westenholz had set up the date, it was mostly Meghan's pals Misha Nonoo and Markus Anderson who were in on the first meeting. (The couple themselves prefer to keep the story of their matchmaker a mystery, even to close friends. Meghan's only clue to pals at the time was that her first encounter with Harry was "serendipitous.")

Markus, a Canadian native and Soho House's global membership director, always made sure Meghan was comfortable at the Toronto outpost of the private members-only club with locations all over the world. Behind the velvet roped-off doorway of the nineteenth-century Georgian building that the club spent $8 million to renovate into an exclusive oasis, Meghan, who would have her own booth reserved on the third floor when she went there for drinks, spent many an afternoon curled up on one of the library's leather club chairs with her MacBook, working away on her blog, or hanging out with her *Suits* castmates.

Markus provided Meghan with introductions to many business and cultural elites—both in Canada and beyond. At a Soho House lunch in Miami, he was the one who sat the actress next to Misha, a budding fashion designer with a vivacious personality and impeccable pedigree. The occasion for the December 2014 Miami trip was Art Basel, a decadent art fair that brings the internationally rich and famous for a week of parties and events of all sorts and sizes. Markus invited Meghan, an art lover, to stay at the epicenter of the action, Soho Beach House, to get some sun, see some art, and have some fun.

A perfect place to make new friends and connections, the Soho House event saw Misha and Meghan hit it off immediately. Born in Bahrain but raised in England, the sunny blond designer, who split her time between New York and London, attended business school in Paris before entering the world of fashion. Her handsome and well-connected husband, Alexander Gilkes, was named to *Art + Auction*'s 100 Most Powerful People in the Art World list after founding Paddle8, an online auction house. An old Etonian pal of Prince William's and Prince Harry's, Alexander met Misha when she was seventeen, and they were married seven years later in Venice with no less than Lana Del Rey performing at their 2012 vows.

Meghan was instantly intrigued by Misha's effortless glamour, and Misha felt similarly about the actress's fresh-faced interest. "She's an impressive woman and so much fun to be around," said Misha.

Before lunch was over, the women exchanged information and tagged each other in photos on Instagram.

The smart and pretty fashion designer spoke about new business opportunities to Meghan, who was eager to expand her social and professional horizons. Meghan loved hanging out with Misha, described by a friend as "one of those undercover, cool, rich aristocratic girls." Anytime that she was in New York, she would stay at Misha's West Village duplex, where the designer and her husband constantly entertained a revolving group of interesting people.

The friendship wasn't one-sided, though. When Misha was named a finalist of the prestigious CFDA/*Vogue* Fashion Fund Awards during New York Fashion Week in November 2015,

Meghan made a huge splash on the red carpet when she wore one of her friend's designs to the awards dinner. The image of Meghan posing in the silver liquid-metal mini dress with a deep plunging neckline was everywhere the next day—a great push for Misha's burgeoning fashion line.

When the two women first met, Meghan was in a serious relationship, even though she was coming off a divorce only a year and a half earlier.

Meghan had been twenty-three years old when she fell for her first husband, Trevor Engelson, a brash, up-and-coming young producer whom *The Hollywood Reporter* named to its Top 35 Under 35 list in 2009. The pair dated for seven years before the thirty-year-old Meghan and thirty-four-year-old Trevor tied the knot on September 10, 2011, in a romantic beachside ceremony in Jamaica.

While they were still dating, Meghan wondered aloud to her closest friends why Trevor didn't always act as if he supported her acting career. After all, he had plenty of connections in the industry. She felt that he liked her being dependent on him. That was the dynamic of their relationship; Trevor was the dominant character. "He was used to being the breadwinner, the one Meghan needed for introductions in the industry," said a friend of their early courtship. But their marriage coincided with her landing a starring role on a hit cable drama. Just months after Trevor proposed to Meghan while on vacation in Belize in 2010, she got the part on *Suits*. "Suddenly the dynamic was changing," the friend continued, "and he didn't like that."

Meghan living in Toronto for the greater part of the year accelerated the decline of their relationship. At first, they made every effort to spend time together. As the months went by, however, the visits became less frequent. When Trevor was invited to the Oscars in February 2013, he didn't bring Meghan to the awards show. He explained that he had only one ticket, but Meghan wondered if he didn't want to share the spotlight. Six months later, the couple, who had appeared deliriously in love on a Jamaican beach just twenty-three months earlier, were divorced. But Meghan never lost faith that she'd find *the one*—even if the first time she decided who he was, she'd been wrong.

When the actress decided to give love another chance, it came in the form of Toronto's number one bachelor, Cory Vitiello, who the magazine *Toronto Life* described as, "known as much for his kitchen skills as for appearing on most-eligible lists." The native of Brantford, Ontario, with the chiseled features always had a different beautiful woman on his arm. Having started his own catering business out of his family home when he was just fifteen, Cory was the owner of one of Meghan's favorite restaurants, the Harbord Room, where the two first met in June 2014. Shortly after, Meghan wrote in *The Tig* about his eatery—and him. "The small-town charm and moral compass of someone who doesn't come from the big city, but dreams big thoughts and makes them happen," she wrote, "that makes his food so approachable yet inspired."

At first, she was attracted to Cory's good looks, but soon she was drawn to his sensitivity, kind demeanor, and entrepreneurial skills. And, of course, food was a huge connection. Although Meghan was already an avid cook and passionate foodie before meeting Cory, he "opened up her eyes to food on a whole different level," according to a friend. By the end of the summer, she and Cory were a confirmed couple, and within a month of their dating, Meghan told friends she was falling in love. "She's careful but does fall quickly when she likes someone," a friend said. "It's the old romantic in her."

From the time she was in high school, through college, and post-divorce, Meghan was never interested in casual dating. She was always looking for commitment. Things with Cory were no different; she wanted to be in a healthy relationship, get married, and eventually have children. Cory's family, with whom she spent Christmas 2015, couldn't have been happier. The whole clan was fond of Meghan, including Cory's mom, Joanne, and they were convinced the pair would soon be engaged.

In reality, though, her relationship with Cory had begun to deteriorate. By the start of 2016, Meghan was confessing to friends that she regretted how quickly things had progressed with him. That was already obvious to some of her closest pals by the fact that although she had moved in with the chef, Meghan had held on to her rental home. But it wasn't until early that May that they officially ended their two-year romance. The problem, according to a source close to the couple, was Cory: he didn't want to settle down. Meghan broke it off with him without any specific accusations, and he didn't put up a fight. "It wasn't a happy time for her," the source said.

Sadness, however, quickly evolved into relief for the young actress. So much so that by the time summer arrived, she was looking forward to her travel plans abroad and ready to have fun. And her new friend Misha thought that summer was the perfect time to set her up on a date or two.

———•———

Prince Harry seemed like a fun guy, even if he was a member of a royal family steeped in protocol completely foreign to an American like Meghan. From the time he was three years old, photographed sticking out his tongue while in the arms of his mother, Princess Diana, who stood next to the Queen on the balcony of Buckingham Palace at the Trooping the Colour, he established himself as the cheeky one. Poking out his tongue at photographers, something he sometimes did as a child, was a particularly rebellious act, since before William and Harry, royal children were pictured only as perfect, quiet, and in the background.

His mother did little to dampen his high spirits. When the boys were in boarding school at the Ludgrove School in Berkshire—first William, then Harry—Diana smuggled Starbursts into their socks when she would visit to watch them play soccer. An avid letter writer, she also liked to send them off-color greeting cards. "You can be naughty," Diana once told Harry. "Just don't get caught."

Harry took that message to heart. More interested in riding or playing sports than in school, he shared his mother's penchant for humor and mischief. Once while playing with his mother's personal protection officer Ken Wharfe, he got past security, snuck out of the palace gates, and radioed Ken on the walkie-talkies.

"Where are you?" Ken said over the radio when neither he nor the palace guards could find Harry.

"I'm outside Tower Records," Harry radioed back to Ken, who ran as fast as he could to Kensington High Street, a half mile away, where he found the small royal in his tiny camouflaged army uniform.

Diana might have forgiven Harry's indifference to the rules in part because the rules of their royal lineage dictated that his brother, William, had a more important title than he did. By the age of four, he was aware of their destinies as "heir and spare." Knowing this, their mother regularly emphasized how she loved her sons equally. Equality was a constant theme in their family unit, because outside of it, that was not the case.

By the time the boys got older, the difference in their positions was clearer. William would have solo meetings with the Queen to learn about his future role, but Harry never did. Diana had tried to imbue in her younger son that he should never let anyone make him feel that he wasn't special just because he would never be king. If anything, she reasoned, he was lucky, because Harry had the opportunity to find his purpose. Titles are both boon and burden.

Not surprisingly, he grew up into a young man most at ease around close friends and people not overly impressed with his royalty. Not one for pomp and circumstance, he never liked certain "stuffy" engagements, like state banquets at Buckingham Palace, or the overly formal attire they sometimes required. To this day, Harry doesn't like wearing a tie. He once confessed to the authors of this book, "We need to liven these things up, make them more fun and interesting."

Part of the reason he fell hard for his first serious girlfriend, Chelsy Davy, was that she loved adventure as much as he did, and she was not overly impressed with his royal pedigree. While he was on his gap year in 2004 after graduating high school, Harry met the smart, lively blonde, who was born in Zimbabwe to Charles Davy, a wealthy landowner and safari operator, and Beverley Donald Davy, a former Miss Rhodesia. Chelsy was just as comfortable riding horses bareback and enjoying the African plains as she was attending high-society events in London. For seven years she and Harry shared a complicated but undoubtedly passionate history. Chelsy was fun-loving but also devoted. Her genuine love for her boyfriend regardless of pedigree was one of the qualities that endeared Chelsy to both Harry and the royal family. Discreet and loyal, she was by Harry's side for all the important moments of his young life, like his 2006 graduation from Britain's elite Royal Military Academy Sandhurst, the 2007 Concert for Diana, and his brother's wedding to Kate Middleton in 2011. Ultimately, though, the constant public scrutiny of her private life proved too much for Chelsy to bear.

Paparazzi lurking in unexpected corners and unflattering tabloid articles also proved the death knell for Harry's next serious relationship, with the actress Cressida Bonas, who his cousin Princess Eugenie introduced him to in the spring of 2012. The willowy blonde traveled in the same aristocratic circles as Harry; her mother, Lady Mary-Gaye Curzon, was one of the heirs to the Curzon banking fortune and her father, Jeffrey, was an entrepreneur.

By the summer of 2016, Harry felt he was ready to be in a relationship. Indeed, he and Chelsy reunited briefly again before he met Meghan—who some of the tabloids would later speculate had still been in a relationship with Cory when she first met Harry. Cory never spoke to the press about his ex, other than to refute the claim that Meghan overlapped boyfriends, stating: "I have too much respect for her and her privacy. She's a wonderful girl."

Misha thought Meghan could be a match for Harry. Her then husband, Alexander, knew him through the social circle of elite young men and women connected to the royal brothers that had been dubbed by the tabloids the Glosse Posse. Included in the circle of friends was also Alexander's brother Charlie, who dated Kate Middleton's sister, Pippa, in 2008 while both were students at the University of Edinburgh. Alexander was a guest at William's 2011 wedding to Kate; Harry went to Charlie's 2014 nuptials in Italy to Anneke von Trotha Taylor (Kate's mother and siblings James and Pippa were also there, but the Duchess of Cambridge, pregnant at the time, had such a bad case of morning sickness she couldn't go).

How would Meghan, a California girl, fit into that scene? "They both have an innocence in their eyes," a mutual pal described of Harry and Meghan. Plus, friends felt it would be good for them both to just get out there and date.

Naturally both participants in this blind date did their homework with a thorough Google search. Harry, who scoped out Meghan on social media, was interested. A friend had shown him an Instagram photo of Meghan in the slinky silver mini dress at the CFDA/*Vogue* Fashion Fund Awards. He liked what he saw but didn't necessarily think of drinks as anything more than a chance to be introduced to a woman he found attractive. He certainly could not have foreseen that she would be the woman he would one day marry.

What Meghan may have seen online could have easily convinced her to call the whole thing off.

In his early twenties, Harry was a regular fixture on the London club scene. He had many wild nights out at trendy spots like Jak's, Funky Buddha, and the Wellington Club. But his reputation as the "party prince" started while he was still a teenager who was known for his drunken antics reported by the tabloids (some true, some less so). There was story after story of Harry seemingly getting out of control. He was kicked out of a pub he frequented a couple of miles from Highgrove, the family residence in Gloucestershire, because of bad behavior. It seemed he took to heart the first part of his mother's message about getting into trouble but couldn't quite figure out how to pull off the second part about not getting caught.

Harry's nadir came when he landed on the cover of *The Sun* in 2005 holding a drink and a cigarette—and wearing a swastika armband. The British tabloid's headline was to the point: "Harry the Nazi." Harry had been one of about 250 guests invited to a costume party at the home of Richard Meade, one of Britain's most successful equestrians, for his son's birthday. The prince's choice of costume, for which he apologized, was unequivocally bad, but the party's timing right before the sixtieth anniversary of the liberation of Auschwitz made it even more egregious.

The other big scandal that pops up in all online searches of the prince was Harry's 2012 Las Vegas trip with his longtime pals Tom "Skippy" Inskip and Arthur Landon. A few alcohol-fueled days (during which Harry challenged twelve-time Olympic medalist in swimming Ryan Lochte to a race at a pool party) abruptly ended when *TMZ* published grainy photos of Harry naked and cupping what the tabloid website called his "crown jewels" during a co-ed game of "strip pool" in his hotel suite. The pictures, which immediately went viral, had forced the Palace to question how this could have happened and who was to blame. "It was a bad moment," said a former royal protection officer. "Everyone was in a lot of trouble."

But the online tales of the "Wild Windsor" didn't put a damper on Meghan's date. Not only was the Las Vegas incident four years old, but the actress, who had her own small taste of tabloid interest during her divorce and relationship with Cory, knew better than most that the media didn't always get the story right.

"She didn't know much about him at all other than what had been written," a friend said. "She knows how wrong the tabloids can be, and she wanted to know who the real Harry was, not what the likes of *TMZ* had said."

The evening of her first date with Harry, Meghan was more pre-occupied with what she would wear than his online reputation. She settled on an outfit and then got started on her makeup in her suite at the Soho House's Dean Street Townhouse property. Meghan had been offered a heavily discounted stay at the five-star Dorchester Hotel but chose the luxurious room secured by Markus instead. As a celebrity and influencer, Meghan was regularly offered free holidays, travel discounts, and the like. But she turned down the Dorchester amid a Hollywood boycott after the hotel chain's owner, the Sultan of Brunei, introduced Sharia law in his country, including death by stoning for those found guilty of gay sex.

In addition to the suite, Markus had a hand in some of the evening's logistics as well. That included other friends being present at the informal gathering, "so it wouldn't be awkward," a source close to Meghan explained. "If that first meeting worked out, then they could plan a proper one-on-one date together."

Soho House's eighteenth-century Georgian building made for the perfect location for the meeting. Before the member's club took over the premises in 2008, it had a history as a meeting place for artists and intellectuals—stretching as far back as the seventeenth century, when the actress and mistress of King Charles II, Nell Gwynn, spent time there. In the 1920s, it was christened the Gargoyle Club and frequented by the playwright Noël Coward, the dancer Fred Astaire, and the screen legend Tallulah Bankhead. By the 1950s, it had been transformed again, into a bar where luminaries such as Lucian Freud and other artists hung their hats.

The club in its current life afforded Harry the privacy necessary for a prince to unwind. The many rooms spread across four floors and two connected buildings made it easy to keep Harry out of sight and away from gawking guests. Markus chose a private dining area cordoned off behind floor-to-ceiling velvet drapes.

From one of the townhouse's thirty-nine bedrooms (many with four-poster beds and Victorian claw-footed tubs), Meghan's home away from home during her London excursion, she settled on a navy-blue sundress and heels for the evening.

Arriving downstairs, Meghan entered the warmly lit room filled with cozy banquettes and familiar faces. She sat down briefly until Harry—dressed in his signature white shirt and chinos—walked in and immediately introduced himself. *Here we go.*

A friend of Meghan's had admitted that the actress was initially nervous about the introduction, as they came from two *very* different worlds. But Misha, according to a source, told Meghan not to worry—they both had "huge hearts." And if all else failed, Markus would be nearby in case the entire evening was a dud.

Harry is admittedly tough to impress, but he almost froze when he walked into the room and saw Meghan. He knew she was beautiful—he had seen the photos on her Instagram account and online—but she was even more stunning in person. "Wow," he later confessed to a friend. "The most beautiful woman I've seen in my life."

Meghan wasn't just beautiful. She was also different from women he was used to meeting, and Harry was intimidated by new situations. Because of his royal birth, he couldn't do a lot of the everyday things most people do, like ride the London Underground or go anywhere without a protection officer. In fact, Harry lived within a bubble of sorts.

And that included the women he usually dated. They were mainly within his small world. Girls at Jak's or Funky Buddha would only need to see that he was Prince Harry to be impressed. He didn't even need to open his mouth.

Meghan, however, threw him off immediately.

It wasn't just her charming freckles, perfect smile, or American accent. Meghan is someone who works a room very well. In social settings, all eyes are drawn to her. She laughs a little louder, glows a little bit brighter. She's self-assured in a way that attracts attention.

Harry quickly realized that impressing Meghan was going to be tougher than just giving her one of his big smiles. "I am really going to have to up my game here," he said of their first meeting. "Sit down and make sure I've got a good chat!"

Perhaps she sensed his nervousness, because the couple was somewhat bashful at first. However, it didn't take long for them to start chatting easily. Very easily. On two individual velvet club chairs, the pair were "in their own little world," a source said.

Over drinks (beer for him, a martini for her), they asked each other questions about their work. Nibbles may have been out on the low table in front of their oversize chairs, but neither touched the food. They were also too engrossed in their conversation, and too involved with each other, to notice the rather rude wallpaper featuring photos of women's private parts that adorned the walls.

Harry talked about his charity work, excitedly telling her stories from his extensive trips to Africa. Their "passions for wanting to make change for good," as Harry described it, was, as Meghan said, "One of the first things we connected on." Meghan lit up when the subject turned to her two rescue dogs. In fact, it wasn't long before she started swiping through photos on her phone like a proud mom.

At the end of the evening, which had lasted almost three hours, Harry and Meghan went their separate ways. Despite the palpable attraction between them, there was no goodbye kiss, no expectation, just a hint that something was there and they hoped to see each other again soon.

Harry wasted no time in texting Meghan, who was back in her hotel room.

His messages were often short and full of emojis, in particular the ghost emoji, which he often used instead of a smiley face. For what reason? Nobody knows. But Meghan found his texting etiquette funny and adorable, just like the prince.

"He definitely didn't hide the fact he was keen," said a friend of Meghan's. "He wanted her to know he was very interested."

3

Courtship in the Wild

While "everyone was hopeful" that Harry and Meghan would have a nice evening together, no one expected what happened next.

"Almost immediately they were almost obsessed with each other," a friend said. "It was as if Harry was in a trance."

Even Misha told friends she was surprised by the quick intensity of the attraction.

The day after her date with the prince, Meghan called one of her girlfriends. "Do I sound crazy when I say this could have legs?" she asked.

That night, Harry and Meghan made plans to meet up again. This time, no friends, no distractions—just the two of them. They returned to Dean Street Townhouse the next evening for a romantic dinner organized by Markus, who the venue staff playfully called "Lady A," because of the way he fretted over making sure every detail was just so.

No front entrance for the pair, they were given directions for how to get into the building using a discreet door away from prying eyes—and familiar only to staff and delivery trucks bringing in produce and fresh fish from Billingsgate Market. A glamorous start, it was not.

Staff did all they could to keep details of the dinner private, allowing just one trusted waiter to serve them the entire evening. As patrons of the members-only club like to say, "What goes on at Soho House stays at Soho House."

According to a friend, Harry and Meghan "chatted a lot" that evening, which ended chastely with Harry returning to the palace. Still, their chemistry had been electric throughout the meal as they both flirted. A touch of an arm here, direct eye contact there.

"Harry knew they would be together at that point," a friend shared. "She was ticking every box fast."

Although she shared much of her London visit on social media, Meghan knew she had to keep her dates with the then fifth in line to the throne a secret. But the clues were there. Around the time of their first encounter, she began to follow a mysterious-looking Instagram account by the name of @SpikeyMau5. With no face visible in the profile photo, just a mouse-shaped helmet, it would have meant nothing to most people. But it was in fact Harry's private account. A big house music fan, he crafted the pseudonym by using part of the name of one of his favorite DJs, DeadMau5. Spikey came from a Facebook alias that Harry used for an account he had under the name of Spike Wells. "Spike" was a nickname sometimes used for the prince, particularly by Scotland Yard officers. Harry's Facebook account (before he shut it down after the Las Vegas scandal) had a profile photo of three guys in panama hats taken from the back in an MGM Grand Las Vegas hotel suite. The account said he was from Maun, Botswana. Prior to that photo, Harry used the image of King Julien, the eccentric lemur from the Dreamworks movie *Madagascar*.

Much bolder was Meghan's public Instagram post the same

night of their first solo date: a photo of a Love Hearts candy with the inscription "Kiss Me" and the caption "Lovehearts in #London."

Whether it had meaning to anyone else, Harry got the message.

The next night, July 3, Meghan left her hotel and got into a taxi like any ordinary citizen. Except as the cab wound through London's dark winding streets, it had no ordinary destination: Kensington Palace.

The car pulled off the main road and drove up the private Palace Avenue that took Meghan to an industrial-looking security gate and guard's office that was a far cry from the gilded palace gates she had imagined. But the humdrum entrance, often used by staff or those visiting the estate for meetings, was the most discreet way in. Meghan tipped the cabdriver like she always does and walked into the office and was met by a protection officer.

Meghan was quickly ushered down a cobbled path of small mews cottages, which she later commented looked so tiny and perfectly appointed with manicured flower boxes and pots that they hardly looked real. She had no idea so many people lived on the grounds of Kensington Palace, but as a working residence, it houses about a dozen royals as well as several retired household courtiers.

"Cute!" Meghan later told a friend of Harry's home, Nottingham Cottage.

Again, the sweet English house was nothing like the imposing stone palace that she had constructed in her mind, inspired by images from childhood fairy tales. When Harry opened the door, there was no large staircase or plush red carpet, no crystal chandeliers or double-height ceilings, no art hanging in heavy gold frames or butler service. Instead, the prince towered in the small hallway with lots of coats hung on hooks and his boots by the door, just like any regular home.

Inside Harry's very cozy house, any nerves Meghan had before her arrival would have dissolved. While Nottingham Cottage, or Nott Cott as regular visitors know it, is a nice place by anyone's standards, it's pretty humble surroundings for an heir to the throne. Clearly, he wasn't materialistic. Plus, Harry had such a big, sweet smile.

Meghan had enough dating experience to know a charmer when she saw one, and Harry was obviously not at all that. If anything, he was unfiltered. While it was clear he wanted to impress her with details about his work, he spoke without overthinking—and he never once mentioned anything about being a royal or a prince. The most he had admitted at that point was that his life was "sometimes a little mad."

Harry was unusually candid for someone with his title, but he was also every bit the gentleman. Wherever they went, and to this day, he gestures for Meghan to go first. The short walk from the living room would have been no different.

With her visit to Nott Cott over, Meghan's trip was sadly coming to an end. She spent her last day in the British capital cheering on her friend Serena Williams in the Players' Box at Wimbledon (where photographers took little note of Meghan, focusing instead on *Vogue* editor in chief Anna Wintour and Pippa Middleton, who were in the same box), she jetted back across the Atlantic to Toronto, leaving in her wake just a few words posted to Instagram: "Gutted to be leaving London." Again, only a few people had any inkling what those words truly meant.

One person in that select group was Doria. Meghan shared the news of her budding romance with her mom almost immediately. There was probably no one more influential in Meghan's life than her mother. "She helped shape Meghan into a strong, powerful, independent woman," Doria's half brother Joseph said of his sister. Their bond had been forged during Meghan's childhood. Practicing yoga, jogging in their LA neighborhood, biking to the La Brea Tar Pits after school, spending time preparing home-cooked dinners with fresh, healthy ingredients, and traveling—Meghan learned to love many of the same things her mom did. Mother and daughter were always very open with each other, and that did not change once Meghan became an adult.

In the following weeks—as Meghan traveled to New York and Boston to publicize the upcoming season of *Suits* and then to Madrid for a quick trip with Misha and Markus, where they drank lots of wine at Taberna Carmencita, visited Museo Nacional del Prado, and danced in bars—it wasn't uncommon to see Meghan typing away on her phone and smiling or giggling to herself. She was texting with her new crush. Harry and Meghan sent each other selfies—nothing untoward, just sweet pics of them going about their day. Meghan also sent pictures of meals she was cooking or when she was hair and makeup–ready for camera on set.

Harry and Meghan were falling for each other fast, despite the fact that trust was an issue for both of them—although for completely different reasons. Meghan was protective of herself. She preferred to play it cool and get to know a guy before committing. That said, when she was sure about someone, she dove headlong into the relationship. Meghan's dream was always to be friends first, then fall in love.

With those he was close to, Harry wore his heart on his sleeve. That's why he protected himself from getting hurt. It took a very long time to earn his trust, because he was never sure about people's motivations when they wanted to be his friend. That concern was only exacerbated when it came to women. Were they interested in him because they wanted to make high-society connections? Did they just want to say they dated a prince? Or did they want to sell a story to the press? His radar was always up, calculating how many questions potential love interests asked about the Palace or the Queen. If Harry could have his way, he would have jumped right in—texting and calling every day—when he found a woman he clicked with. But being a prince, he was raised to be wary of the intentions of others.

The correspondence continued through early August, when

Meghan traveled to New York for her college friend Lindsay's wedding to the British businessman Gavin Jordan. From New York, Meghan jetted to the Amalfi Coast for a long-planned holiday with Jessica. Camped out at Le Sirenuse Hotel, a chic five-star hotel in Positano, Meghan and Jessica spent most of their trip poolside, sipping negronis, Bellinis, and champagne while sunbathing. They called it "cocktails o'clock" as the two girlfriends caught up on their lives. With the azure crystalline waters of the Tyrrhenian Sea and Capri visible in the distance, Meghan spoke about everything, including the prince. As Meghan documented every moment of her trip on social media, dubbing it the "Eat Pray Love" tour of the Amalfi Coast, in a cheeky nod to her new love interest, Meghan posted a photo of a red leather-bound volume titled *Amore Eterno*.

Jessica was one of the few people in the world who knew Meghan's secret; she was soon meeting Harry again in his home city. Just six weeks after their first date in the city, the prince was taking her on a trip. Harry planned everything for the five-day adventure. He told her to just arrive in London, and he'd handle the rest.

Their destination was Africa—a continent that had great personal significance for him.

A few weeks before, Harry had told Meghan he was planning to go to Africa soon—as he did every summer—and asked her if she would like to come along. He said he'd love for her to join him, since it was the perfect chance to spend time together in a place he was confident they wouldn't be followed.

When Meghan asked about plans, like finding a place to stay, the prince said, "Leave it with me."

This wasn't Meghan's first trip to Africa. In January 2015, she traveled with UN representatives to Rwanda to visit the Gihembe refugee camp and spend time in Kigali with female parliamentarians.

The trip had its roots in a *Tig* post from July 4, 2014, where Meghan connected Independence Day and individual independence: "Raise a glass to yourself today—to the right to freedom, to the empowerment of the women (and men) who struggle to have it, and to knowing, embracing, honoring, educating, and loving yourself."

Her *Tig* post caught the attention of an executive at HeForShe—the United Nations' global campaign for gender equality—who reached out to enlist Meghan in their efforts. Her increasing profile as an actress meant more to Meghan than just red carpet invites or free clothes. She wanted to stretch herself intellectually and morally. She had seen how actresses such as Angelina Jolie had advanced humanitarian goals and similarly wanted "to use whatever status I have as an actress to make a tangible impact." So, she agreed—even offering to intern for a week during her upcoming filming hiatus from *Suits*. It was very much in character for Meghan, who, before taking on a commitment, likes to be fully prepared.

Rwanda is the only country in the world with a 64 percent female majority in Parliament. This female empowerment grew out of the ashes of the country's 1994 genocide, which killed between eight hundred thousand and one million and left the population 60 to 70 percent female. Passed in 2003, the country's new constitution declared that women must hold 30 percent of the seats in Parliament. In the election, though, voters surpassed the quota, raising it to 48 percent of the seats, a number that went up to 64 percent in the following election.

Almost a year after her first trip, she returned to Rwanda in February 2016, this time with World Vision, a Christian humanitarian organization dedicated to working with children. The purpose was to witness firsthand the importance of clean water. While visiting a school in the country, Meghan taught students to paint with watercolors, using water from a newly installed pipeline in their community. The students created pictures based on their hopes for the future. "It was an amazing experience, taking water from one of the water sources in the community and using it with the children to paint pictures of what they dream to be when they grow up," Meghan said. "I saw that water is not just a life source for a community, but it can really be a source for creative imagination."

It was an experience Meghan talked about with Harry on their first date. He also shared many of his own feelings about Africa—a place where he has said many times he feels "more like myself than anywhere else in the world."

Harry fell for Africa following the tragic death of his mother, Princess Diana, in 1997—over the years it had quickly become his home away from home, but his first visit will always be as clear as day. Days after a fifteen-year-old William and twelve-year-old Harry followed their mother's coffin from St. James's Palace to Westminster Abbey, Prince Charles, due to make his first trip to South Africa, encouraged his sons to come along to escape the public mourning that surrounded them.

Diana's death was a big turning point in Charles's relationship with his sons. The Prince of Wales always tried to be the best father he knew how to be, but he had been raised with a strict sense of formality. While he showered affection on his sons when compared to what he experienced as heir to the throne, Charles was incredibly stiff and not at all used to the kind of world Diana created for the boys.

As a result of her parents' divorce and difficult childhood, Diana was committed to creating a normal family home filled with love and laughter at Kensington Palace. Diana, one of the first royals to make the kitchen a place for the family and not just the staff, loved it when their chef, Carolyn Robb, cooked with the boys. Carolyn had a cake recipe that called for digestive biscuit crumbs, for which she enlisted Harry and William in pulverizing the cookies in Ziploc bags.

Charles was never going to fill the role of his sons' mother, but after Diana's death, he realized that he had to finish the job of raising his boys. That came before everything else, even his relationship with his longtime love, Camilla Parker-Bowles. Two weeks before they were set to make their public debut at an Osteoporosis Society function, Diana was tragically killed. They weren't seen in public together for another two years, as Charles shifted his priorities to focus on his children.

On that trip with his father right after his mother's death, Harry went on safari and was able to meet Nelson Mandela (as well as the Spice Girls). At a time in his life when he was most vulnerable, he made his very first visit to the countries of Lesotho and Botswana. The beauty of the animals and their natural habitat was something the thirteen-year-old would never forget.

As soon as Harry was old enough to travel by himself, he made sure to spend at least two to three weeks in Africa every summer. He also focused some of his charitable works on protecting the native wildlife and habitats that make the continent so special. "We need to look after them," he said, "because otherwise our children will not have a chance to see what we have seen. And it's a test. If we can't save some animals in a wilderness area, what else can we do?"

Thanks to his dad, Harry was an environmentalist long before it became a mainstream movement. Prince Charles has been talking about climate change and plastic use since the seventies, noting he was considered "rather dotty" when he first brought up these issues. An advocate of sustainable farming, he manages his estate at Highgrove under "the strictest sustainable principles," including a reed-bed sewage system and rainwater that's collected in tanks for some of the toilets and watering the fields.

When Harry and William were growing up, the Prince of Wales was constantly on them to turn out the lights and also took them to pick up litter while on holiday. "I used to get taken the mickey out of at school for picking up rubbish," Harry said in a documentary to mark his father's seventieth birthday. Despite the teasing, the brothers both took up their father's environmental activism, launching their own initiatives in that charitable space.

Harry's conservation efforts, however, were not his only work in Africa. He was also inspired to continue his mother's work fighting the AIDS epidemic. Just five months before her death, Princess Diana made a private visit to South Africa to visit her brother Charles Spencer, who was living there at the time. While in the country, she fulfilled a longtime wish to meet Nelson Mandela in Cape Town to discuss the threat of AIDS. "She went for the sort of charities and organizations that everybody was scared to go near, such as landmines in the Third World," Harry said of his mother. "She got involved in things that nobody had done before, such as AIDS. She had more guts than anybody else.

"I want to carry on the things she didn't quite finish," said Harry, who spent part of his gap year in 2004 in Lesotho, which had the second-highest rate of HIV and AIDS in the world.

Harry's mentor Captain Mark Dyer—who served formerly as an equerry for Prince Charles and had stepped in as a second father figure to William and Harry after their mother's death—had suggested he visit the impoverished African country when the prince said he hoped to learn more about his mother's work.

Lesotho's statistics were bleak. Unemployment was at a staggering 50 percent, and life expectancy was less than forty years old for nearly 70 percent of the population. Nearly 25 percent of the adult population was infected with HIV—a number that rose to upward of 35 percent for childbearing women. Poverty, gender inequality, and the stigma associated with the disease all stood in the way of prevention and treatment of HIV and AIDS.

Harry—who spent two months with the orphaned children of Lesotho experiencing firsthand the widespread effects of the AIDS crisis—made a connection with Prince Seeiso of the country's royal family, who had recently lost his mother, Queen Mamohato.

Together they came up with the concept of Sentebale, an organization they officially founded in 2006 to support "the mental health and wellbeing of children and young people affected by HIV in Lesotho and Botswana." Both princes viewed Sentebale, which means "forget me not" in the country's language of Sesotho, as a way to honor their late mothers. Forget-me-nots were Diana's favorite flower.

Among all the subjects Harry and Meghan talked about that first night in Soho House, Africa was the one that they instantly bonded over. Meghan said that she'd love to go back and see more of the continent—and Harry had clearly been listening.

After Meghan said yes to the trip, a friend said she was "excited" but also wondering, "Is this crazy to go away like this?"

"It wasn't something she had done before," the friend continued. "But in the short time she had spent with him, and their daily phone conversations and text chats, she knew he was a good man. And a gentleman at that. Sometimes you just have to allow yourself to get swept up in these things—and that she did."

Having flown in from Toronto, Meghan spent one night with Harry at Kensington Palace before boarding an eleven-hour flight from London to Johannesburg the next morning. That was followed by two hours on a private light plane to Maun International Airport. Then they jumped into a 4×4 sport utility vehicle for a seventy-five-mile drive along the A3 National Route deep into a place many refer to as Africa's last Eden.

When it came to Africa's natural beauty, in Harry's mind nothing beat the Okavango Delta—the stunning 5,800-square-mile wetland at the center of Botswana's safari country, one of the last remaining wildlife habitats, and where he was secretly taking Meghan. He had visited the same part of the world before with Chelsy—first traveling the waterway on the houseboat the *Kubu Queen* in 2005 and again in 2009 for three nights at the five-star Shakawe River Lodge. For his romantic getaway with Meghan, he chose Meno A Kwena (translated as "teeth of the crocodile"), a safari camp on the edge of Makgadikgadi Pans National Park.

Six miles from any other safari camp (rare for the area), Meno A Kwena provided the couple with maximum privacy, not only from press but also from other tourists. On the wall of the resort is a framed photo of Harry's grandparents the Queen and Prince Philip from when they made a state visit to Botswana in 1979. Also on the wall: a portrait of Sir Seretse Khama, the first president of Botswana, and his white, English wife, Ruth Williams. The couple created a furor when they married in 1948. (Their story was made into a film, *A United Kingdom*, starring David Oyelowo and Rosamund Pike, in 2016.)

Harry and Meghan spent much of their trip in one of the $1,957-a-night deluxe tents. The word "tent" might be somewhat of a misnomer for the fully serviced accommodation at Meno A Kwena. With teak king-size beds covered in cozy hand-woven comforters for when the temperature drops at night, the rooms at the campsite are far more akin to luxury cabins. Each tent has its own private terrace and a fully equipped en suite bathroom, featuring solar-powered hot water on tap, pressurized showers, and Egyptian cotton towels, making this a rather plush camping experience. The comfortable space always made for a welcome sight after a day out on safari for the couple.

A typical outing started with an early breakfast served on the deck outside their room—usually bacon and eggs for Harry, and fruit and yogurt for Meghan. They then packed up their essentials for the day ahead, including boxed lunches provided by the camp kitchen. Meghan made sure to pack sunscreen for both (especially handy for Harry, who burned easily and often forgot to use SPF protection).

The couple also spent nights away from the site on a specially organized safari of the Makgadikgadi Pans. Although Meghan is a well-traveled and an adventurous woman, a friend said she did find that sleeping outside took a bit of getting used to. Hearing random calls of birds or the grunt of a hippo or other animals in the middle of the night did not lend itself to a great night's sleep. Harry was used to the sounds of the bush and so was the perfect person to have by her side.

Meghan could be forgiven if she didn't find sleeping in the heart of a truly wild and remote part of Africa easy at first because she proved to be a versatile traveler, which Harry loved. In fact, she brought only one backpack on the trip (albeit a large one). Extremely organized, Meghan immediately impressed Harry with her packing skills. She has always taken pride in being a great packer—going as far as layering dryer sheets in between her clothes to keep them smelling fresh and no matter her destination always bringing tea-tree oil for bites, cuts, and pimples—and her skills were appreciated by the prince.

"The fact that Meghan has always been so comfortable with doing away with luxuries and embracing natural surroundings is something that Harry has always really loved about her," a friend of the couple revealed. "I remember Meghan once joking that she can manage to pack even less than he does when they go away!"

If he worried that he was bringing along a high-maintenance Hollywood actress on safari, Harry was delightfully surprised by Meghan's down-to-earth attitude. While camping, she cleaned her face with baby wipes and happily wandered into the woodlands if she needed a bathroom break. Spending five days of uninterrupted time together gave the new couple a chance to get to know each other and discover that they shared a curiosity about the world and a laid-back nature.

"It's this love of adventure and sharing these exciting experiences that brought them so close together in the first place," said a close friend of the couple. "The fact that they're both as happy as just throwing on a backpack and going out to explore . . . I honestly think these experiences will never stop for them."

After Harry and Meghan's visit to Botswana, Meghan went home by herself and Harry moved on to Malawi to spend three weeks working with the organization African Parks, which manages an ecologically diverse portfolio of national parks in Africa.

After Meghan had departed for home, Harry worked alongside volunteers, veterinarians, and experts in one of the largest and most significant elephant relocations in history, moving five hundred elephants.

Harry helped safely move elephant herds from Majete and Liwonde to help replenish stocks in the Nkhotakota Wildlife Reserve. "Elephants simply can't roam freely like they used to, without coming into conflict with communities, or being threatened by poaching and persecution," Harry said. "To allow the coexistence of people and animals, fences are increasingly having to be used to separate the two and try to keep the peace."

The wildlife conservationist and veterinarian Dr. Andre Uys rode in a helicopter with Harry that flushed elephant families from woods onto a floodplain. Andre safely tranquilized them to move them almost two hundred miles away to a safer place, and Harry would tag the elephants using a nontoxic temporary spray paint. "Harry's dedication to conservation is admirable. His passion for helping preserve wildlife clearly comes from the heart," Andre said, adding that Harry "got involved like everyone else. One of the team."

When Meghan returned from Africa, a friend said, "She came back smiling and just completely spellbound." Her phone was *full* of photos—the nature they had seen, candid snaps of herself, and selfies with Harry. According to the friend, if Meghan didn't have to return to Canada for work and Harry to his life in London, "they would have happily spent the entire summer there together." It wasn't just the beauty of the place that had made the trip so idyllic. Meghan said that she and Harry talked so much, about things she rarely shared with anyone.

"I've never felt that safe," Meghan told her friend, "that close to someone in such a short amount of time."

4

The World Gets Wind

Harry felt that familiar buzz of excitement when his flight from London touched down at Toronto's Pearson International Airport on October 28. Once again, after another agonizingly month-long separation, he was just minutes from being reunited with his girlfriend.

With months of clandestine meet-ups under their respective belts, with no one the wiser, they had their undercover dating routine down pat. The prince took commercial flights, as he always did. (Although he was usually the last on the plane and the first off.) But in an effort to maintain a low profile, he flew into Toronto with just one plainclothes protection officer instead of his normal two. And he'd seen to it that a generic-looking sedan would be waiting just outside the terminal to whisk him the twelve miles to Meghan's two-story wine-colored townhouse in the city's Seaton Village neighborhood, their safe haven.

Ever since the couple's trip to Africa, their romance had been on a fast track. "Technically the getaway was just their third date," said a friend about Botswana, "but by then, they were each already dancing around the idea that this just may be a forever thing."

For Meghan, she was all in. Nothing could get her to slow down, not even a friend who cautioned her about getting involved with Harry. The British pal warned her from the prince because of the tabloids. "They hate royal wives and girlfriends. They will come after you," he said. "Look at Diana." But so much had changed since the time of Diana, Meghan reasoned: "How bad could it be?"

Another friend warned her off because of the tabloids, but for a very different reason: Harry's wild reputation as portrayed in the media. The British press, which had connected him with a different girl almost every month, made him appear as though he wasn't settling down anytime soon. That was enough for the friend to tell Meghan to "be careful." But Meghan couldn't reconcile the tabloid persona with the earnest man she felt so close to now. "He's a really nice guy," she insisted. "Very sweet, very genuine."

Even though Harry was a prince, he was just like any young adult in that he had gone through experiences that pushed him to face adulthood. By the time he met Meghan, Harry had undergone a huge evolution through his experience in the military.

Military service is a rite of passage for male members of the British royal family. Prince Charles served in the Royal Navy, as did his father, Prince Philip. Prince William completed more than seven years of military service. (He was an active Search and Rescue pilot when he married Kate.) For Harry, though, the military was much more than just a rite of passage—it was a chance for him to see the world as a normal human being, and it provided a source of great purpose.

Ever since he was a little boy riding atop a tank while accompanying his parents on an official engagement, Harry had wanted to serve his country. After completing his training at Sandhurst, there were debates both publicly and privately about whether

Harry could serve in the war in Iraq, already several years old at that point. There was a need for forward air controllers like himself in the conflict zone, but his high profile presented a host of complications. Yet Harry was adamant he wouldn't be "held back at home twiddling my thumbs." And in February 2007, it looked as though he was headed to the front lines when the UK Ministry of Defence and the Palace issued a joint statement that Harry would be going to Iraq to take up a "normal troop commander's role involving leading a group of twelve men in four Scimitar armored reconnaissance vehicles, each with a crew of three." But Iraqi insurgents issued their own statement that quickly put the kibosh on Harry's deployment.

"We are awaiting the arrival of the young, handsome, spoilt prince with bated breath and we confidently expect he will come out into the open on the battlefield," said Abu Zaid, the commander of the Malik Ibn Al Ashtar Brigade. "We will be generous with him. For we will return him to his grandmother—but without ears."

In public, Harry had put on a brave face. Privately his dreams had been dashed. Everything he worked for had been jeopardized because of his Royal birthright. Harry was devastated. His commanding officers knew something needed to be done.

The patriotic royal wouldn't be sent to the Middle East as a soldier for another year. After a media blackout was negotiated so the Taliban wouldn't be alerted to Harry's whereabouts, it was none other than his grandmother the Queen and commander in chief of the British Armed Forces who delivered the news. "She told me I'm off to Afghanistan," said Harry, who on December 14, 2007, boarded a C-17 military aircraft in Oxfordshire bound for Kandahar, Afghanistan.

Two days later he was aboard a Chinook helicopter with Special Forces headed to Forward Operating Base Dwyer in the Helmand province. Close to the Pakistan border, it was one of the most dangerous places on the planet. In the military, Harry was known as Second Lieutenant Wales. Once he hit the ground in Afghanistan, he was simply "Widow Six Seven."

Like the rest of the soldiers, Harry could be called to duty at any moment, scrambling out of the makeshift canvas tent from which the British flag hung in the dead of night. "One minute you're in bed asleep," he said, "six and a half minutes later you're speaking to someone on the ground who is being shot at."

As Christmas approached and the media blackout continued, the rest of the world had no idea Harry was due to join the Gurkhas at Forward Operating Base Delhi, a military expeditionary base occupied by the United States Marine Corps, in Garmsir.

While Harry patrolled the dusty, bombed out terrain of Helmand—the camp had been repeatedly attacked by RPGs, mortars, and machine gun fire from the Taliban since the British took over the base—his grandmother gave her annual Christmas address praising the British troops in Afghanistan. "I want to draw attention to another group of people who deserve our thoughts this Christmas," she said in the televised recording. "We have all been conscious of those who have given their lives, or who have been severely wounded, while serving with the Armed Forces in Iraq and Afghanistan." It was not a safe place for a British prince, and certainly not the third in line to the throne.

Ten weeks into his fourteen-week tour of duty, an Australian tabloid breached the news embargo by revealing that Harry was secretly serving in Afghanistan. Evacuated from the war zone within the hour, a deflated Harry was met by his father and brother when he touched down at RAF Brize Norton back in the UK.

While Harry described being "broken" by the experience of leaving his soldiers not of his own accord, he almost immediately started working on making his way back to the front lines—this time as an Apache helicopter pilot.

At the start of 2009, Harry enrolled in the Army Air Corps

to begin training as a helicopter pilot at RAF Middle Wallop in Hampshire. The prince was committed to the grueling training and examinations required to get his pilot's license. By mid-2009, Harry passed the first phase of his training, which he described as the "easiest way of getting back on the front line, maybe safer, maybe not safer, I don't know." In the summer of 2010, he enrolled in the second phase. The prince had impressed his commanding officers enough that he was afforded the opportunity to train as an Apache pilot, which only two percent of British pilots achieve. The attack helicopter, equipped with antitank missiles, rockets, and a chain gun, was used in thousands of battles and rescue operations in Afghanistan because of its lethal nature.

He flew to the United States in October 2011 to complete the final phase of his training. Harry spent the last days of his training at the Naval Air Facility in El Centro just north of San Diego (often referred to as the Top Gun school) and the Gila Bend Auxiliary Air Force Base in southern Arizona near the Mexican border. The desert training—which prepares pilots with air-to-ground bombing skills, rocket firing, and mobile land target practice—is as close as pilots get to actual air combat. NAF El Centro is the most rigorous training in the world and prepares Naval and Marine Corps military personnel as well as Army Green Berets and Allied pilots from Britain, France, Germany, and Italy. When it was over, Harry was cleared to return to Afghanistan.

Harry arrived back in the Islamic Republic in September 2012 as a copilot gunner with the 662 Squadron, 3 Regiment Army Air Corps. This time, it was with full knowledge of the public, and within a week of his arrival, nineteen members of the Taliban, armed with rocket-propelled grenades, mortars, and automatic weapons stormed his fortified base camp. Inside the camp, the gunmen started firing their RPGs and Kalashnikov AK-47s in a gun battle that lasted for more than five hours.

A few days earlier, the Taliban had announced "Harry Operations," which was just as its name sounded. Their goal was to kill or injure the prince. Under the cover of night, the insurgents, pretending to be farmers from a nearby maize plantation, got past the floodlights and armed guards keeping watch from towers to breach the thirty-foot wire fence topped with barbed wire. "We attacked that base because Prince Harry was also on it," a Taliban spokesman said.

While it had been assumed that a plan for emergencies was in place to shuttle Harry to a "panic room," a source close to the prince shared that there were zero special arrangements made for Harry on the base or anywhere in theater. Should he be attacked, his response would be the same as any other serviceman. After all, he was trained to fire a gun for a reason. "Harry was aware of the risks against him, and the blackout deal was brokered to try to ensure that the enemy had no idea where he was, so that he would not be specifically targeted," said the source.

Despite the obvious danger, Harry was grateful to be allowed to finish his twenty-week tour of duty. The military provided Harry with much needed structure, camaraderie, and anonymity. In Afghanistan, Harry lived like every other soldier at Camp Bastion where he was stationed. In the confined space of a dusty VHR (Very High Readiness) tent, the prince made his own bed and passed the time by playing Uckers, a board game popular with Royal Navy personnel, and *FIFA 07* on the Xbox. Harry tried his best to lie low, even going to the base's canteen late, after most of the other soldiers had cleared out, so there were fewer people to gawk at him during mealtime.

"My father's always trying to remind me about who I am and stuff like that," Harry said when he returned home in January 2013, "but it's very easy to forget about who I am when I am in the army." Never a fan of the stuffier side of royal duties, Harry, better known as Captain Wales, was at home in the no-frills, hands-on world of a soldier.

It's not surprising, then, that when he made the "tough decision" to end his ten-year career with the British Army in 2015, Harry found himself at loose ends. Anger and anxiety started to bubble to the surface, and neither emotion fit into the official persona of a prince. At royal engagements, he suffered panic attacks. In the most proper and officious of settings, such as a reception by MapAction to mark Harry's new patronage of the humanitarian emergency response charity, the flight-or-fight instincts of an Apache helicopter pilot kicked in. A source remembered that when Harry left the event held at the Royal Society in London, "He just started taking in deep breaths.

"The people, the cameras, the attention," the source said. "He had just let it get to him. He was on the edge."

Harry described the phenomenon himself. "In my case, every single time I was in any room with loads of people, which is quite often, I was just pouring with sweat," he told the UK army channel Forces TV, "my heart beating—boom, boom, boom, boom—literally, just like a washing machine."

During both his tours, Harry saw the kind of action that doesn't leave a soldier's mind even long after he or she has come home. His first tour in Afghanistan, when he was serving as a joint terminal attack controller on the ground, he directed the support aircrafts in an emergency medical evacuation when the Afghanistan National Army came under fire from the Taliban and took heavy casualties.

The seriously injured were in the process of being airlifted back to camp by a Chinook when suddenly Harry's position came under attack from the Taliban. Harry was ordered to dig in and take cover as the rockets rained down. One exploded to devastating effect a mere fifty meters from where the prince was.

The photographer John Stillwell, part of the Press Association team embedded with Harry in Afghanistan while he was on operational duties, initially thought Harry would be shielded from some of the more dangerous missions. But that notion was totally dispelled when he and everyone else in the prince's tank found themselves to be sitting ducks for a sniper's bullet as they waited for help in a riverbed.

Stillwell, riding in the prince's tank, remembered coming around the outskirts of a town and about to cross the creek when the lead vehicle in their convoy spotted an IED in the road.

"Before I went to Afghanistan I thought, 'Oh, Harry will be at Camp Bastion, thirty feet underground, miles away from danger,'" the photographer said. "I was totally wrong. He was in very real danger a lot of the time, but he took it all in his stride.

"When you think of him being a prince, the Queen's grandson, he could have had a cushy office job," Stillwell added. "But he chose to do the hard stuff, go out on the front line."

While the prince's heroism earned him accolades from the public and his fellow servicemen, it wasn't without a price. After retiring from military service, when Harry wasn't suffering from anxiety, he had bouts of rage. "I took up boxing, because everyone was saying boxing is good for you and it's a really good way of letting out aggression," he said. "That really saved me because I was on the verge of punching someone, so being able to punch someone who had pads was certainly easier."

Boxing, however, wasn't a sufficient bandage for the internal conflict raging within him. Harry was, as he put it, "very close to total breakdown on numerous occasions when all sorts of grief and lies and misconceptions are coming to you from every angle."

While his experiences on the front lines contributed to his emotional state, it wasn't the complete answer to his issues. And the worst part was, he didn't know what exactly was happening. "I just couldn't put my finger on it," Harry said. "I just didn't know what was wrong with me."

If the struggle was hardest on anyone other than Harry, it was William. The brothers were bound not only by blood and royal titles but also by the unique tragedy of losing their mother at such a young age and in such a public way. "Every year we get closer," Harry told reporters in 2005. "Ever since our mother died, obviously we were close. But he is the one person on this earth who I can actually really . . . we can talk about anything. We understand each other and give each other support."

That mutual support between brothers took many forms—everything from renting a cottage together when both were training at a Shropshire flight school in 2009, to both becoming helicopter pilots, to setting up the Royal Foundation, the umbrella organization for all their philanthropic work, the same year. Even once William got married and started a family, the two still found time for fun. According to a source, the brothers enjoyed sneaking out for drinks and food at a place called Mari Vanna about a mile away from the Palace. The Russian restaurant is a favored locale for some the world's wealthiest oligarchs, but it's also a very private place. "Most of the look-at-me action takes place across the road at Mr. Chow," said a staffer. Inside the restaurant, gaudily decorated with glass chandeliers, Russian dolls, looming bookcases full of antique tomes, and lounge chairs, the brothers were afforded a rare bit of privacy. One night in early 2016, they both got "totally drunk," according to the source. But it wasn't until Harry went outside to smoke that there was a problem. "He fell into a little bush. Someone tried to take a photo of him on their phone and Harry's protection officer literally jumped to block them from taking it," the source said. "Harry was none the wiser. He just went back in to William, so they could carry on drinking."

Each brother wanted real happiness for the other. It was precisely because of this that William confronted his brother in 2015 about his mental health. As Harry later recounted in a podcast interview with the columnist and friend Bryony Gordon, who herself has obsessive-compulsive disorder, he said, "You really need to deal with this. It is not normal to think that nothing has affected you."

Those words broke through to Harry and spurred him to begin the daunting process of true soul-searching, including therapy, which is no small thing for a member of the House of Windsor.

In his open, honest manner, the prince revealed how before he came to terms with his own pain he had felt completely overwhelmed by the demands of public life. For two years, Harry said, he was in "total chaos."

It didn't take many conversations about his feelings for Harry to realize that he had a lot of unprocessed grief from his mother's death. It was a trauma that he never had the chance or ability to cope with before then. When he lost his mother at the age of twelve, his sorrow had been immediately subsumed by the grief of an entire country, which turned into conspiracies and other national obsessions. Meanwhile, Harry and William had to put on brave faces for all of England and the world. The first and only time he let himself cry over his mother was at her burial on September 6, 1997, on the island within the lake on the grounds of her family home, Althorp Park.

Harry described himself as having "shut down" all thoughts and feelings about his mother's death for nearly two decades. "I thought that thinking of her was only going to make me sad and not going to bring her back," he said, reasoning, "right, don't ever let your emotions be part of anything."

Talking about his feelings turned out to be the best medicine— and part of the inspiration for the single biggest project the princes had ever undertaken together.

In April 2016, William, Kate, and Harry launched Heads Together, a campaign to reduce the stigma surrounding mental health. The goal was to change the conversation about mental health so millions might feel safer getting the help they needed. William, Kate, and Harry hoped that if they opened up about mental health, others in the UK, where the British stiff upper lip prevailed, would feel they had permission to do the same.

William and Harry credited Kate for the initiative's genesis, saying the original concept was scribbled on the back of a cigarette pack one night. With much of her humanitarian work focused on early-childhood development and addiction, the Duchess of Cambridge had become an outspoken proponent of mental health awareness. She believed the root of many unresolved adolescent problems could be traced to mental illness, which, if left untreated, often manifested as greater societal problems later in life.

While Heads Together, a flagship initiative for the Royal Foundation, might have been Kate's brainchild, it was Harry's radical public admission of his personal struggles during one of the darkest periods in his life that imbued the mental health initiative with real impact. A year after the launch of the charity, Harry stunned the world when he bravely shared his decades-long repression of grief over his mother's death, his subsequent anger and anxiety issues, and the confusion he felt about the source of his problems on Bryony's podcast, which brought a lot of publicity for his cause but also broke with convention.

William and Harry had never spoken so candidly about their mother, and certainly they had never shared in the press the immense pain they felt in the aftermath of her death. It was a watershed moment that defied the stereotype of the royal family.

It was a brave and bold decision for Harry to open up about the anguish he suffered over the years. He was helping untold millions with his candid confession. Yet some Palace courtiers privately questioned whether the "soul baring" had gone a step too far, setting the wrong precedent and exposing William and Harry in the future. After all, the royal family normally revealed very little and certainly never addressed such intimate struggles.

At the time, his father didn't comment on his son's confession, although in 2019, Prince Charles said he was "proud" of his son's work to remove the stigma of mental health struggles. Though there was no public response from the Queen to his admission, the mere fact that Harry was launching a public mental health campaign with his brother and sister-in-law implied that he had the tacit approval of his grandmother. Harry's personal revelations weren't a break from protocol; they were a move forward for the monarchy within the confines of its rules.

Only Harry, however, could have gotten away with such an admission. It had nothing to do with playing favorites. There were stricter confines for his brother, because he was direct heir to the throne. The same dynamic was true for Prince Andrew, who had been continually given chances after making major missteps or lapses in judgment. Until his association with American financier and convicted sex offender Jeffrey Epstein, Andrew got to keep going on as a working member of the royal family after behavior that would never have flown with Charles. There is a different level of protocol for direct heirs to the throne.

Harry was proud of the two and a half years in which he not only prioritized his royal duties but was "able to take my private life seriously as well." Three months later, when he joined his brother at a private service at Althorp House to rededicate Diana's grave on what would have been her 56th birthday, Harry could honestly say that he was a changed man. By his own admission he put "blood, sweat, and tears into the things that really make a difference," both for himself and others.

But even as he hit his stride as a public figure, Harry still struggled to find a soul mate. His brother, William, had been lucky enough to settle down with a woman he first met at the age of nineteen, while Harry had two failed long-term relationships and a history of bad headlines. William and Kate's successful courtship and marriage, however, was more than just luck. William went to university, which allowed him to meet new friends in a protected environment. At St. Andrews, in Fife, Scotland, he developed his social skills without intrusion from the press, because of an agreement with the British media, including tabloids, that he would be left alone while at university. In that safe space, he met Kate, who, except for a three-month split in 2007, has always been someone William could lean on and trust.

In a committed relationship, William didn't always understand Harry's interest in London nightlife. He checked out the scene with Kate now and then, but it was a very different experience as part of a couple.

During his 2013 tour of Afghanistan, Harry admitted being "very jealous of my brother . . . back home he gets to go home to his wife and dog." Whether he was "stuck playing PlayStation in a tent full of men" while on active duty or playing *Call of Duty* and ordering pizzas from PizzaExpress (a favorite of the princes) to his modest Kensington Palace apartment that he moved into once he returned, Harry led a relatively solitary life. His longing for his own family only grew as William and Kate expanded theirs with a second child after the birth of Princess Charlotte on May 2, 2015.

All combined, Harry had changed, from the impulsive prince Meghan had been told about by the friend who cautioned against dating him, to the man, ready to find love, in front of her.

Bringing Meghan to Botswana, one of the most sacred and special places in his life, was a symbol of how he felt about her. She was smart, independent, adventurous, optimistic, and beautiful. But perhaps most important to Harry, Meghan came across as authentic. With Meghan, he knew she wasn't trying to impress him. He felt as though he was getting the real Meghan from day one.

Just three months into their relationship, a Meghan pal said, they had already begun swapping the words "I love you." It was Harry who said the three little but very loaded words first, but Meghan immediately replied, "I love you, too." From there it didn't take long for them to begin talking in non-oblique terms about their future.

In another display of affection, Meghan left inside jokes and references littered across her Instagram feed. There was her July reference to a "date night for one," on the evening she spent alone in her hotel room during one of the first trips when she met Harry, and her posting a photo of two kissing matches with the caption "Sunday kind of love" on July 17. Then came the pretty displays of peonies that were presumably a gift from one Captain Wales. "Swooning over these," she wrote on July 1. More flowers came two weeks later. "Because I'm spoiled rotten," she said, alongside the hashtag #theynevergetold.

Harry also showed his feelings by traveling to Toronto three times between August and October. Fearing his famed ginger locks would be an easy spot, they had both largely avoided going out to her favorite haunts, such as Bar Isabel and Terroni, preferring to hunker down at the three-bedroom, two-bath house she began renting in the summer of 2013, right around the time of her divorce.

When Meghan moved in, it was the largest place she had ever had to herself—and to furnish. Meghan decorated like she dressed. She was a big fan of mixing high- and low-end products. While she may have had some decent art to hang on the walls (it was an occasional payday treat to pick up a small piece for her growing collection), for some of her furniture and home accessories she often turned to affordable places such as HomeSense, IKEA, and even Home Depot. "Money in the bank doesn't mean money to spend" was the advice her father gave her as a teen, and she still took that to heart.

She eventually treated herself to the ceramic kamado-style Big Green Egg barbecue she had had in her Internet bookmarks for a year; the large patio space was perfect for entertaining. With its deck, beachy décor, and large open windows to the rear, the space reminded her a little of California. Friendly neighbors, mostly families, lived in the closely grouped houses centered around a good public school and dog park where Meghan's rescue dog, Bogart, could frolic.

Although Meghan didn't grow up with pets, Bogs, as she called him, became the object of her devotion and in heavy rotation on her Instagram feed. But she credits Ellen DeGeneres as the reason she adopted the Lab mix.

Meghan was cuddling with Bogart at the animal shelter that had rescued him and his brother in Los Angeles when the daytime talk show host walked in with her wife, actress Portia de Rossi.

"Is that your dog?" Ellen asked Meghan.

"No," Meghan answered.

The two women had never met. And although Meghan, of course, knew Ellen, Ellen had no idea who she was. Still, the famous comedian said to her, "You have to take that dog."

"Well, I'm deciding . . ."

"Rescue the dog!" Ellen ordered.

Ellen left the rescue center, but as soon as she walked outside, she tapped on the window and yelled to Meghan, "Take the dog!"

How could she refuse? "It's sort of like if Oprah tells you to do something," Meghan said. "I brought him home. Because Ellen told me to."

She didn't regret the decision. In fact, two years later, she adopted another rescue—a beagle she named Guy after meeting him at an adoption event organized by the Ontario-based charity A Dog's Dream Rescue.

Now her sweet dogs ran underfoot as Meghan whipped up her signature roast chicken for the prince sitting in her sleek, all-white chef's kitchen.

While Harry and Meghan kept a low profile, the prince's presence could not go unnoticed in her neighborhood. It didn't take long for Harry's visits to become an open secret among the residents of Seaton Village. As one of Meghan's neighbors said, "When a black SUV was parked with guys inside wearing headsets and eating burritos, we'd say, 'Hey, Harry's in town!'" But the news never went further than the Seaton Village community Facebook page, typically devoted to discussions about shoveling snow and dog poop. Toronto doesn't have the kind of paparazzi presence of New York, LA, or London, because there is not a large Canadian celebrity media industry to serve.

But Harry and Meghan didn't just spend time together in London and Canada. Letting their closest friends in on their secret had been key. Not worried that any of their dearest confidants would out them, they instead found themselves with a multitude of accomplices willing to help them hide.

One of Harry's oldest friends, Arthur Landon, offered the couple the use of his LA home for a week. The son of the late brigadier Tim Landon—known as the White Sultan, or Landon of Arabia, because of the peaceful coup he is said to have helped organize in Oman and the fortune he made there—Arthur is one of the wealthiest young men in Britain. The onetime model and filmmaker, who had always tried to look out for Harry since the two became friends at Eton College, called the woman who sold the naked photos of the prince during the trip they took together to Las Vegas "despicable."

Knowing firsthand what lengths people would go to in order to get a picture of Harry and his personal life, Arthur told the prince that the best place he could stay in LA while visiting with Meghan was his house. Arthur's bohemian-style West Hollywood spread sits in the lowest part of the Hills, with a pool and views of Sunset Boulevard. It was a prime, and private, location from which Harry had his first chance to visit Meghan's native city. The trip—during which they spent almost the entire time at the house in hiding—is also when Harry met Doria for the first time.

Unable to venture to Doria's two-bedroom house in the neighborhood of Windsor Hills, Harry and Meghan invited her over to their temporary LA digs. (Although the couple was holed up, that didn't stop Meghan from having Harry taste dishes from some of her favorite local restaurants, including Sushi Park, which she said has "the most delicious sashimi," by using a delivery app.) While

Meghan may have been nervous for her mom to meet Harry for the first time, Doria was as cool as ever. It takes a lot to faze the yoga instructor, although she later told a colleague at the mental health clinic where she worked that the experience of meeting a prince who also happened to be dating her daughter was "a little surreal."

Although she talked with Doria about the guys she dated, Meghan didn't make it a habit of introducing them to her mom until the relationship was further down the line. But she wanted to put Doria at ease and show her that even though Harry was a worldwide public figure, he was also a good man. "Meghan didn't want her worrying about anything," says a source. "She wanted her mom to see the real Harry. The man she was falling in love with."

Harry also wanted to impress Meghan's mother when he first met her. Not with gifts, but through his words and actions. Often one to worry what others think of him, he wanted to prove that he was different from the royals depicted in the British tabloids. And it worked. Doria came away impressed by his compassion, empathy, and level of activism. As a friend said, "She could see he was genuine."

During those first months of their relationship, when their news was still a secret, Meghan went to the UK at least three times. Each time she arrived at the airport, Harry made sure a driver was waiting for her—no fancy Rolls-Royce or chauffeur in uniform, just someone from a local corporate taxi company that he and other members of the royal family used on occasion.

Markus, however, could always be counted on to find a cozy, luxurious, and hidden spot for the couple. He put them up at a private four-bedroom cottage tucked away from the main members' Soho Farmhouse. In Oxfordshire, barely an hour and a half outside of London, it was the perfect retreat from the city. Although the stone house stood on one hundred acres of English countryside, they still enjoyed sashimi and other Japanese dishes delivered to their cottage from Pen Yen, one of the restaurants on the property.

During a fall visit Markus arranged for the couple to spend a weekend at Babington House, an eighteenth-century manor house in Somerset that Soho House had converted into one of their vacation properties. Harry and Meghan's accommodations included a roaring open fire and a butler—another secret getaway the press never found out about.

It wasn't long before Meghan was feeling so confident in their pairing, so emboldened by their ability to hide in plain sight, that she even had Harry join her as she walked her dogs along their favorite paths through Toronto's Trinity Bellwoods Park. A hoodie and a baseball cap were enough to obscure Harry's famous face during his visit to the city. Most Canadians never looked twice anyway at the young couple wearing matching beaded blue bracelets they picked up in Botswana. (Bracelets are a signature item of the prince's, and each has its own meaning and importance. A silver band with engravings that he's worn religiously since 2001 came from his 1997 trip to Africa after his mother died. William has been photographed wearing a similar bracelet.)

They especially didn't feel like spending Halloween weekend in hiding, as there was much to celebrate. Some four months into their relationship, they were madly in love and eager to take part in the fun of one of their favorite holidays. The evening of October 29, with Harry in town, the couple decided to go to a big costume party being thrown at Soho House in Toronto. Harry and Meghan both had on Venetian-style masks, hiding their true identities to other partygoers.

Surrounded by the establishment's exclusive clientele and confident due to a rule that discouraged patrons from surreptitiously snapping pictures with their phones, Harry and Meghan felt at ease. It wasn't their first time at the club. During a previous visit, they had stepped into the bar's photo booth together, keeping the strip of snapshots as a souvenir.

They also weren't alone. The pair turned up at the Halloween bash with Harry's cousin Princess Eugenie and her longtime boy-friend, Jack Brooksbank, who was in Toronto for work as a brand ambassador for George Clooney and Rande Gerber's tequila brand, Casamigos. Harry and Meghan had already been out on two double dates with them.

Eugenie had always been more than just a cousin to Harry. They were also the closest of friends. Out of all the Queen's grand-children, Harry and Eugenie have one of the most natural con-nections. Like Harry, Eugenie is loyal, honest, and great fun. The two had many nights out together in London, sneaking into back entrances of clubs, such as Mahiki, where Jack once was manager, or Tonteria, where in one of the VIP cave areas, they downed shots from Mexican skull-shaped glasses and a giant frozen margarita (with multiple straws). Harry had so much fun at the club co-owned by one of Harry's close childhood pals, Guy Pelly, he partied there four nights in one week of July 2014.

Although they grew up in different places (she at Royal Lodge in Windsor Great Park, he at Kensington Palace in London), the close relationship between their mothers brought them together. Sarah Ferguson would often bring her daughters to tea with Diana, William, and Harry at Kensington Palace. After both women's di-vorces were finalized in 1996, the single mothers took their kids on vacation together to the South of France. (It was Harry who later ensured that his aunt Sarah was invited to the wedding ceremony and first reception—quite the feat considering that Prince Philip reportedly once said he never wanted to be in the same room as her again.) Like Harry, Eugenie also struggled to carve out her own identity growing up. Not being in a senior role meant that she had to go out into the world and find her own path, which she had done, moving to New York in 2013 to work at Paddle8, the auction house run by Misha's husband and Harry's friend Alexander.

Harry had always confided in his cousin when it came to the women in his life. Not only did he trust her implicitly, but friends say that she gives great advice and has always been "beyond wise" for her years. It's not surprising, then, that Eugenie was one of the first in the family to know about his relationship with Meghan. Although she was the one to introduce Harry to her good friend Cressida (they used to double-date as well), she was nothing but encouraging about his new relationship. In fact, Eugenie, who'd long wanted to see her cousin settle down and be happy, told friends she loved Meghan and that she was "just the tonic" for him.

On that late October night in Toronto, Harry was happy, and so was Meghan.

A cocktail or so into the party, they were both feeling relaxed, absorbing the Halloween spirit.

It was possibly the perfect night out—until they received a call from one of Harry's aides at Kensington Palace. It wasn't good news.

The Sunday Express was going to run with the story of their relationship—and the tabloid was rumored to have been tipped off by an employee of none other than Eugenie and her father, Prince Andrew.

With the news about to blast out to every corner of the Internet that everyone's favorite bachelor was off the market, Harry and Meghan's night of revelry threatened to turn into a melee.

Harry and Meghan left the party and returned to her house. Their main worry was that her place would be besieged by photographers within twenty-four hours. They had a little time to think, because there were only a couple of paparazzi in Toronto. (One of them had already texted Meghan to ask if the news was true; she didn't reply.) But it wouldn't be long before photographers flew in from New York and LA, all hoping to get that first picture of the happy couple. Another outlet, *Us Weekly*, had also confirmed their pairing and knew that they were together in Toronto but agreed with the Palace to hold off reporting the news until Harry had returned home.

Harry's phone wouldn't stop pinging with word from the Palace. Aides suggested it would be best for Harry to cut his trip short and quietly return to London, his minimal security now something of an issue. But the prince wasn't having it. He wasn't budging. If things were going to get tricky, there was nowhere else he'd rather be than at Meghan's side.

5

A Prince's Stand

When Harry and Meghan arrived at Jessica and Ben Mulroney's house the morning of October 30, they had at least slept through the craziness of the news blowing up.

They had made the decision to head to the Mulroneys' Upper Canada home the night before, after Harry was advised by an aide to stay somewhere discreet, somewhere no one in the media would think to look. Meghan had already been texting Jessica (or Jess, as friends called her) throughout the evening for moral support when her pal suggested that they were welcome to hide out at their place. Harry and Meghan agreed it was the perfect plan and decamped from Seaton Village early the following morning with bags packed.

It wasn't the first time they had been at the Mulroneys'. Before the world knew that Harry and Meghan were a couple, they had often visited the couple's home in the quiet, upscale neighborhood where Harry's security was less visible.

It was there that Meghan got a firsthand glimpse of how Harry might be as a father, falling hard as he expertly won over the Mulroneys' then six-year-old twins, Brian and John, and three-year-old daughter, Ivy. Already experienced in charming little ones, he never turned up empty-handed, instead arriving with small presents each visit. But it wasn't just his generosity that endeared him to the kids. Harry was also willing to get on the floor with them to play or smush up his face against the window, his funny expressions never failing to earn a giggle.

Now that the world knew Harry and Meghan's secret, they convened around the countertop in the open living room/kitchen space, so Jess and Ben could hear everything.

Meghan felt somewhat bittersweet about the situation. On the one hand, she was disappointed that their secret was out. It was no longer just the two of them. While Meghan, before she met Harry, had occasionally set up a paparazzi photo here and there or let info slip out to the press, she did everything in her power to protect the privacy of her relationship with the prince. She knew that keeping things quiet meant that they could get to know each other without pressure or further worries that came from reporters covering and commenting on their burgeoning romance.

But there was also a part of her that was relieved. She had struggled to keep the secret from friends and colleagues (only a handful of castmates and production staff at *Suits* knew) and didn't like lying about the purpose of her trips to London.

Harry knew this day was "inevitable" and had told Meghan as much soon after they met so they could, he explained, "make the most of this time we have." Of course, Meghan couldn't really understand what it would mean to be famous on the level Harry had been for his entire life. "We were very quietly dating for about six months before it became news," Meghan said later in *Vanity Fair*. "And right out of the gate it was surprising the way things changed."

After they were outed, Meghan received close to one hundred

messages in twenty-four hours from people she hadn't spoken to in months, even years. Everyone wanted to know: *Is the news true?*

Meghan's mother and father knew about her and Harry, of course, long before they were exposed. She had told Doria as soon as she returned to Toronto from her trip to London where they first met, and she had introduced her mother to the prince in Los Angeles. Meghan's dad didn't hear about her boyfriend until later that summer, after her visit to Botswana. In a *Good Morning Britain* interview, Thomas later shared, "She said, 'We'll have to call him "H" so no one knows.' I eventually spoke to him, and he was a very nice man, a gentleman, very likable." A source confirmed that Harry had spoken to her father several times over the phone in the first year of their relationship.

But for the rest of the world, this was major news. In addition to friends and acquaintances, Meghan also received messages from a few journalists she had swapped details with over the years. She didn't reply to anyone.

For the next three days—while friends, neighbors, and particularly *Suits* cast members texted Meghan to warn her of reporters and photographers appearing all over—the couple stayed at the Mulroneys'. Then Harry had to go back to London for work, leaving Meghan in Toronto to deal with her new life of constant scrutiny.

Every move she made became front-page news, including attending classes at Moksha Yoga or shopping with Jessica at their favorite department store, Hudson's Bay, where they used to be able to spend uninterrupted hours.

Universal Cable, *Suits*'s production company, provided security to escort Meghan to and from the large studio in North York, near downtown Toronto. But the paparazzi quickly became familiar with her daily routines. Prior to meeting Harry, the only time she experienced cameras were on a set or a red carpet. The few paparazzi images of Meghan taken before she started dating Harry were mostly taken cooperatively.

The security was necessary. Shortly after the news broke, a photographer from an LA-based photo agency had scaled the fence into her back garden and waited for Meghan by her car, hoping to get a picture before she headed out to run errands. Meghan was terrified and immediately called the police. "This is how it's always going to be, isn't it?" she said to a friend at the time.

Not even a week after her romance was splashed across countless newspapers, magazines, and websites the world over, Meghan was back in the VIP section of Toronto Pearson, en route to London and Harry. Now that she knew photographers were on the hunt for her, she felt uneasy. Apart from the occasional *Suits* fan asking for a selfie, Meghan has always traveled undisturbed. This time, she decided upon a disguise. Nothing dramatic, just a Yankees baseball cap pulled down to shade her eyes. It seemed to do the trick.

After Meghan described how nerve-racking it was to travel now that she was officially the prince's girlfriend, Jessica arranged for her to use the private jet of the Canadian real estate power couple Krystal Koo and Michael Cooper. Jessica's longtime friends, the couple had run interference in the past for Harry and Meghan and were more than happy to help. Fancying a trip to London themselves, Krystal and Michael joked about hiding Meghan in one of the new suitcases that Meghan had bought when it became clear that there were to be a number of transatlantic trips in her future.

Traveling with familiar faces helped ease a bit of Meghan's anxiety, and once she landed in London, where she stayed with Harry at Kensington Palace, she was met with a sense of comfort. Starting to consider Britain as a potential future home, she began to establish her own life there.

A regular runner, she took to jogging through Kensington Gardens and then nipping out to the nearby Whole Foods to pick up whatever supplies she needed for dinner at Nottingham Cottage, which Meghan had already warmed up with a few little touches like Diptyque candles and a potted plant. (His garden with a little hammock was minimal, as "neither of them are green fingered.")

Arriving home laden down with shopping bags, she never had to worry about fumbling around for her ID. While your average Kensington Palace visitor must show two forms of legal identification to get through the gates, Meghan was now able to breeze past the guards without a second thought. She had ingratiated herself early with a polite handshake and an insistence that they refer to her only as Meghan. All that "Ms. Markle" nonsense was not her style. (Harry called Meghan "Meg," and she always referred to him as "H.")

It was clear to everyone who knew her how happy Meghan was—even her hair colorist. While she was living in Toronto, the actress went to Luis Pacheco every month for a touch-up or some gold highlights or chocolate brown lowlights that gave her hair a "rich, healthy, and reflective" look on and off camera. When Luis saw Meghan in November 2016, he noticed, "There was something really different about her. She looked so sweet and tender—she had this glow about her." He didn't know that the reason was Harry, or the fact that she was about to hop on a plane to see him again in London.

Whether Meghan was lunching at one of her favorite restaurants like Kurobuta, which served tapas-style Japanese on the Kings Road, perusing antiques and homewares at Portobello Market, or simply grocery shopping, Harry made it clear she didn't need to hide out behind the palace walls. Unbeknownst to her, the Whole Foods near the palace was a lunch spot for *Daily Mail* reporters since it was located right next to the tabloid's offices. While shopping there one day, she was spotted by a reporter who tailed Meghan back to the gates of the palace, snapping a picture on his phone. It was front-page news the following day: "Harry's Love Is in London!"

The British tabloid press was, in fact, having a field day with Harry's new girlfriend. Not that most publications ever seemed to need permission to go after someone before, but to them Meghan presented herself as particularly fair game. She had lived much of her adult life in the public eye, occasionally in sexy outfits, such as when she was on *Deal or No Deal*, which the papers had quickly unearthed. But it was the hints she left on her social media accounts—like the image of two spooning bananas she posted the day after her relationship with Harry went public—that made certain sections of the media think she was perhaps purposefully teasing them.

In royal circles, there is an unspoken code of silence expected from royal girlfriends who are expected to conduct themselves with the same discretion as members of the royal family itself. The press closely followed Meghan's various social media accounts and found lots of material they felt broke with this code. There were the matching bracelets, photos of trips to the Cotswolds, and more. Harry, known for his wicked sense of humor, enjoyed Meghan's coy posts. But the press came away with a different message: you can't plea for privacy *and* tease the media.

No matter how Meghan conducted herself online, there was never any justification for the racism that didn't take long to appear in stories about her. A headline in the *Daily Mail* in the first week of November referred to Meghan's upbringing as "Straight Outta Compton," going so far as to call her mother's neighborhood "gang-scarred." Three days later, the same British tabloid wrote that Meghan would have failed the "Mum Test." The article breathlessly detailed how "the Windsors will thicken their watery, thin blue blood and Spencer pale skin and ginger hair with some rich and exotic DNA." It went on to describe Meghan's mother as a "dreadlocked African-American lady from the wrong side of the tracks." These publications had sunk to a new low. Subtext turned into outright race-baiting as each day certain tabloids went one step further. A newspaper wrote that Meghan was "not in the society blonde style of previous girlfriends."

Racism in the UK takes a different form than it does in the United States, but there is no mistaking its existence and how engrained it is. A major theme of racism in the UK centers on the question of who is authentically "British." It can come through in subtle acts of bias, micro-aggressions such as the Palace staffer who told the biracial co-author of this book, "I never expected you to speak the way you do," or the *Daily Mail* headline, "Memo to Meghan: We Brits Prefer True Royalty to Fashion Royalty." While their columnist was criticizing Meghan for her *Vogue* editorials, there was another way to read it, and that was that to be British meant to be born and bred in the UK—and be white.

With anti-immigration sentiments rising amid fears of the country losing its British identity through its diverse elements, the idea of a nonwhite person moving into the House of Windsor ruffled feathers. Some took to Meghan's Twitter and Instagram accounts to express racist feelings that were anything but subtle, including calling her the N-word or a "mutt." Members of the royal family had dated and even married commoners, but no senior royal, apart from Princess Diana post-divorce, had ever publicly dated anyone who was not white. This was a real first.

Harry was incandescent with rage. For the prince, Meghan was his personal introduction to the ugliness of racism. While it might have been new territory for Harry, bias—both unconscious and intentional—had always been a part of Meghan's life.

The issue of skin color started for Meghan even before she was born, with her parents' marriage. Their romance was at once ordinary and radical since Thomas, the youngest of three boys from Newport, Pennsylvania, was white, and Doria, raised in LA, was black. "Growing up in a homogeneous community in Pennsylvania, the concept of marrying an African-American woman was not in the cards for my dad," Meghan wrote. "But he saw beyond what was put in front of him in that small-size (and, perhaps, small-minded) town."

The predominantly white community of Woodland Hills that Meghan lived in when she was a toddler was not always welcoming to Doria. Meghan described her mother's hurt at often being confused for her nanny because her skin tone was darker than her daughter's.

Meghan grew up being taught to embrace both parts of herself. When she was seven, Meghan awoke Christmas morning to find a large box, wrapped in glitter-flecked paper. Tearing open the gift, Meghan said, "I found my Heart Family: a black mom doll, a white dad doll, and a child in each color." Her dad had bought a number of Barbie family sets, taken them apart, and carefully created one that accurately reflected his daughter's reality. Her parents, as Meghan said, "crafted the world around me to make me feel like I wasn't different but special."

But they couldn't entirely keep ugly truths from infiltrating Meghan's childhood. One of her memories is from the 1992 riots in South-Central, sparked by the acquittal of the police officers involved in the brutal beating of Rodney King a year earlier. Eleven-year-old Meghan, home from school early because of the riots, watched the ash from street fires sift down on suburban lawns.

"Oh, my God, Mommy," she said. "It's snowing!"

Being biracial proposed a whole special set of obstacles. In the seventh grade, Meghan was asked to identify her ethnicity, either white or black, on a census in her English class. She didn't know how to answer. "You could only choose one, but that would be to choose one parent over the other—and one half of myself over the other," Meghan wrote. She left the box blank. Her father told her, "If that happens again, you draw your own box."

The last place she thought she would encounter ignorance was at college, but that was exactly what she found during her very first week at Northwestern. When one of her dorm mates asked leading questions about her black mother and white father and their divorce, Meghan sensed the woman's underlying judgment. In her nonconfrontational way, she extricated herself from the conversation. But she was left with a terrible feeling of having been forced to justify her very existence.

It was after college, though, that Meghan described her most jarring experience of hate. She was back home in LA when she witnessed her mother called the N-word as they pulled out of a parking space.

"My skin rushed with heat as I looked to my mom," she wrote. "Her eyes welling with hateful tears, I could only breathe out a whisper of words, so hushed they were barely audible: 'It's okay, Mommy.' I was trying to temper the rage-filled air permeating our small silver Volvo."

Emotions swirled inside her. She worried about her mother and their safety.

"We drove home in deafening silence, her chocolate knuckles pale from gripping the wheel so tightly."

It wasn't just big moments like the one in the parking lot that helped define Meghan's character; it was countless small ones as well. She came to despise the question "Where are you from?" Not easily identified, she knew what people were really curious about was her skin color. But Meghan didn't want to be defined by that.

"While my mixed heritage may have created a gray area surrounding my self-identification, keeping me with a foot on both sides of the fence, I have come to embrace that," she wrote in *ELLE*. "To say who I am, to share where I'm from, to voice my pride in being a strong, confident mixed-race woman."

Meghan might have fully accepted her unique identity, but there was no way she was going to accept attacks on her background and, more specifically, on her mother. With photographers camped out in front of Doria's home, some of the tabloids continued to publish inaccurate stories that rested on racist stereotypes of the struggling African American woman and completely ignored her mother's 2015 masters in social work and her position as a senior counselor within the geriatric community.

Harry refused to accept this either. The press wasn't Harry's only source of confrontation about Meghan being biracial. When he first started seeing her, Harry, sensitive to even the slightest hint of prejudice, had fallouts within his own tight circle. When some questioned his new relationship, and whether she was suitable, he would wonder, "Is this about race? Is it snobbery?"

An old friend of Harry's spent an afternoon gossiping about Meghan, making disparaging remarks about her Hollywood background. Word got back to Harry, and the prince immediately cut him off.

If he was willing to confront those close to him, when it came to the media, Harry was poised for outright war.

The international media frenzy around Meghan, which attracted daily clicks and newspaper sales in the high millions, reopened old childhood wounds. "Because she's been attacked so publicly, there must be a part of him that is reliving what happened to his mother at the hands of the tabloid press," a former senior courtier said.

The pain of the paparazzi's involvement in their mother's death hadn't diminished over the years for either prince.

"One of the hardest things to come to terms with is the fact that the people that chased her into the tunnel were the same people that were taking photographs of her while she was still dying in the back seat of the car," Harry said in a documentary released shortly before the twentieth anniversary of Princess Diana's death. "She'd had a quite severe head injury, but she was very much still alive in the back seat. And those people that caused the accident, instead of helping, were taking photographs of her dying in the back seat, and those photographs may have made their way back to news desks in this country."

Both Harry and his brother had a constant reminder of what their mother went through because of the daily intrusion in their own lives by the press. As a former senior courtier said, "They're seeing it play out again and again."

Harry, the source said, would do anything to defend Meghan's reputation and protect her privacy, but he was "frustrated by the limits to his ability."

While he hadn't been able to do much to protect his previous girlfriends from the press, whom he credited with contributing to the ends of those relationships, Harry was determined that this relationship would not meet the same fate.

To figure out just what he should do, Harry reached out to the only person he knew who would understand the complexity of his situation—his brother.

Meghan first met William at Kensington Palace in early November 2016. As she walked up the seven freshly jet-washed concrete steps to Apartment 1A with Harry, she wasn't thinking about the future king of England but her boyfriend's older brother, and one famously protective of his younger one, who had experienced more than his fair share of emotional wounds. Meghan thought that William would no doubt want to know everything about her—and her intentions. She was self-aware enough to understand that the brothers were wary of women who were more interested in their titles than their well-being. And she couldn't have come from a more different world than that of William, his wife, and most of their friends. Because of all this, she had thought the entire meeting through, as she told a friend. "She prepared herself for a grilling," a confidant said.

But she needn't have worried. As soon as William opened the black double doors to welcome Meghan into his home, he said, "I was looking forward to meeting the girl who has put that silly grin on my brother's face."

On the console tables in the foyer, Meghan took in the framed photos of the brothers with their late mother, Diana, family moments with the Queen, and cute snaps of George and Charlotte. Although she had never met the people in the photos before, she had heard a lot about them from Harry. The three of them walked straight past the drawing room, with its neutral color palette accented by important antiques and artwork, and straight to the rear of the first floor and the heart of the Cambridge family home: the kitchen. No fuss, no servants, just the three of them and the tea they were about to drink.

Meghan was disappointed she didn't get to meet Kate, who was with the children at Anmer Hall, the couple's Norfolk estate home near Sandringham. But having gotten along so well with Harry's brother, she didn't think much more about that. William made his feelings known to his brother when he shared how he was happy to see Harry smiling.

Now seeing his brother in so much pain, William agreed that things had gone too far. There was no doubt in Harry's mind that he needed to act, but how they should proceed remained a question.

The press had no intent of letting up, since Meghan got a lot of clicks online and was a guaranteed boost to newspaper sales.

On the front cover of the country's highest selling tabloid, *The Sun*, a headline screamed "Harry's Girl on Pornhub." A shocking claim, it was simply based on the fact that a user had uploaded a love scene from *Suits* to the pornographic website alongside movie and TV clips of other Hollywood stars, including Nicole Kidman and Jessica Biel. "Meghan felt sick to her stomach when she saw that," a friend said. "She wanted to cry. She wanted to shout . . . She was upset and angry."

Doria was under constant siege in her own home. When a tabloid published a set of unflattering photos showing her on her way to the laundromat, pushing the narrative of a struggling African American woman in a rough part of LA, Meghan remained silent publicly. But behind the scenes she was in tears. Within the confines of Nottingham Cottage, Harry tried to console her. Worried he might lose Meghan, he frantically wanted to protect her.

On Monday, November 7, as he ventured out of his cottage, the thirty-nine-degree crisp chill in the air did nothing to dull Harry's already heightened anger as he made the short walk to his mother's old apartment in Kensington Palace, the current location of the household offices. He had been accused in the past of being impetuous, wearing his heart on his sleeve. But this was too much.

He climbed the elaborate white wooden staircase—the walls adorned with old masters' paintings and elaborate crown moldings—to his mother's former home. At the top of the landing to the right was Diana's old study, where she kept her famous desk in front of two large picture windows that allowed her to gaze out at the cherry blossoms where Harry's Nottingham Cottage sits.

Directly ahead was her sitting room, which overlooked a cobbled courtyard. An antique mahogany dining table from the Palace's extensive Royal Collection archives sat in the room that backed up to a kitchen used by staff for cups of tea. Beyond those two rooms, which served as reception spaces for events, were the press offices at Kensington Palace that looked after William, Kate, and Harry.

The princes first got their own office back in 2008. With growing profiles, both in their military careers and charitable endeavors, the Queen and Prince Charles agreed that it was time. Up until that point, the young men's affairs were handled at St. James's Palace by Charles's trusted communications secretary Paddy Harverson, who for more than ten years had guided William and Harry.

Miguel Head—the smart thirty-year-old Ministry of Defence press officer who had engineered the press strategy with General Richard Dannatt during Harry's tour in Afghanistan—was plucked from the MOD to serve as the brothers' first press secretary. The office also included former SAS major Jamie Lowther-Pinkerton, their former principal private secretary who had agreed to remain available as a sounding board to the brothers, alongside office manager and personal assistant Helen Asprey, who ensured every detail in their lives ran smoothly. The Queen also appointed one of her most trusted diplomats, Sir David Manning, who had served Her Majesty's Government as British ambassador to the United States, to join as an advisor and intervene when necessary as the young princes started to take increasingly more high-profile roles both at home and abroad.

Several years later, William and Harry had made the decision to move their offices into the home they had shared with their mother. It was a difficult one that the brothers did not take lightly. The place evoked many memories, to be certain, but at the same time inspired them to carry on their mother's charitable work.

The princes' office was a communal space Harry frequented often, popping by sometimes just to have a chat with Jason Knauf, his capable press head. On this early November day, however, the meeting was far less casual.

Jason—who had navigated William and Kate's media efforts for family privacy and been instrumental in crafting the royal trio's highly successful Heads Together campaign in May 2016—had often given Harry good advice. And it didn't hurt that he was also American, with an understanding of the press on both sides of the Atlantic. The Texas-born head of communications was approachable, liked by the royal press pack, and savvy to the ways of social media.

Harry would also periodically seek out the guidance of Paddy Harverson on privacy issues. Harverson, who oversaw communications for the Prince of Wales from 2004 through 2013 (Prince Charles married Camilla Parker Bowles in 2005) was widely credited with the growth of Charles and Camilla's popularity. Although he founded Milltown Partners, a strategic communications and reputation management firm, after leaving Clarence House, Paddy remained close to both William and Harry and was well equipped to advise when the media had run amok.

Sitting down in his mother's old apartment, Harry said, "I'm not in my twenties anymore. I'm thirty-two, and this is a woman I could marry one day."

The prince wanted to directly address the racism and sexism directed toward Meghan in the press. As a general rule, however, Palace courtiers loathed aggressive, harshly worded statements to the press. They also rarely commented on the personal lives of family members, never engaged on security matters, and were cautious when issuing any type of quote.

Typically, statements from Buckingham Palace or Clarence House were a few sentences in length—and for the more controversial subjects, the royal household would elect not to respond at all.

While not the norm, the kind of aggressive stance Harry was suggesting did have a precedent.

Just a year earlier, William and Kate had contended with outrageous tactics by paparazzi following Prince George. One photographer had gone so far as to hide in the trunk of a car as the boy played in a park. The threatening behavior raised alarm bells, and lawyers quickly got involved. William and Harry detected a worrying pattern with the press, who had backed off for a while after Diana's death but were now reverting to their old mercenary ways. At William and Kate's direction, Jason issued a harshly worded statement in August 2015 condemning the paparazzi targeting Prince George.

"In recent months, there have been an increasing number of incidents of paparazzi harassment of Prince George," the statement read. "And the tactics being used are increasingly dangerous."

The document, distributed to media outlets around the world, recounted the methods used to get images of George, including stalking the two-year-old heir, monitoring movements of other members of the royal family, and chasing cars.

In some ways, Kensington Palace's more modern, forceful strategy suited the shifting media landscape driven by a hunger for 24/7 digital content. But courtiers at both Clarence House and Buckingham Palace were not all in agreement that this more vocal approach was the most effective way to move forward.

William and Kate were concerned only with the welfare of their children. And the same went for Harry's concern for Meghan when he, along with his aides and brother, decided to issue an equally forthright statement.

The only stumbling block was Prince Charles. On an important three-nation diplomatic tour in the Middle East, the Prince of Wales and the Duchess of Cornwall had just arrived in Bahrain to meet the country's King Hamad bin Isa al-Khalifa. It was a critical moment in history that had been in the works for months. A statement from Kensington Palace condemning the press and, in the same breath, confirming Harry's new girlfriend would all but eliminate coverage of Prince Charles's tour of the Gulf.

The Palace decided to go ahead with the statement nonetheless, much of which was drafted by Harry himself. Charles learned of the statement just twenty minutes before it went out. Sure enough, as soon as Harry put out his declaration, the statement dominated the news cycle. The team at Clarence House, which had spent months putting together Prince Charles's tour in the hopes that it would be covered significantly, was crushed. While disappointed that his son didn't wait for him to come back, Charles also understood intimately that the situation with Meghan had reached a tipping point. Harry had felt the need to prioritize the woman he loved over duty to the greater royal family. The personal and professional were often in conflict for members of the monarchy. In this case, however, Charles recognized that Harry wanted to protect the loved ones in his life. His son had already lost the person he had once loved the most—his mother.

Harry's statement lambasted sections of the press for the "abuse and harassment" of the American actress, making particular note of the "racial undertones" of some coverage. "Prince Harry is worried about Ms. Markle's safety and is deeply disappointed that he has not been able to protect her," the statement read. "It is not right that a few months into a relationship with him that Ms. Markle should be subjected to such a storm."

Meghan was scared of opening a Pandora's box by trying to take on the press. "Shouldn't we just ignore it?" she asked. But Harry had made up his mind.

In the unprecedented release, Harry not only officially confirmed his relationship with Meghan but also made it clear that he was the one behind this bold protest, "in the hopes that those in the press who have been driving this story can pause and reflect before any further damage is done."

6

Culture Shock

On November 27, 2016, Prince William released his own statement in order to put rumors to rest: "The Duke of Cambridge absolutely understands the situation concerning privacy and supports the need for Prince Harry to support those closest to him."

Though the purpose of William's follow-up statement was to make it clear that he supported his brother's relationship with Meghan, two weeks later, the press reported on tensions between the princes over Harry's decision to speak out. Behind the scenes, courtiers and some members of the royal family had questioned whether Harry's statement was too strong. Staffers, who thought what Harry was doing was irrational and hotheaded, fed the news cycle on background. On the record, however, Kensington Palace quickly debunked any suggestion that the Duke of Cambridge wasn't in full agreement with his brother's actions. It would not have been a good look. And while he had in fact privately voiced concerns to aides about the speed at which Harry's relationship was developing with a Hollywood actress he hadn't known for long,

William did worry about press intrusion and wanted his brother to feel supported on that issue.

Meghan was hurt and stunned by the reactions in the press and online. In conversations with friends, she admitted that while thankful to be with someone as protective and understanding as Harry, she was "emotionally drained."

Making matters worse, Harry's royal duties meant the couple were apart in the immediate aftermath of his statement defending Meghan. Days after its release, Harry took on a fourteen-day, seven-country tour of the Caribbean to celebrate the Queen's ninetieth birthday. Youth empowerment, sports for social development, and conservation were the areas of focus during the prince's itinerary, which included the Commonwealth Realms of Antigua and Barbuda, St. Kitts and Nevis, St. Lucia, St. Vincent and the Grenadines, Grenada, and Barbados, as well as a visit to Guyana on behalf of the Foreign and Commonwealth Office.

Even though it meant being apart from Meghan when she needed him most, it was a tour that established Harry as a force within the royal family. (Trips like this are planned six months to a year in advance, and there was no way he could have seen this coming.) From assisting in the release of baby turtles to the sea for the Nevis Turtle Group to handing out honors while sailing on RFA *Wave Knight* to St. Lucia (a job usually reserved for the Queen, Prince Charles, and Prince William), he won over the people of each country he visited. The prince's easy rapport with children made #HarryWithKids a trending hashtag on Twitter. Pictures of Harry meeting a wheelchair-bound seven-year-old named Tye while learning about the work of the Child Development and Guidance Centre in St. Lucia melted hearts around the world.

He found that at most places he went, people wanted to talk about Meghan. When he visited Kingstown's Botanic Gardens to see the national bird, the Vincey Parrot, trainers attempted to get the bird to say Meghan's name for the prince—without success.

On the first day of the tour, Gaston Browne, the prime minister of Antigua and Barbuda, teased Harry, "I believe we are expecting a new princess soon.

"I want you to know that you are very welcome to come on your honeymoon here," the politician pitched the prince. "We have been voted consistently as the best honeymoon destination in the Caribbean, and one of the best in the world, so there will be nowhere in the world as special to spend your honeymoon, when that day arrives."

Throughout the tour Harry and Meghan, who was in Toronto working and dodging paparazzi, spoke almost every day via Face-Time. No matter how hard things were for her, Meghan understood the importance of Harry's mission, best exemplified in his visit to Guyana and Barbados to mark the fiftieth anniversary of the nation's independence.

It was in Barbados that he and the singer Rihanna took HIV tests in a clinic in the country's capital, Bridgetown, on World AIDS Day.

"I want to say to everyone who hasn't been tested—get tested, regardless of who you are, your background, culture, or religion," said Harry, who, like his mother before him, has long campaigned to end the stigma of HIV. In the 1980s, when many were afraid of those infected with the disease, Princess Diana made headlines for being the first member of the royal family to have direct contact with people suffering with AIDS.

As soon as the Caribbean tour was finished, Harry's first stop—in a break from protocol—was to see Meghan. Palace policy dictated that "working visits should not be combined with personal travel." Harry came under fire from the press for not taking the British Airways flight to London from Barbados that he had been booked on, instead traveling straight to Toronto. If Meghan hadn't already fully understood that every small detail of a royal's life was under the microscope, she did now.

Although Harry had once warned Meghan that his life was "surreal," even he had been blindsided by the kind of coverage she elicited.

While Harry was traveling and Meghan was home in Toronto, she made her affections known in subtle ways. While running errands around town on December 3, she wore her newly purchased $300 The Right Hand Gal necklace, a delicate fourteen-carat-gold chain bearing both the initials "M" and "H." That same day, she also dressed her beagle, Guy, in a Union Jack sweater, posting the snap to Instagram. The message was received by Harry, who turned up outside her door not twenty-four hours later.

Two days after Meghan was photographed buying flowers at her usual florist, wearing her new initial necklace, she received a phone call from a senior Kensington Palace aide. She was advised that wearing such a necklace only served to encourage the photographers to keep pursuing such images—and new headlines.

She said little during the call, choosing instead to simply listen to the counsel. But after hanging up, she felt frustrated and emotional. While she knew the aide had good intentions, the surreal experience of having someone from her boyfriend's office tell her what kind of jewelry to wear or not to smile at a photographer was too much.

Meghan immediately called one of her close friends, close to tears as she waited for her pal to pick up.

"I can't win," she said, completely distraught. "They make out like I'm to blame for these pictures, that it looks like I'm encouraging them, that me even acknowledging the cameras may not be sending the right message. I don't know what to say. It was only yesterday people online were saying I look miserable in pictures, because I was trying to just ignore [the photographer]." She felt damned if she did and damned if she didn't.

Another one of Meghan's good friends, Jessica Mulroney, had had a similar conversation with her friend Sophie Grégoire Trudeau in 2013, after her husband, Justin, set his sights on becoming Canada's prime minister. According to a source, Jessica told the future First Lady of Canada that unfortunately that kind of intrusion into her behavior was something she had to get used to if she wanted a life with a public figure—and she should trust that people around her husband just wanted the best for both of them.

It was Sophie who ultimately offered Meghan the same advice. Jessica introduced the women in 2016, knowing that the two now had a lot in common. Sophie had given up a career in television, where she had been working as a correspondent on CTV's *eTalk*, to take on a more formal role alongside her husband as he hit the campaign trail.

The pair became fast email friends, Meghan was interested to hear how Sophie had successfully made the move from an entertainment news correspondent to much-beloved First Lady, all while skillfully dodging controversy.

"Sophie would have made it clear that every single aspect of Meghan's past would be dug up, so the most important thing was to be honest with Harry—tell him everything," said a close Trudeau friend and former cabinet member. "Sophie's a smart woman and the perfect brain for Meghan to pick. She knows how difficult something like this is. Few people can relate or truly sympathize. For those of us that knew about their friendship, it was amazing to see the change in Meghan that followed."

Still, Harry and Meghan had to transition to a new way of life.

"Both of us were totally surprised by the reaction after the first five or six months of when we had it to ourselves, of what actually happened from then," he said later in a joint interview with Meghan for the BBC. "You can have as many conversations as you want and try and prepare as much as possible. But we were totally unprepared for what happened after that."

"We were just hit so hard at the beginning with a lot of mistruths that I made the choice to not read anything, positive or negative," Meghan said of the narrative of her as a scheming social climber from "the ghetto" whose main goal in life was to marry up. "It just didn't make sense. And instead we focused all of our energies just on nurturing our relationship."

That was the public line, but privately the couple couldn't help but stay abreast of what was written in the newspapers and online, thanks to press aides having to ask for comments or explanations. Meghan told friends that looking at any websites or comments sections on her social media accounts made her feel sick, especially when her ethnicity was under attack.

"It's a shame that that is the climate in this world," she said. "At the end of the day I'm really just proud of who I am and where I come from, and we have never put any focus on that. We've just focused on who we are as a couple. And so, when you take all those extra layers away and all of that noise, I think it makes it really easy to just enjoy being together and tuning all the rest of that out."

Still, after fighting back, the couple was exhausted. They had been together publicly for only just over a week, but it felt more like a lifetime. The adversity only made their love for each other stronger, and a family friend said that it strengthened Harry's mission to protect Meghan.

No matter how much Harry tried to put it in context, she often spoke to friends about how difficult it was not to take it personally when the press and public questioned her suitability as a royal bride and compared her to the aristocratic girls Harry had dated in the past.

Being an actress in Hollywood certainly helped Meghan start off her new role more adeptly than the other women in Harry's life. But the tabloid controversies did all they could to derail her poise.

"There's a misconception that because I have worked in the entertainment industry that this would be something that I would be familiar with," Meghan said. "But even though I'd been on my show for, I guess six years at that point, and working before that,

I've never been part of tabloid culture. I've never been in pop culture to that degree and lived a relatively quiet life, even though I focused so much on my job. So that was a really stark difference out of the gate."

While she might not have been prepared for the intensity of being catapulted from TV stardom to the royal stage, as an actress she was used to a level of criticism most people aren't. She also possessed a comfort level in front of photographers that doesn't come as easily to Harry.

Meghan was now in a role that never had a hiatus. Like another American actress, Grace Kelly, who married Prince Rainier of Monaco, she had the potential to make the royal family more accessible to a wider swath of the public in the UK and abroad. The price for Meghan, however, was that now every word uttered, every gesture made, every piece of clothing worn, would instantly be scrutinized and analyzed for subtext. She had to move with a level of decorum that no normal life demands.

The transition wasn't just culture shock for Meghan. Kensington Palace's royal courtiers also had a period of adjustment exacerbated by the relentless twenty-four-hour digital media cycle. Most of the team began work at the household after William married Kate in 2011, so they missed the early days of the couple's relationship and the British tabloid's incessant harassment of Kate, as they criticized her and her mother, Carole, digging up every trace of her and her family's past.

"When Harry introduced Meghan as his girlfriend, a serious girlfriend, it was a new experience for everyone," a former palace aide revealed. "When Harry formally introduced her to his team [in August 2016], he was already certain of their future. I think dealing with the extreme and sudden level of interest in Meghan and teaching her how to deal with it was something many of them had to learn on the job. There is no training you can do to prepare for that."

Learning on the job inevitably involves making some mistakes or at least having some rocky moments. Meghan expressed frustration to friends over aides "flip-flopping" between decisions. Case in point were the numerous discussions Harry and Meghan had with staff about the right time and place to first be photographed as a couple. Taking her to an engagement was off-limits, as that would go against royal protocol. But perhaps Harry could bring Meghan to a sporting event as a guest spectator in the stands with him, so they could be seen together without appearing to court attention. The goal of the photo was to softly introduce Meghan to the public while keeping the paparazzi at bay.

Meghan had a good idea about how the pap game worked, but now she was in Harry's "overwhelming and confusing" world and so deferred to him and his staff. "There was an element of 'I'm just going to be quiet and see what everyone else thinks,'" a friend said of Meghan's attitude.

As to the timing of their first photo together, Harry wanted to take a "sooner the better" approach, and Meghan agreed. Heads nodded all around on one idea, only to have an aide at another household dismiss the entire plan as a bad idea the very next day.

If there was this much debate over a photo, what was going to happen if Meghan wanted to speak her mind about something? If she wanted to fully enter the royal sphere, she had to remain apolitical, which made her previous level of activism impossible. (She had previously spoken out against Brexit and called Donald Trump "misogynistic" and "divisive.") Silencing herself was no small sacrifice.

It took some months before she felt comfortable with the guidance provided by Harry's team, including Jason and the prince's private secretary, Edward Lane Fox, known as Ed or ELF to friends and journalists. Ed, Harry's "right-hand" man, was a former captain in the Blues and Royals, a regiment of the Household Cavalry, who had served in Iraq and Bosnia. That was where he and Harry first met, before he joined Harry's team in April 2013. Hugely involved in the Invictus Games, Ed had become a close friend of Harry's during the prince's solo travels over the years. The team trained Meghan and the people most important in her life on how to protect themselves from the increased attention. Having the palace acknowledge her friends and their presence in her life was a relief to Meghan, who at one point wondered if there would be pressure to move away from those in her "old" life.

There were conversations about social media conduct, and specific advice to Meghan's friends, all who had one-on-one time with Jason to learn the dos and don'ts of Twitter and Instagram (for example: how to avoid leaving clues that revealed Meghan's location to the paparazzi, who were monitoring anyone associated with Meghan's accounts). "It was a little bizarre," one of the friends who spoke to Jason said. "But it made sense. This wasn't about the royal family; it was simply about her safety. That's how it was laid out. It was good to know there was someone to talk to if we had been pestered by tabloid journalists or paps."

Calls between Meghan and Kensington Palace aides quickly became the norm. And while she still got a little annoyed at the advice sometimes, Meghan grew to realize the importance of their support and experience as she navigated Harry's world, which was quickly becoming her own.

7

Tropical Storms

As 2016 came to an end, a more confident—and careful—Meghan was emerging. She changed her phone number for the first time in years, sending out the new UK digits to just a small group of people. It was yet another step toward leaving behind her non-royal life.

What hadn't changed was her conviction that Harry was the one. Their feelings ran in tandem. Harry told friends he was excited about how natural things felt with Meghan, how their relationship moved organically—"like it was just meant to be," he confided to a friend over drinks in London at the start of December. Two weeks later, Meghan booked a last-minute Air Canada flight to London, because she simply couldn't bear to wait until their planned rendezvous later in the month. After all, this was to be their Christmas celebration together.

While Harry and Meghan were serious, their relationship was still far too new for her to earn an invite to the Queen's spouses-only formal affair at Sandringham. So while Harry was in the countryside at the Queen's home in Norfolk, Meghan planned to spend the holidays in Los Angeles with Doria and the family of her good friend Benita Litt, an entertainment lawyer turned founder of a carryall line, who had traveled with Meghan and Misha to Spain earlier that summer. Meghan loved spending time with Benita and her husband, Darren, especially when her "fairy goddaughters," Remi and Rylan, were around.

If the last-minute London visit was the couple's holiday celebration, they were determined to live it up. A day after her arrival at Heathrow Airport, they turned up at Pines and Needles in Battersea Park on the hunt for their first shared tree. (The Christmas shop, just two miles from Kensington Palace, was also a favorite of Madonna's and Elton John's.) After fifteen minutes of browsing, they made their pick: a six-foot Nordmann Fir that Harry and Meghan tucked under their arms and carried out to the car by themselves.

Back home they hunkered down, trimming the tree and cooking meals, leaving only once to fit in a quick workout at Harry's nearby KX gym before stocking up on groceries for dinner. On December 14, eager to leave the cottage after two days indoors, they decided to spend an evening out on the town. They had accepted last-minute tickets to see *The Curious Incident of the Dog in the Night-Time*. But having gotten a late start driving out of the palace, they were afraid the Piccadilly Circus traffic they were now stuck in would keep them from making the 7:30 p.m. curtain call. So, they hopped out of the nondescript minivan they had taken to avoid drawing attention to themselves and started to walk briskly, heads down and holding hands, toward the Gielgud Theatre.

The West End was bustling, and the couple knew if they moved quick enough, they could get into the theater without being spotted. Both were quite excited by the idea of running through the busiest streets of London, knowing full well that the entire world wanted to see them together. It was a brief moment of freedom they hadn't experienced in a while, even if it lasted for only sixty seconds at the most. For that small amount of time, they felt as if they were just another of the many couples powering down the sidewalk. It was exhilarating and fun. When they breezed through the door of the theater like regular patrons, the usher waiting to take them to their VIP box seats was somewhat taken aback. Harry and Meghan exchanged a look that showed they couldn't believe it either.

Ironically, their brief moment of anonymity as a couple turned out to be the first captured for all the world to see. What Harry and Meghan were unaware of at the time was that a photographer had followed them from the Palace gates and had snapped their every move as they dashed to make it to the theater before the lights went down.

The release of their first pictures together was decidedly *not* the planned affair Kensington Palace had hoped for. They only found out about the paparazzi when Harry received a text message from a press aide at 10:35 a.m. the next day with a photo of the front page of *The Sun*. "WORLD PHOTO EXCLUSIVE!" the cover line blasted. "Harry and His Meg: 1st Snap of Prince with Love." The couple were unbothered, knowing that such an article had been bound to happen eventually—although Meghan wasn't crazy about the fact that the two had been followed without their knowledge. "That was creepy," she told a friend.

What did bother Meghan, to the point of being reduced to tears, were an alleged series of topless photos posted by the tawdry gossip site *Radar Online*. Although the celebrity website claimed the pictures were taken during her 2013 Jamaica wedding to Trevor, Meghan insisted they weren't of her. Her lawyers took legal action, but the lackluster apology they received on the website did little to ease the pain. Coupled with the paparazzi now constantly staking out Doria's LA home—an intrusion that forced the mother and daughter to change their Christmas plans and spend much of the holidays hiding out in Toronto—the latest barrage of media attacks left her feeling shaken.

To lift her spirits, Harry planned a New Year's trip where they could really get away from it all. He rung up his pal Inge Solheim, a Norwegian adventure guide Harry had befriended during a Walking with the Wounded charity trek back in 2011. Inge had gone all out for Harry when he was with Cressida, arranging a top secret 2014 ski trip to Kazakhstan. "It's always my pleasure to help a friend like Harry," said Inge, who arranged for Harry and Meghan to spend a week in a cabin in Tromsö at the very tip of Norway in the Arctic Circle, where there was absolutely no chance of being bothered by photographers. There, Harry and Meghan enjoyed seven days of dog sledding, whale watching, dining on local delicacies, and snuggling to watch as the aurora borealis lit up the skies.

From the Arctic Circle, the couple returned to London, where Meghan finally met Kate, the Duchess of Cambridge. The January 10 get-together at the Cambridges' Apartment 1A home was brief, but Harry wanted to make sure the two had a chance to connect.

Despite the fact that Harry was a regular guest in her household, Kate had seemingly not shown much interest in finding out who this woman was who had made her brother-in-law so happy. But that indifference wasn't necessarily directed toward Meghan. "The Duchess is an extremely guarded person," a friend explained. After she married William, she was careful about letting others in to her social circle. Her friends today—including Lady Laura Meade and Emilia Jardine-Paterson, both of whom married friends of William's—are for the most part the same ones she had on her wedding day. Like her husband, Kate ran in a tight group.

Meghan brought a present for the duchess, who had celebrated her birthday just a day earlier. The soft leather Smythson notebook helped to break the ice, as did Meghan's cooing over then twenty-month-old Charlotte. The meeting ended with Kate letting Meghan know that she was always welcome to contact her if she needed anything. Having been through the experience of being a royal girlfriend herself, Kate knew how trying it could be to suddenly have one's personal life laid bare.

On January 17, Meghan arrived in New Delhi for a five-day visit to India with the international relief organization World Vision. As one of its global ambassadors, she was in the Indian capital to learn about the myriad issues, such as obstacles to healthcare and education, facing local impoverished women and children. After she successfully completed the trip she had been researching and planning for months, Meghan returned again to be with Harry in London.

Although the pair weren't expressly living together, she spent most of the winter of 2017 at Harry's Kensington Palace apartment. Having already left her mark on the décor, Meghan now had a wardrobe assembled from pieces she purchased in London, from the likes of J.Crew and Stella McCartney, as well as clothes she had brought over on previous trips.

London was starting to feel like home. On many nights, she and Harry curled up in his modest living room, binge-watching TV (*Game of Thrones* and *Breaking Bad* were favorites). They also had the same taste in films. Fans of Disney, they loved to watch movies like *Moana* and *The Lion King*. And thanks to the arrival of awards season in the United States, Meghan was also in possession of a stack of screeners sent out to voters and SAG-AFTRA members. Because Meghan was a member, the pair were able to view the year's best cinema from the comfort of their own home.

They emerged from time to time, visiting the Notting Hill movie theater the Electric Cinema to see *Hidden Figures* or grabbing a bite to eat. They had their tried-and-true spots, including Soho House, the site of their first meeting, and the Sands End, a rustic style gastropub in Fulham owned by Mark Dyer. The former Welsh Guards officer—who accompanied Harry on his gap year—had always been on hand to offer the prince advice and support.

Harry and Meghan were at ease in those places, but that wasn't the case when they headed off to Jamaica in March for the wedding of Harry's pal Tom Inskip, who had been in Las Vegas for the infamous trip back in 2012. Montego Bay's Round Hill Hotel and Villas was more open than felt comfortable, but the couple received assurances that all 110 acres of the resort would be closed to the public for the entire three-day affair. And so, Harry booked a villa on the far corner of the resort, tucked beneath the lush vegetation and the couple hopped a flight for the Caribbean.

On the first day, gloriously sunny skies and turquoise waters put all the wedding guests in a celebratory mood. The festivities went far into the night as old friends stayed up late, tossing back cocktails and exchanging memories.

But just twenty-four hours in, the trip soured for Harry and Meghan. Protection officers accompanying the pair to Jamaica discovered a photographer from a Los Angeles–based celebrity photo agency on the grounds. They were promptly tossed out of the resort, but not before capturing the couple in a steamy embrace on their private balcony and Meghan in her tiny swimsuits frolicking in the water with the prince.

While Meghan was horrified by the intrusion, Harry was apoplectic. During a heated call to the palace, he laid out his instructions in no uncertain terms. These photos were *not* to see the light of day. "Do whatever needs to be done," the prince said.

His communications secretary assured Harry that the situation was being taken care of. Subsequent calls to the company, using such language as "outrageous violation of privacy," ensured that the revealing balcony photos were never offered up for purchase and didn't turn up anywhere, even in the darkest corners of the Internet (they still have never seen the light of day). But the agency still planned to sell pictures of the couple in the water, including dozens of frames zoomed in on Meghan's body.

In their villa bedroom, Harry was angry and shouting while Meghan was concerned. She more than understood his feelings about media intrusion, how that deep distrust had formed after his mother's death and had never gone away, bubbling up each time a reporter took their efforts to get a story too far. But she had never seen him like *this*. In past incidents with the paparazzi, Meghan had usually been able to find the right words to soothe his anger. Often, she was the only one able to calm Harry down when he got into one of his moods. In Jamaica, however, he remained frustrated for days. He was in such a state that even his buddies remarked on his dour mood. Although Meghan had never seen this side of Harry before, she wasn't put off by it. Instead, she was sad to see him so affected.

Unfortunately, it was hardly the last time the press would ruin their plans. Intense media scrutiny was the reason Meghan shuttered her lifestyle blog, *The Tig*, in April, announcing that her once-beloved passion project had run its course. It wasn't so much that her blog was criticized as it was used to fuel false speculation about her personal life with the prince. All of her old posts became news stories. If she and Harry weren't seen in three days, someone at a gossip blog would pull up her recipe for acai bowls and write a story that that was what she was serving her new man. Or her post about the benefits of green juice: Was this the diet she was making Harry follow? No, it was some article Meghan had written three years earlier. It all got very silly and no longer fit with the life of a royal girlfriend.

After taking a moment to share some of her favorite quotes from the site (including "Being yourself is the prettiest thing a person can be," "Of this be sure: you do not find the happy life . . . you make it," and "Travel often; getting lost will help you find yourself"), she addressed her readers.

"After close to three beautiful years on this adventure with you, it's time to say goodbye to *The Tig*," Meghan wrote in a farewell letter online. "What began as a passion project (my little engine that could) evolved into an amazing community of inspiration, support, fun, and frivolity. You've made my days brighter and filled this experience with so much joy. Keep finding those Tig moments of discovery, keep laughing and taking risks, and keep being 'the change you wish to see in the world.'

"Above all, don't ever forget your worth—as I've told you time and time again: you, my sweet friend, you are enough."

More attention followed when Meghan made her first outing at an official society function. On May 6, she appeared in the royal box at Coworth Park to watch Harry play polo for charity, though the throng of photographers led to Harry and Meghan hiding out from cameras behind cars in a VIP parking area, making for a very awkward and frustrating moment for the couple.

The media frenzy that followed their every move made them somewhat of a reluctant addition to the guest list for Pippa Middleton's vows on May 20, 2017. Both the bride and her mom, Carole, privately harbored concerns that the American actress's presence alongside Harry might overshadow the main event.

Meghan put careful thought into her outfit, leaning heavily on Jessica to pull together an ensemble that was stylish without being splashy when walking into the church with Harry. Her determination not to make a misstep at Pippa's wedding was just one in many actions she took befitting a woman on track to becoming royalty.

Despite her best efforts, Meghan's presence at Pippa's wedding did pose a problem—but it had nothing to do with her clothes. The day of the nuptials, *The Sun* ran a cover story, "It's Meghan v Pippa in the . . . Wedding of the Rears," accompanied by a rearview paparazzi picture of Meghan in yoga pants leaving a central London yoga studio that week side by side with the infamous photo of Pippa from behind during Kate's 2011 wedding ceremony.

Harry and Meghan agreed that she couldn't possibly turn up at the church, only fifty meters away from a specially arranged media pen, after such a crass cover story. If they worried their arrival might create a media circus despite taking every precaution, now they had no doubt that it would. Meghan's church outfit, and Philip Treacy hat, would have to be worn another time.

While in the days after the affair it was assumed that Harry had headed out to St. Mark's Church in Englefield, Berkshire, solo, before returning to London to grab Meghan for the reception on the grounds of the Middletons' Bucklebury home, logging some 150 miles of travel, the pair had actually come up with a clever work-around.

The morning of the vows, the couple made the hour-long drive out to Berkshire together. Harry dropped Meghan off at the Airbnb a close friend and fellow wedding guest had rented before continuing on to the chapel. While all the other guests were at the ceremony, Meghan changed into a decidedly unflashy long black gown and did her own makeup. (A hairdresser had been dispatched to Kensington in the early morning.)

Following the 11:30 a.m. service, Harry returned to the rental home to have lunch with Meghan before driving them over to the reception site in a black Audi, the pair arriving just as a Supermarine Spitfire fighter plane was launching into an aerial performance for guests. Sitting together in the custom glass marquee that had been erected on the eighteen-acre property should have been a fun night for the couple, but, per Pippa's request, no couples sat together. Harry sat with his pal and TV news anchor Tom Bradby, clapping as Pippa and James entered the room. Across the room, Meghan sipped the 2002 Dom Ruinart champagne and dined on trout and lamb, chatting to her new posse of friends for the evening, which included Roger Federer's wife, Mirka. With DJ Sam Totolee at the turntables after dinner was over, Harry and Meghan were reunited near the dance floor. The old Harry would have certainly closed out the bash with the rest of his friends. Instead, he and Meghan spent most of their time chatting about their evening apart. They called it a night close to 2:00 a.m., a protection officer driving them back to Kensington.

8

Voicing Disapproval

Every detail had been meticulously organized ahead of their August 4 arrival in Botswana, a trip Harry planned to coincide with Meghan's thirty-sixth birthday.

Unwrapping the first of several surprise gifts from Harry on the final leg of their turbo propeller-plane ride, Meghan couldn't help but smile when she noticed the corner of the canvas painting poking out of the carefully prepared bubble wrapping packaging.

Just two months after they had started dating in the summer of 2016, Harry had given Meghan one half of a Van Donna diptych, which depicted a young boyfriend and girlfriend holding hands. He had picked up the $4,500 artwork during a private visit to the Walton Fine Arts gallery in Chelsea, London, and kept the second piece, which simply featured the title of the work, *Everybody Needs Somebody to Love*, for what would be their first anniversary. It seemed he had always known that they would go the distance.

As they hit the tarmac at Maun Airport, both immediately felt a sense of relief and excitement. The vacation wasn't just in celebration of Meghan's birthday; it was also a milestone of their relation-ship. The trip stood as a full-circle moment for the couple, a return to the country they had snuck off to just four weeks after meeting in 2016. They were excited to camp out again in the Botswana wil-derness under the stars as they had done almost a year earlier to the day.

The festivities began the moment they touched down. They were quickly whisked away in blacked-out SUVs to their first lo-cation: a night at the home of Harry's friend Adrian Dandridge, a former jewelry designer he first met during a trip to Botswana in 2004. There, at a rustic guesthouse nestled next to a nearby chili farm in the community area of Tsutsubega, was a surprise birthday party set up and waiting for Meghan. Ravenous after the fifteen-hour journey from London, Harry's and Meghan's faces lit up when they were greeted by the smell of flame-grilled fare on a large barbecue and a variety of local foods prepared by Adrian's wife, Sophie, including Harry's favorite local dish, seswaa, a beef stew cooked with onion and peppers and served over thick polenta.

For Meghan, it was moments like these that defined Harry. No matter where they were, or who they are with, he always did all he could to make her feel important and included. And there was always some sort of thoughtful surprise.

Earlier that summer, when the couple escaped, completely undetected, to Turkey for a five-night stay at a private villa over-looking the Yalikavak Bay and surrounding mountains in Bodrum, Meghan noticed a jewelry store in town that carried a designer she liked. Kismet by Milka, known for delicate handmade pieces in gold, is popular with the likes of Beyoncé, Madonna, and Cameron Diaz. The couple browsed inside the store, which the owner (upon realizing it was Harry and Meghan) quickly locked down so they could look around in peace. When they left, Meghan told Harry that she liked a couple of things and wanted to come back. The next day, Harry popped into the boutique to buy two pieces. "He said, 'I would like to surprise her,' and picked out the items," the designer Milka Karaagacli said about the Hamsa ring and yellow gold seed dots bracelet.

Harry's latest gesture during the ad hoc birthday party in Africa was simpler but no less thoughtful. Watching him smile as he carried out a small birthday cake, Meghan felt more loved and in love than ever.

The next morning, the couple needed no alarm clock as they woke to the sound of a raucous flock of birds in a joyful dawn chorus. Then they excitedly hurried through breakfast, before jumping into an open-top Jeep to travel forty miles east to the remote Makgadikgadi Pans National Park.

Harry and Meghan were back at Meno A Kwena, the luxury resort they had visited the prior year. Now they could enjoy alone time.

Not that it was ever really just the two of them. Joining them on the romantic trip were two of Harry's personal protection officers, or PPOs, as they are commonly referred to. The SAS-trained, plainclothes bodyguards from the SO14 Royalty Protection Group of the Metropolitan Police Service routinely carried 9mm Glock 17 pistols, radios, and first aid kits—and were never more than a few steps away. They had only one job: to keep the prince safe at all times and at all costs. Meghan used to find the extra presence on dates a little awkward, but, as the Duchess of Cambridge once told friends, "There comes a point where you don't notice."

With no likely threats in this secluded area, the security team was moved to their own quarters on another side of the resort, leaving Harry and Meghan with more than enough privacy. They were also free of digital distractions, rarely checking their phones except to take the occasional photo.

In Botswana, Harry and Meghan's days were spent getting closer to nature and their evenings, closer to each other. Every night, after a dinner of steak or game stew prepared by longtime resident chef Baruti, the couple moved to the resort's campfire area, sinking into low canvas chairs and sipping local wine in front of a crackling fire.

During these starlit evenings, the couple took a deep dive into whatever was on their minds. Meghan's thoughts had recently been on her job, which no longer fit into the life she was building with Prince Harry. She was under pressure to let her network bosses know whether she would be returning to *Suits* for an eighth season, but she didn't want to rush into any rash decisions. After all, this was a job most actresses dream of.

Although she and Harry didn't have a formal commitment to each other, Meghan felt as though she could talk to him about anything. In the calm of the delta's gateway, their conversation interrupted only by the occasional roar of a lion, she opened up about her hopes for the future and where Harry fit into them. For Harry, the subject was an easy one: they had made a promise to never leave each other's sides, and it was a promise he intended to keep.

If the prince realized on the first date that he wanted to date the actress, it was some three months later when he knew he wanted to make her his wife. "The fact that I fell in love with Meghan so incredibly quickly was confirmation to me that all of the stars were aligned," Harry later said in his engagement interview. "Everything was just perfect. This beautiful woman just tripped and fell into my life; I fell into her life."

Their courtship had been a smooth one. They enjoyed a lot of the same activities, such as traveling and fitness, although Meghan, the type of girl to grab a smoothie after a hot yoga or Pilates session, pushed Harry to up his game. Her morning ritual started with a cup of hot water and a slice of lemon, followed by her favorite breakfast of steel-cut oats (usually made with almond or soy milk) with bananas and agave syrup for sweetness. For snacks in between meals, she opted for apple slices and peanut butter. It was a far cry from Harry's bachelor days of eating takeout pizza, but he had already taken an interest in healthy living and it was fun to do it together.

The couple were both fans of self-help books, with Harry counting *Eight Steps to Happiness* as a favorite, while Meghan read *The Motivation Manifesto*.

They shared the deeper values that are the backbone of a marriage, including the importance of giving back to those less fortunate and being conscientious stewards of the environment. (Extremely eco conscious thanks to the teachings of his father, Harry always avoided plastic wherever possible, including making sure plastic lids weren't put on his coffee or forgoing the plastic wrapping on his dry cleaning.)

Harry often took the lead on romantic gestures, but Meghan made sure to show her appreciation and return the affection. Taking note of his likes, she tried to surprise him with his favorite things whenever he visited her in Toronto. During one trip, she cooked him a traditional British Sunday roast lunch, even though it was a weekday, because Harry told her it was his favorite meal. "There's never a wrong time for a roast," she later joked.

Meghan expanded Harry's spiritual world, introducing him to yoga through her own practice and buying him a book on mindfulness that, like all her gifts, came with a handwritten note. Harry soon began, at Meghan's encouragement, a daily meditation practice.

By June 2017, she and Harry weren't talking about their wedding as a possibility so much as an absolute. They even went so far as to bring the Palace into the conversation, consulting with the prince's aides about the best time for a ceremony.

Although Harry had yet to propose, he had started to tell most of his inner circle that it was something he planned to do. Unbeknown to most, he already had an engagement ring in the works. That May, Harry traveled alone to Botswana in his role as patron of

Rhino Conservation Botswana. While in Africa, he did a little secret diamond scouting with a close friend who helped him to source the perfect conflict-free stone.

Not everyone felt as sure of this match as Harry did. A month after his own wedding, Skippy sat down with his childhood friend to voice a concern: Harry and Meghan were moving too quickly. He was "pretty blunt" with Harry about whether he was "rushing into things," according to a source.

Skippy, who, like the majority of Harry's close friends, didn't know Meghan well, advised Harry to "be careful."

Skippy advised they live together before "doing anything more serious." He said his words came from a good place, but Harry didn't totally see it that way. It felt like his friend was implying that Meghan couldn't be trusted and had ulterior motives. "It really hurt him that someone he was so close to would not trust his judgment," the source said.

Skippy and Harry, who always texted or talked regularly, didn't speak for some time after the failed heart-to-heart.

Both William's and Harry's friends were concerned with the pace of his relationship. In a way, Meghan wasn't being treated differently to anyone else—male or female—who entered their orbit. Since Diana's death, the princes had been extremely cautious of anyone who might try to take advantage.

Around the same time that Skippy took Harry aside, Prince William decided to confront his brother over his own concerns.

"A happy and content Harry is rare, so to see him practically skipping around was a delight," a source still in regular contact with the brothers said. "But at the same time William has always felt he needs to look out for Harry, not as a future monarch but as an older brother. Their whole adult lives he's felt he should keep an eye on Harry and make sure he's not in trouble and on a good path."

Having met Meghan only a handful of times, William wanted to make sure that the American actress had the right intentions. "After all, these are two brothers that have spent their whole lives with people trying to take advantage of them," the source said. "They've both developed a radar to detect that type of person, but as William didn't know a whole lot about Meghan, he just wanted to make sure that Harry wasn't blindsided by lust."

Like all royals, William straddles two roles. When it comes to Harry, he is not only his brother but also heir to the throne—and as the future king, it was his job to assess the risk of any newcomers into the Firm. This was an institution with dozens of staff involved in the lives of their bosses, some of whom were whispering words of alarm into the Duke of Cambridge's ear. By nature, senior Palace staff and courtiers are people who, having dedicated their entire lives to the institution of the monarchy, do not like outsiders upsetting the carefully balanced machine. It is their job to spot the potential crises when outsiders are coming into the Firm, whether it's a new staffer heading up a charity initiative or someone marrying into the family.

Meghan was totally foreign to this group of advisors, who sometimes tended to be even more conservative than the institution they guarded.

This was the backdrop when William sat down with his brother to discuss his relationship with Meghan.

"Don't feel like you need to rush this," William told Harry, according to sources. "Take as much time as you need to get to know this girl."

In those last two words, "this girl," Harry heard the tone of snobbishness that was anathema to his approach to the world. During his ten-year career in the military outside the royal bubble, he learned not to make snap judgments about people by their accent, education, ethnicity, class, or profession.

Removing Meghan from the equation, Harry was also tired of the dynamic that had become established between him and his older brother. There had come a point when Harry no longer felt as though he needed looking after. There was a thin line between caring and condescending. Just because he went about his life differently than his brother didn't make it wrong.

William may have felt he was acting out of concern, but Harry was offended that his older brother still treated him as if he were immature. "Harry was pissed off," another source said. "Pissed off that his brother would ask such a thing. Some felt it was an overreaction. But then, this totally sums them up as people—William the calm and rational one, and Harry, who can't help but take things far too personally."

"Harry has a heart of gold, but he's also incredibly sensitive," a longtime family friend said.

Though another friend added, "Harry could see through William's words. He was being a snob."

Harry was taken aback, even angry, despite the fact that William was simply looking out for his brother. He didn't really know Meghan yet. He was concerned that Harry had isolated himself from many of their old friends. "But perhaps he just didn't want to accept that Harry had grown up and become his own man," said a source.

William told an aide he was "hurt" that his brother didn't see that he really was simply watching out for Harry's best interests. The two brothers had spent a lifetime, after all, relying on each other in the wake of their mother's death.

"William and Kate love Harry. They felt that they looked after him. William brought his brother up a lot of the time, provided a parental role and what that actually meant," said a source close to the Cambridges.

At least two other family members also voiced concerns to each other over the pace at which Harry's relationship was moving. Meghan had often been the topic of conversation and gossip among them. When she first arrived in the prince's life, one senior royal referred to the American actress as "Harry's showgirl." Another told an aide, "She comes with a lot of baggage." And a high-ranking courtier was overheard telling a colleague, "There's just something about her I don't trust."

Harry was "aware of the talk," a close friend of his said. "He's extremely protective of Meghan. He understands that a lot of people are against them, and he will do everything he can to keep her safe and away from getting hurt—even if that means distancing himself from those people."

In the months after William talked to Harry about the relationship, the two hardly spoke. The brothers went from always making time for each other to barely spending any time together. Harry had always loved popping across the grounds of the palace to see Charlotte and George, bringing them gifts that included an electric SUV for his nephew and a tricycle for Charlotte. But those visits came to a virtual halt by that summer of 2017. In fact, Harry had spent less time with Prince Louis than the others because of the growing tension between him and his brother after the baby's birth on April 23, 2018. The distance came from both directions. Harry spent less time going over to see the children, but the invites from William and Kate were the first to dry up.

Though not necessarily her responsibility, Kate did little to bridge the divide. She was fiercely loyal to her husband and his family.

Although Kate and Meghan were close in age, they weren't meeting each other at the same point in their lives. Kate had been deeply embedded in the royal family ever since she met William in college. A mother of three (and mother of the heir to the throne), her life revolved around family and duty to monarchy and country.

Kate and Meghan came from different backgrounds and have had vastly different life experiences. Kate was never interested in having a career, while that was always a driver for Meghan. They also had different personalities. While Kate was shy and quiet, Meghan was an extrovert.

Harry didn't care what his family thought or said. "Nothing was going to get in the way of his happiness," a source close to Harry and Meghan said. "He knew Meghan was right for him. Their love was real, and their feelings for each other were genuine. Everything else was noise."

While Harry was battling those in his private life who didn't think he should propose, Meghan was fending off public inquiries on the very same subject.

The possibility of a royal wedding was the top question for the press when Meghan took her place alongside the rest of the *Suits* cast at the June 11 ATX Television Festival in Austin, Texas. There to promote the series' one hundredth episode, she nonetheless found herself dodging questions about the possibility of her marrying a prince. Meghan offered nothing but a smile when one reporter outright asked if she was eager to marry Harry.

Her castmates tried to help by filling in the blanks. "Meghan is super happy," said Patrick J. Adams, her on-screen romantic interest. "She is so deserving of all the great things that happen for her in this world."

The series' executive producer Aaron Korsh later revealed that while he never asked about Meghan's relationship status, he had quietly been planning for the exit of her character, Rachel, from the show from the start of 2017. "Collectively with the writers, we decided to take a gamble that these two people were in love and it was going to work out," he told BBC Radio 4.

Meghan didn't discuss her marriage plans with anyone, but to her closest friends it was clear how she felt. Perhaps that was why Jessica was so keen to shift course in the middle of a June fitting that had been intended to be for personal evening events as well as upcoming scenes on *Suits*. Eyeing some bridal gowns on a nearby rack, the stylist suggested Meghan try on a few. While the studio hadn't shared a script yet, the pair knew there was going to be an upcoming wedding scene for Meghan's character, Rachel. It may have been for work, but the two couldn't help but giggle as Meghan tried a couple on. Meghan looked breathtaking in each one.

Harry and Meghan weren't only moving forward with their relationship privately. In late June, with Harry's consent, Meghan invited Sam Kashner, a high-profile *Vanity Fair* writer, to her Toronto townhouse. She was ready to talk, but it was going to happen on her terms.

For a couple who had pleaded with the press for privacy, this was a risky move. Though Meghan had been falsely accused in the past for courting the press, this time there could be no mistake: Meghan was sitting down with a reporter *with* Harry's blessing. Never had a royal girlfriend spoken so publicly about her relationship and, most surprising, declared in a glossy magazine that she was in love.

Meghan's only request for the photo shoot with the photographer Peter Lindbergh was that her freckles not be photoshopped away. She wanted to look natural and show her real self. She was more than pleased with the results, even sending handwritten thank-you notes to then editor in chief Graydon Carter and other team members involved in the feature. "I loved it," she wrote.

Prior to the writer's arrival, Meghan prepared a lunch of field greens, pasta with chili peppers, and warm bread. Her favorite peony blooms sat alongside assorted books, including a *Vogue* anthology, Grace Coddington's memoir, and, fittingly, a thick coffee table book of *Vanity Fair* portraits through the years. Her white couch was scattered with British throw pillows and a strategically placed blanket so that her beloved pooches, Bogart and Guy, could lounge without dirtying the furniture.

In the interview, Meghan claimed that Harry was the reason she kept her sanity despite the media frenzy. "It has its challenges, and it comes in waves—some days it can feel more challenging than others," she said. "And right out of the gate it was surprising the way things changed. But I still have this support system all around me, and, of course, my boyfriend's support."

When Meghan's cover story hit newsstands on September 7, it was groundbreaking in how frankly she discussed her relationship with Harry. "I can tell you that at the end of the day I think it's really simple," she said. "We're two people who are really happy and in love."

She argued that dating Harry hadn't changed who she'd always been—an independent woman not defined by the men in her life. The only thing that was different was "people's perception" of her.

"I'm sure there will be a time when we will have to come forward and present ourselves and have stories to tell," she said, "but I hope what people will understand is that this is our time. This is for us. It's part of what makes it so special, that it's just ours. But we're happy. Personally, I love a great love story."

Theirs was a love story that took hold in Africa—where now Meghan, on the last day of an incredible three-week stay, stretched her body into the perfect warrior pose.

She quietly took in her surroundings from the grounds of their final home away from home on this trip, a modern villa in Livingstone, Zambia, just under ten miles upstream from Victoria Falls. The rising sun washed over her makeshift yoga garden, while an exotic flock of birds that looked as if they had just had their tails dipped in pots of colorful paints serenaded her.

Harry and Meghan's return to the place they had fallen in love a year earlier had been a magical one. The pair had explored Botswana's wildlife with the help of Harry's friend and fellow conservationist David Dugmore, who runs Meno A Kwena. From driving trips across the Makgadikgadi Pans, one of the largest salt flats in the world, to scoping out passing zebra, warthogs, and hippos during romantic boat trips along the Boteti, each day brought a different kind of excitement. Just waking up in their tent was an experience in wildlife, with elephants, giraffes, and zebras all part of the incredible view from the window opposite their bed.

Harry once likened his life in London to that of a caged zoo animal, so it was no wonder that witnessing the likes of lions, elephants, and cheetahs surrounded by space and wilderness made him feel free, too. "I have this love of Africa that will never disappear. And I hope it carries on with my children as well," he said, adding that he welcomes any "opportunity to give something back to a country that has given so much to me."

Harry was a tireless supporter of Botswana's efforts to preserve its natural habitats, including his becoming a patron of the Rhino Conservation Botswana charity in January 2017. During the second week of their trip, he showed Meghan the charity's work. Its director, Martin "Map" Ives, took the couple out to see some of the critically endangered black rhino, which Harry helped move and fit with electronic tracking devices in September 2016.

"Harry has seen at firsthand the cruel and senseless damage inflicted on these endangered animals by poachers," Map said. "Rhino conservation is a deadly serious business, and Botswana cannot do it alone—we need everyone to help us fight this battle."

That Harry brought Meghan to see his work with RCB was another testament to the depth of their relationship. He wanted to share everything important in his life with her. "There is a conservation angle to [their relationship]," Map said, "but it's also an emotional attachment."

During the trip, Harry had also introduced Meghan to Dr. Mike Chase, who founded Elephants Without Borders, which supports local communities to coexist with elephants. The couple spent some time with Mike and his partner, Kelly, who showed an awestruck Meghan how to affix a satellite-tracking collar to a ten-thousand-pound mammal.

As Meghan continued her morning yoga practice by the green riverbanks of the Zambezi River, it was difficult not to lose focus.

She had never imagined she would be laying out her mat as wild Cape buffalo grazed across the water and fishermen's boats returned to their ports after the morning's catch.

Nor did she ever dare dream that during this magical trip that the man beside her, the fifth in line to the British throne, would promise to make her his wife. During those soul-baring moments under Botswana's blanket of stars, Harry made his intentions very clear and she wanted nothing more. On their final day in Botswana, they felt more connected to each other than ever—best friends, partners, soul mates.

And Harry quickly proved himself to be a man of his word. Shortly after their return to London, he made his promise official. As Meghan prepared dinner at Nottingham Cottage, which had quickly started to feel like home, he got down on bended knee and asked for her hand in marriage. It was a moment they would never forget. But it would be some time before they shared the news with the world. For now, it would be their little secret.

9

Boom!

Now that they were engaged, there was plenty of discussion at Kensington Palace about the couple making their public debut before the 2017 Invictus Games. But with Harry's international sporting event for wounded, ill, and injured members of the armed services and veterans taking place in Toronto, the September competition became a natural place for their public coming out. (Despite reports claiming otherwise, it was sheer coincidence that the Games were in Meghan's adopted hometown; the host city had been chosen in May 2016.) What could be better than combining a public declaration to each other with perhaps Harry's most important legacy?

The Invictus Games had their genesis when Harry returned from his first tour of duty in Afghanistan profoundly affected by what he had seen.

"In February 2008 I found myself boarding a plane at Kandahar airfield, Afghanistan, that had been delayed due to the loading of a Danish soldier's coffin," he wrote in an essay pegged to the first games. "Three of our own were flying back with us, all in induced comas and with different scales of injuries . . . Many of us on that flight were relieved to be flying home to loved ones, but this was also when the reality of the conflict hit home. Sure, I'd heard about it, expected it, called in many medical evacuations for it, but I had never seen it first-hand. By 'it' I mean the injuries that were being sustained largely due to improvised explosive devices. Loss of life is as tragic and devastating as it gets, but to see young lads—much younger than me—wrapped in plastic and missing limbs, with hundreds of tubes coming out of them, was something I never prepared myself for. For me, this is where it all started."

His advocacy was also inspired by a 2013 White House meeting with Michelle Obama, which the First Lady described as "focused on honoring the sacrifice and service of our veterans and military families." Mrs. Obama, along with the Second Lady, Dr. Jill Biden, created the Joining Forces organization to support veterans and their families by providing education and other opportunities for transitioning service members.

While in Washington, Harry also visited Walter Reed National Medical Center to observe the groundbreaking work of the medical teams aiding many of the most severely injured veterans, including those missing limbs and suffering from TBIs (traumatic brain injuries).

Harry then traveled to Colorado Springs to participate in and lend the Royal Foundation's support to the Warrior Games, a competition for service members organized by the US Department of Defense, which became the inspiration for his Invictus Games. By the time Harry left the States, his goal to honor his fellow soldiers had crystallized into a specific plan to, as Harry put it, "steal" the concept of the Warrior Games for wounded, sick, and injured service members and bring them to London. It was a daunting task, but Harry was filled with a sense of renewed purpose having found his calling. The Invictus Games and the Invictus Games Foundation were born.

William and Harry long had strong ties to the military community not just through their own service but also in their charitable efforts. In 2012, their Royal Foundation created the Endeavour Fund to inspire wounded servicemen and women to pursue physical challenges that supported their recovery. The brothers had also made public and private visits to Headley Court, the UK Department of Defence's medical rehabilitation center, to meet with soldiers learning to live with new prosthetic limbs after being injured in Iraq and Afghanistan.

In September 2014, Harry hosted the first Invictus Games. Aside from his two tours of duty, it was arguably his most important military legacy to date. The Paralympic-style event, in London's Queen Elizabeth Olympic Park, brought 400 competitors from thirteen different nations to compete in nine different adaptive sports. There was everything from wheelchair basketball to archery to wheelchair rugby, which was so fierce it was jokingly referred to as "murder ball." The Games were a chance for people who had suffered from the traumas of war, both visible and invisible, to proudly represent their countries in a new and powerful way.

Harry's compassion often drew comparisons between him and his late mother. Whether cheering on a competitor struggling to finish a wheelchair race or offering words of encouragement to swimmers missing limbs hoisting themselves onto swimming blocks before a race, Harry appeared very much his mother's son, the People's Prince. The association with Diana has never been a burden on Harry; it drove him.

In 2016, Prince Harry redoubled his efforts for the second tournament in Orlando, Florida. During a busy spring promoting Invictus, Harry turned to the president of the United States and Mrs. Obama to help drum up interest in their country for the Games.

In April 2016, the Obamas made their last visit to the UK before the end of the president's second term. They enjoyed lunch at Buckingham Palace to celebrate the Queen's ninetieth birthday and later made a private visit to Kensington Palace for an informal supper with William, Kate, and Harry. A week after their visit, the president and First Lady responded to a challenge Harry made to American athletes via Twitter to "bring it" at the Invictus Games.

"Hey, Prince Harry," Mrs. Obama said in the video. "Remember when you told us to bring it at the Invictus Games?"

Laughing next to her, the president said, "Careful what you wish for!"

"Boom!" a serviceman added as the coda.

Oh, it was on.

"Mrs. Obama came to us with the challenge and I genuinely, I didn't know what to do. She dragged her husband into it, who happens to be the president," he said. "Who can you call to top the president?"

There was only one answer: his grandmother.

"I didn't want to have to ask the Queen because I didn't want to back her into a corner," admitted Harry, ever the gentleman. "But when I showed her the video and I told her, she said, 'Right. What do we need to do? Let's do this.'"

And when Queen Elizabeth II says, "Let's do this," you do it.

In their reply, Harry is seen showing his grandmother the Obamas' challenge. The Queen, who has a wicked sense of humor, simply responds, "Oh, really. Please." On cue, Harry looks at the camera, dryly smirking, and then: "Boom."

The video instantly went viral—and all in service of the Invictus Games in Orlando, where Mrs. Obama appeared at Harry's side for the opening ceremonies.

The 2017 Invictus Games in Toronto posed a whole new kind of challenge with Meghan's introduction as the prince's girlfriend.

Rather than Harry and Meghan basing themselves at her home for the event, Harry's protection officers insisted that the couple stay at a hotel where it would be easier to provide protection and privacy (including hiding the fact that Meghan's mother, Doria, had also secretly flown in to join them for the Games).

Harry and Meghan shared the Royal Suite at the Royal York Fairmont, where not only the Queen and Prince Philip but also Harry's great-grandparents King George and the Queen Mother once stayed. Downstairs in the wood-paneled, marble-floored lobby, a portrait of his grandmother hung proudly. Hardly inconvenienced, the couple had a floor to themselves, except for Harry's protection officers and staff, as well as Meghan's mother. Doria had a suite on the same floor to allow the three to spend some quality time together. It was her first time seeing the couple since they got engaged and there was much to celebrate.

Although Harry had more than a full schedule hosting the Games, he still took time to visit the set of *Suits* to see Meghan's workplace, since it was unclear if he would ever have another chance.

For obvious reasons, things hadn't been the same on set since Meghan started dating Harry. In the early months, Meghan whispered to some of her coworkers that the new boyfriend she'd been flying off to see was actually the prince and began speaking about their time together in code, once mentioning offhandedly to her on-screen dad, Wendell Pierce, that she had just arrived in from London. As of late, though, she had felt the need to pull back and act more reserved around the people she'd known for the better part of the decade.

That hadn't been easy for everyone. While Meghan was invited to her costar and friend Patrick J. Adams's December 10 wedding to the actress Troian Bellisario—a whimsical weekend-long affair that saw guests sleeping in tents and attending a ceremony in the woods of Santa Barbara—she decided in the end that it wouldn't be a good idea for her to attend. Paparazzi flying over the ceremony in helicopters to take pictures of her would have ruined the day for everyone.

Meghan, who had her name excised from shoot schedules to avoid any paparazzi getting word of her location, also began showing up to set with discreet bodyguards. On top of that, crew members she'd toiled alongside for some seven years were issued stern warnings by production not to provide any information about Meghan to reporters and informed that should they disobey, they risked losing their jobs.

While it was hard not to take offense, the team also understood why such precautions were necessary.

"It did make things awkward at the beginning, and there was certainly a little jealousy from some people when she suddenly became the jewel in the crown of the show," a *Suits* crew member said. "But to most of us she was still the same old Meghan, who would bring fun snacks to set to share or hang around after filming to chat with fans outside the studio."

Perhaps that was why, one afternoon before the Games began, castmates and crew were so gracious when the prince slipped into the closed set in the North York section of Toronto to meet the people who had helped keep a secret for the past year.

"He came in quietly, and a lot of people didn't even know he came until after the visit," a production staffer said. "He kept saying how proud he was of Meghan, but he also just seemed curious to see how it all works. He wanted to see the props department, and Meghan was more than happy to take him on a little tour with some of her close friends from the show."

The day before the Invictus Games' opening ceremonies, however, Harry had a packed schedule of official duties. His first stop was Toronto's Centre for Addiction and Mental Health, which Princess Diana had visited twenty-six years earlier. He met with medical personnel to discuss post-traumatic stress disorder, depression, and "invisible injuries" such as mental illness, which veterans, including himself, often struggled with when they returned from service. Harry also held meetings with the new First Lady, Melania Trump, who led the US delegation to the Invictus Games, and the Canadian prime minister, Justin Trudeau.

Before the opening ceremonies, Harry did a walkthrough with aides, familiarizing himself with the facilities and practicing his speech on the teleprompter. While this was his third Invictus Games, tonight was special, as his love would be in the stands, making her first appearance at an official royal engagement.

As Harry prepped for his speech that night, Meghan was figuring out the right look for her public debut with Jessica, who had traveled to the hotel through its underground entrance with numerous dresses for consideration. The good friends knew that every photographer in the Pan Am Sports Centre that night would have his or her lens trained on Meghan. The pressure was on.

As with Kate before her, women around the world looking for style inspiration were turning to Meghan. The "Meghan Effect" was in full swing. That afternoon, she looked at several outfits with Jessica before settling on a burgundy Aritzia midi dress with chiffon pleats and a Mackage leather biker jacket draped over her shoulders. It ticked the right boxes—not too dressy, not too dressed down.

Finally ready, Meghan left for the stadium. Her plus one for the evening was her good friend, Markus. It was only fitting that the man who had introduced her to many of her friends in Toronto, and helped organize some of those early dates with the prince would be on hand to witness such a special evening. Like Jessica, he was one of the few people to know the couple's big secret.

At the ceremony, Harry was seated with the other international dignitaries. But he snuck glances at his wife-to-be, who sat just eighteen seats away from him. (It would have been considered a breach of royal protocol for Meghan to join Harry while he was seated next to Melania Trump and Justin Trudeau.)

As the Games continued for the next day and a half, the royal correspondents assembled there were beginning to wonder if the couple would actually make their public debut.

Kensington Palace routinely communicates with the same group of approximately twenty reporters who cover the royal family about upcoming events. Much like the White House press corps, it's a close but essential relationship. When William and Harry play polo for their charitable interests, it's the Palace that will often guide the "pack" so the obligatory photos and information can be taken from a safe distance without any violation of privacy. There is a pool of print reporters, television correspondents, and photographers who rotate so that each event is covered by one person from each medium (filing back to other members of what's called the "royal rota"). Naturally, everyone wants to be there for the magic moments—births, weddings, engagements, and, in this case, Harry and Meghan's carefully choreographed coming out.

But this time was different. Harry had instructed staff not to provide information to the press about Meghan's appearance during the Invictus Games as he didn't want a media circus to take away from the athletic competitions. To Harry, detracting from the stories that mattered the most was a no-no. He would sometimes even instruct aides not to put his name before others on press releases, "Because it's not about me. It's about them."

Still, the buildup to their big moment had been mounting since the opening ceremonies, and rumors went into overdrive when a somewhat agitated Ed Lane Fox breezed into the wheelchair tennis arena instructing officials to prepare two seats courtside. *Was this the moment?* If so, many of the royal photographers who followed

Harry weren't present at the tennis match. Only a few British reporters were even in the vicinity.

At 1:45 p.m. on September 25, Rhiannon Mills from Sky News, one of Britain's biggest news outlets, received a call from Jason.

"Rhiannon," Harry's private secretary said, "Prince Harry and Meghan Markle are going to make an appearance in ten minutes."

She was the only UK television journalist who had a crew near the tennis venue, but there was still barely enough time to get her crew in place and ready for what was arguably one of the biggest royal stories of the year.

At 1:55 p.m., in sweltering eighty-six-degree heat, flanked by two protection officers and trailed by Jason, Harry and Meghan made their entrance, fingers intertwined, toward the tennis courts. With Harry's aides meticulously planning their top secret entrance down to the most minute detail, the couples' public coming out, designed to appear low-key, was anything but.

Meghan was dressed casually in a pair of ripped MOTHER Denim jeans, Sarah Flint flats, a bag by Everlane, and, in a cheeky nod to their secret, a white pearl button-down blouse called "the husband shirt" designed by Misha. (Unsurprisingly, the $185 shirt from Misha's collection instantly sold out, and the outfit quickly became a trending topic online.)

Meghan gazed adoringly at her fiancée as they made their way to their seats, where they sat among the Aussie and New Zealand families cheering on the players. The couple were at ease as the cameras captured every move, from Meghan stroking Harry's arm to his putting a protective one around her.

Kylie Lawler, whose husband, Sean, was competing for the Australian team, joked that her spouse probably would never forgive her, because, seated next to Harry and Meghan, she said, "I missed half the match.

"She was excited . . . and lovely," Kylie said. "They seemed really relaxed as a couple."

Kylie had in fact learned about the couple's attendance before the press. Informed by a protection officer a half hour before the couple's appearance, she told her son to go change his shirt, since he was going to sit next to "a future princess."

Harry tried to make time for every veteran and every family member who stopped to thank him. He was gracious about taking photos with the teams. However, after a long day as the focal point of a major sports event, he had no interest in going to a restaurant that night to have people interrupt or stare. At the Invictus Games a year earlier in Orlando, he had spent much of his downtime in the privacy of his hotel rather than venturing out to the city's restaurants and clubs. At this stage of his life, Harry had grown to prefer a night in with close friends, where he could be himself.

So he was looking forward to an intimate dinner at the Mulroneys' home with Justin and Sophie Trudeau as well. But just as Harry and Meghan were preparing to leave the hotel, they got a call about paparazzi staking out Ben and Jessica's house. Local photographers had started to gamble on watching the Upper Canada property in case the couple paid a visit. The dinner was called off.

At least the closing ceremonies were a celebration. Doria and Meghan joined Markus and Jessica in Harry's skybox, where, after the prince delivered a speech, he joined them. He was spotted by photographers tenderly kissing the woman who had captured his heart and listening intently to his future mother-in-law, who later danced in the private box as Bruce Springsteen brought the audience to their feet.

By welcoming Doria at an official royal engagement so publicly, particularly after all the ugly, racist commentary, Harry was consciously showing the world that this was what his future family would look like.

As if the importance of Meghan in Harry's life needed any more reinforcement, when Barack Obama, Joe Biden, and Joe's wife, Jill, attended the last day of the Invictus Games, the former president asked after the prince's lady love.

Hayley Stover, an eighteen-year-old student from Toronto who sat next to the prince at the wheelchair basketball game he attended with President Obama, overheard the former president letting Harry know that Meghan had watched the tennis matches with him.

"Harry was really smiling when he said it," Hayley said. "He looked really happy. It was cute."

President Obama wanted to know how things were going with Meghan's work, and Harry asked how the First Lady was doing. It was just an ordinary conversation between two men talking about their lives.

Before they parted, Harry added, "Send my love to Michelle."

10

Farewell Toronto

Meghan was feeling a little emotional as she looked around the boxed-up living room of her Toronto home. With endless late nights on the *Suits* set and so many farewells, it took more than three weeks to pack her life into the boxes that now surrounded her in early November 2017. A moving team had just left, marking furniture with different labels for overseas shipping or storage, and sheets were wrapped around her white cotton sofas, leaving nowhere left to sit.

With all the packing and changes in routine, her two beloved rescue pups, Bogart and Guy, were currently staying with a friend. Due to Bogs's old age, Meghan was warned that flying seven hours to the UK with him could be dangerous and so he would have to stay behind in Canada with a close friend. (Three years on—and a few visits from his original owner later—and he is still "a very happy dog," a pal shared.) The cozy corner where they slept every night was now empty. The house felt eerily quiet.

Some of her best memories from living in Toronto were made in that space—Thanksgiving dinners with her costars, giggling into the early hours over rosé with girlfriends on warm summer nights, preparing al fresco dinners for Harry when they didn't want to venture out.

But now she'd hosted her last dinner party and marked her final day on the set of *Suits*, where, as her costar and pal Sarah Rafferty had pointed out, they'd all logged more time together than they had with any friends from high school or college.

Although the news was not yet public, Meghan was exiting the long-running legal drama at the end of the season. Her costar Patrick later told *The Hollywood Reporter* that while a lot had gone "unsaid" with Meghan at the end of their run, they left on good terms.

"We grew up together over the course of the show," he explained. "There was this natural sense that we both knew that the time had come for both of us. It went unspoken and we just enjoyed the hell out of the last few episodes that we got to shoot. We both knew that we wouldn't be coming back. It made every one of our scenes that much more special. We had a great time. We could laugh through it. Even the things that might have frustrated us about the show, they became things that we could have a good laugh about and compare notes on just how crazy this thing had become."

Her last few weeks of shooting, culminating in a wedding scene with Meghan's and Patrick's characters, Rachel and Mike, finally tying the knot, had been filled with nostalgia. But she had known for some time that she was ready for a new chapter.

Wendell Pierce, who played her father on the show, gave his on-screen daughter some advice before wrapping on her final scene. "I just wanted her to know that even if we lose touch because of the new life she was about to take on, I would always have her back and be there for her," he said. "We all felt like that. It was emotional to see her leave but also very exciting . . . like sending a child off to college. This was her graduation."

Being on a hit show for seven years was the kind of achievement few in the industry could boast.

"Once we hit the one-hundredth-episode marker, I thought, you know what—I have, I have ticked this box," Meghan said. "I feel really proud of the work I've done there."

She knew that the moment she gave up her role on *Suits* and moved to London, her acting career would be over. Forever. No turning back. In some ways, it came as a relief. As she got older and saw more of the world and saw she had more power to help change it with her platform, she began to think about moving away from acting and toward a career that was more meaningful.

Leaving acting, something she had spent so long working to achieve, was also "terrifying," as she admitted to friends. At one point she *had* dreamed of moving into movies and meatier roles. As she moved into her mid-thirties, however, her dreams and aspirations started to change. A voice inside her kept telling her she could be doing so much more with her platform. That was one inspiration behind *The Tig*. But she also looked up to actresses like Angelina Jolie, who had become a force of her own in the charitable space, focusing mostly on humanitarian projects that she interspersed with the more commercial ones, and funding her life with the occasional brand deal. At one point that was Meghan's career model. But then she met Harry. If she was going to have a real future—and family—with him, she had to give up acting altogether.

Meghan was ready now, especially since a month earlier she had cleared the first hurdle: a formal meeting with the Queen.

Despite a very brief encounter with Her Majesty earlier in the year ("she and Harry literally bumped into her," a source laughed), Meghan was still nervous to meet his grandmother—it would be the first time she was sitting down with the monarch as Harry's fiancée. Though Harry had already obtained formal permission from his grandmother to marry, history had not been kind to divorcées in the royal family. King Edward VIII caused a constitutional crisis in the House of Windsor when he abdicated the throne in 1936 to marry Wallis Simpson, the twice-divorced American who captured his heart. When Princess Margaret asked for permission to marry the divorced Group Captain Peter Townsend in 1955, shortly after Elizabeth had ascended the throne, the Queen was advised by senior courtiers that her sister marrying a divorced man was untenable now that she herself was not only Queen but also head of the Church of England.

Townsend, an accomplished RAF pilot, had been awarded the Distinguished Flying Cross and later served both King George as an equerry and Queen Elizabeth. He also spent time as deputy master of the household. Still, his honors did not change the fact that he was divorced. Princess Margaret was asked to postpone any engagement while Townsend served as an attaché in Brussels, and she later abandoned her plans to marry him.

It was by no means a certainty that Harry's grandmother would grant approval of Meghan but much had changed since the fifties. Three of the Queen's four children have gone through divorces, and Charles was even able to marry Camilla, who was also divorced in 2005. The truth was that the sovereign was simply delighted for Harry.

Days before the October 12 meeting, Meghan and Jessica had discussed what an appropriate outfit would be for the all-important meeting with Her Majesty. As they often did, they went back and forth over iMessage, with photos and voice memos. At one point Jessica kept a second phone only Meghan had the number for— it meant they could chat safely and securely without any worries about hacks. After reviewing dozens of ideas, they settled on a conservative pastel dress.

Meghan, in the middle of filming *Suits*, had flown in and out of London for this meeting only. (A couple of days later she was back on the set in Toronto.) With the paparazzi often staking out the gates of Kensington Palace, Harry and Meghan took no chances getting caught visiting the Queen. Instead of riding in one of the usual Range Rovers, they hopped in a blacked-out four-door Ford Galaxy, a minivan more consistent with moms than with the Firm.

The couple made the one-and-a-half-mile drive to Buckingham Palace. After being waved in by the armed Scotland Yard police guards that man the front gates, the car drove discreetly to the side of the palace and pulled up next to the glass-covered sovereign's entrance. The hundreds of tourists who were gathered outside were none the wiser.

Harry and Meghan rode the Queen's elevator—a stunning wrought-iron lift from the previous century—up to the monarch's private entrance. Exiting the elevator, Meghan saw Paul Whybrew, one of Her Majesty's closest aides.

Page of the Backstairs, tall, slender, and with prominent cheekbones, Paul had been serving the Queen for more than forty years. Meghan recognized him immediately as the man who escorted Daniel Craig (as James Bond) to see the Queen in the video that was created to open the 2012 London Olympics.

The inner sanctum of the Queen's private apartment was not at all what Meghan expected. Not that she really knew what to expect. Harry kissed his grandmother on both cheeks as they walked into her sitting room. Meghan knew she needed to curtsy and had practiced a dozen times before that day.

The maroon-and-cream Aubusson carpet accented with a floral-and-scroll pattern complemented the gilded picture frames around the Old Master paintings hanging on eggshell blue walls. It was a paler shade of Tiffany blue with the most spectacular ornate crown moldings that Meghan had ever seen. Was she really meeting with the head of the Commonwealth?

Today, however, it was just "Granny," as Harry called the Queen, who sat down on the silk, upholstered straight-back chair. Two crescent-shaped wooden tables sat on each side of the white fireplace. On top of one was William and Kate's engagement photo. Other family photos along with stunning displays of white and pink blooms in crystal vases sat beneath the gorgeous paintings.

The meeting took place at 5:00 p.m., the Queen's favorite time to have tea. Meghan loved afternoon tea in Britain. It was a tradition she had come to adore. The Queen always drinks her own blend of Darjeeling and Assam tea, nicknamed the Queen Mary's blend.

Whatever insecurities Meghan had were put to rest when the Queen's corgis took to her right away. Nestled at her feet, Willow realized he had a friend in Harry's future wife. Vulcan and Candy, the Queen's two dorgis (a mix of dachshund and corgi), who also followed Her Majesty around wherever she went, soon followed Willow's lead. Harry would later share in his engagement interview, "I've spent the last thirty-three years being barked at. [Meghan] walks in, absolutely nothing."

As the dogs lay at her feet and wagged their tails, Meghan was also put at ease by the Queen, as warm and loving as Harry had told her his grandmother would be. The conversation flowed naturally before Meghan had to leave—a full ten minutes after their one-hour time slot. The Queen, arguably the busiest woman in the country, never ran over schedule. It was a good sign.

On November 20, a little over a month after her meeting with the Queen, Meghan landed in London, knowing the British capital was no longer just where her partner lived. It was now her home. While the past few weeks had been challenging, this felt right. She was excited.

Harry felt guilty that she had to give up so much—her home, her career—to fit into his world. He was always worried about disrupting her life. Privately he harbored fears about the road ahead. What would the press be like? Would he have to deal with prejudice from more people in his own circle and the institution? He wanted to protect Meghan, to wrap her up and shield her from all the negativity, but he knew that was impossible. He worried about her turning to him one day to say, "I love you, but I can't live like this." Meghan assured him she was strong and ready to "become a team."

After she moved her things into her new home with Harry, the cozy three-bedroom Nottingham Cottage, the plan for the days ahead were shrouded in secrecy. For Harry, as a working member of the royal family, it was business as usual as he continued to attend regular engagements, including a reception for Walking with the Wounded on November 21, the day after she arrived, at the Mandarin Oriental hotel, which was just a few minutes up the road from the home he now shared with Meghan. A big supporter of the veterans charity since 2010, having taken part in their treks to the North Pole in 2011 and the South Pole in 2013, Harry told the organization's co-founder Simon Daglish after he delivered his remarks to the room, "Life is very good."

There was work to be done on the domestic front. During her previous stays in London, Meghan left clothes and a few decorative touches, but now she had to find room for all her belongings. Her natural eye for design had gone a long way toward dressing up the house, but there wasn't really anything she could do to change the size. There were parts of the second floor where the drop ceilings were so low that Harry was forced to stoop his six-one frame to avoid hitting his head. And Meghan's wardrobe nearly filled one of the bedrooms. But a little crowding was hardly a problem. After months of long-distance, Meghan was thrilled to finally be sharing a zip code, W8 4PY, with her partner.

Meghan extended her personal touch beyond the walls of their cottage. She kept a box of disposable hand warmers she ordered from Amazon in the house so that whenever she went past the security gates on cold winter days, she could give a few to the guards.

Meghan always liked to make the places she lived in as comfortable and chic as possible, and she'd moved often due to the nature of her work. This time, however, her domestic bliss was partly a way to cope with the major shift her life had taken, both geographically and internally. She felt at home at Nott Cott with Harry—she's always been able to bloom where she was planted, but she hadn't moved to London to start a new job. She had moved to London to start a new life. And although she was used to living thousands of miles from her mother, her constant source of support, there was something about being in London that felt just that little bit farther away. They spoke on the phone or via text message most days, but it wasn't as easy because of the eight-hour time difference. Plus, she hadn't moved to the UK like any typical member of society; she was going to become a member of the royal family, and that was a change that no one can truly be prepared for.

With Harry and Meghan holed up in their love nest, rumors of their engagement hit a frenzy—chatter not quieted by the fact Kensington Palace aides were more tightly lipped than ever. Media requests for comment on their engagement status were met with no response or a promise of "nothing to report." But the evidence was mounting. When Harry and Meghan took a sudden two-hour meeting with Jason, Harry's head of communications, and Ed Lane Fox, his private secretary, on November 22, it was clear that *something* was happening.

Media speculation continued to mount when BBC staff members and cameramen started to spread the word that they had been contacted by the Palace to capture the couple's first interview as future husband and wife.

Something *had* happened. But one thing was for sure: no one in the couple's circle was about to leak the news early—especially after keeping it secret for so long. The only ones who Meghan had explicitly told were her parents and her best friends, including Jessica, Markus, and Lindsay. To some of her closest girlfriends, she had more recently announced the news simply with a photo of her hand bearing her engagement ring.

"Keeping it a secret was easy for Meghan," a longtime friend said. "It was something she could keep to herself with Harry. And an opportunity to enjoy the moment before it became public news."

If the rest of the world was eager to know the status of Harry and Meghan's relationship, the couple was content to spend most of their time at home at Nottingham Cottage, enjoying, as a friend described it, "cozy nights in front of the television, cooking dinner." They socialized with friends, including Charlie van Straubenzee and his girlfriend, Daisy Jenks, sometimes heading over to the London home Lindsay shared with her husband, Gavin Jordan, for dinner. But the couple spent the majority of their time doing ordinary things like shopping for groceries at Whole Foods, picking up flowers at Kensington Flower Corner, cooking favorite dishes together like pasta with zucchini and "lots of parmesan." (Their laundry, however, was taken care of—and they had a regular housekeeper.)

Nottingham Cottage might have been a quiet space where Harry and Meghan mainly enjoyed every day of domestic life. But it was also where Harry popped the question.

Meghan later revealed during her engagement interview with the BBC that the prince proposed as they were "trying" to roast a chicken for dinner, with Harry adding, "Here at our cottage; just a standard typical night for us."

"It [was] just an amazing surprise, so sweet and natural, and very romantic," she said. "He got on one knee."

"She didn't even let me finish," Harry said with a laugh.

"Can I say yes? Can I say yes?" Meghan said, interrupting and hugging him.

Meanwhile, Harry hadn't even given her the ring yet.

"Can I . . . can I give you the ring?" he said to her.

"Oh yes, the ring!" she said.

Marriage proposals are hard to carry off as planned, but Harry was pleased with how the whole thing went down. "It was a really nice moment," he said. "It was just the two of us, and I think managed to catch her by surprise as well."

Meghan loved the ring—a two-and-a-half-carat cushion-cut conflict-free diamond from Botswana flanked by two roughly three-quarter-carat diamonds from Diana's collection. It was not only a gorgeous piece of jewelry but a meaningful nod to his late mother. "Just the level of thought that went into it," she told one female pal. "I can't get over that."

Harry felt that Meghan and Diana would have been "thick as thieves, without question," he said. "She would be over the moon, jumping up and down, you know, so excited for me."

The thought of his mother, however, turned the happy moment bittersweet.

"Days like today," the prince said in the interview, "[are] when I really miss having her around and miss being able to share the happy news. But you know with the ring and with everything else that's going on, I'm sure she's with us."

Once Harry asked Meghan for her hand in marriage, he had talked to her about how the entire process of marrying a royal would work. He guided her through the necessary protocol that would follow their engagement—including Her Majesty's public declaration of her approval of the union.

Although the Queen had already privately given their engagement her blessing, the Queen's approval wasn't formalized until the following year, when she signed the Instrument of Consent, which read, "Now Know Ye that We have consented and do by these Presents signify Our Consent to the contracting of Matrimony Our Most Dearly Beloved Grandson Prince Henry Charles Albert David of Wales, K.C.V.O., and Rachel Meghan Markle."

The rule that the monarch must approve marriage for the first six in line to the throne has existed since the Royal Marriages Act of 1772, which was ordered by King George III, whose younger brother, the Duke of Cumberland, secretly married Lady Anne Horton, considered to be the disreputable widow of a commoner.

Queen Elizabeth II's declaration approving Harry and Meghan's marriage was made at the meeting of the Privy Council on March 14, 2018, but was not publicly announced until early May.

As Harry explained all of this to Meghan, they also discussed the roles she might take on as a future duchess. Meghan, always a high achiever, was ready and willing to jump to whatever her platform as Harry's wife afforded her. Wanting to attend engagements with Harry immediately after the announcement, she quietly began researching British charities and organizations where she would have the most impact. At the beginning, it was simply her aim to understand the UK's philanthropic landscape rather than just the organizations that dealt with issues close to her heart. This was a chance for the woman who had spent her life up to that point doing work in areas she felt passionately about—to effect real change—and she saw no need to delay the process until after they'd been named husband and wife.

Harry had shared the details of these conversations with Doria while both were in Toronto to attend the Invictus Games.

He hadn't done anything as conventional as ask Meghan's father for her hand in marriage. Meghan, after all, was a strong-willed, independent woman in her mid-thirties whose feminist ideals centered around the simple fact that both genders should be on an even playing field. The only person who had a say in whether she could marry Harry was Meghan herself.

As the days after Meghan's move to London ticked by, a group of dedicated media outlets had permanently gathered outside Kensington Palace. The press set up cameras and lighting equipment starting at 6:00 a.m. every day, waiting for that much-anticipated moment.

Finally, on November 27, 2017, a frozen Monday morning following the US Thanksgiving weekend, the news everyone had been waiting for was announced. The father of the groom, the heir to the throne, Prince Charles directed his office at Clarence House to reveal the happy news: "His Royal Highness The Prince of Wales is delighted to announce the engagement of Prince Harry to Ms. Meghan Markle."

Sixteen months after meeting her prince, and just over three months after their secret engagement, Meghan was announced as the next royal bride.

11

The Fab Four

The Queen and Prince Philip were quick to follow the news of the engagement from Clarence House with their own message that they were "delighted for the couple," wishing them "every happiness."

Charles, who like the other family members had known since the summer, added that he was "thrilled," and Camilla, the Duchess of Cornwall, jovially declared, "America's loss is our gain."

Meghan's parents also came together, with help from Jason, to add their own congratulations in a joint comment: "We are incredibly happy for Meghan and Harry. Our daughter has always been a kind and loving person. To see her union with Harry, who shares the same qualities, is a source of great joy for us as parents."

William and Kate were characteristically appropriate in their response. "We are very excited for Harry and Meghan," William said in a statement. Kate later told reporters at an engagement, "It has been wonderful getting to know Meghan and to see how happy she and Harry are together," even though, in reality, the two women still didn't really know each other that well.

At the outset of her romance with Harry, Meghan had fully expected Kate to reach out and give her the lay of the land on everything an outsider to the Firm needed to know. But that was not how things turned out. Meghan was disappointed that she and Kate hadn't bonded over the unique position they shared, but she wasn't losing sleep over it. According to a source, Kate felt they didn't have much in common "other than the fact that they lived at Kensington Palace."

Anyway, now that she and Harry were engaged, Meghan had a lot to occupy her mind.

There was a moment after Harry proposed when Meghan realized that moving forward, she would never be able to go anywhere or do anything without letting a protection officer know. Just that thought alone momentarily took her breath away. It didn't feel real. But she quickly embraced this new truth and accepted it as part of her new life.

Within seconds of learning the news, media outlets from around the globe stationed in London raced to the tightly organized photo op at the Sunken Garden in Kensington Palace, where Princess Diana would often chat to the gardeners after morning jogs around Kensington Gardens. Harry had long ago accepted the inevitability that any woman he picked to be his wife would be compared to his mother. His sister-in-law, Kate, was also measured against her. The late princess's legacy set a high bar with the British public, and Harry was okay with that. He felt that in marrying Meghan, he had picked a partner with the same level of warmth and humanity his mother had possessed.

When the couple walked down the stone steps in front of the garden's lily pond, taking position in front of the cameras on a small chalk cross marked on the ground by a Kensington Palace assistant, Meghan paired her white belted coat with an emerald green dress by the Italian designer Parosh, which had been packed and shipped over with help from Jessica before the announcement, alongside an entire "engagement wardrobe."

With a permissive nod from Kensington Palace aides, a few questions from the press were allowed.

"When did you know she was the one?" one reporter called out.

"The very first time we met," Harry replied, without hesitation.

"Was it a romantic proposal?"

"Very," Meghan said with a smile, holding up her hand to show off her diamond engagement ring.

Harry thanked everyone for coming before they returned to within the private confines of the Palace, holding hands as they walked inside, to prepare for their first television interview.

Filmed in the modest living room of Nottingham Cottage, their time spent with the BBC news presenter Mishal Husain gave a remarkably sincere and affectionate insight into their sweet romance. With the nerves of the photo-op subsiding, both Harry and Meghan were feeling loose, even joking with crew members as they prepared the shoot.

The couple recounted the details of their whirlwind courtship, from the first date to the months of their transatlantic relationship jetting between London and Toronto. "Coming over here four days or a week, and then going back and then straight into filming the next day. Four a.m. wakeup calls, on a Monday, straight into set," Harry said. "Just trying to stay as close as possible. But, you know, on two different time zones. And five hours apart does have its challenges. But we made it work, and now we're here. So, we're thrilled."

Whether everyone in Britain and around the world was equally thrilled or ready for a confident, unapologetically feminist, mixed-race duchess to occupy a position in the House of Windsor still remained to be seen. However, for the monarchy to truly survive, it must adapt—and rejecting a woman because she was divorced, an actress, or biracial was no longer tenable, despite whatever misgivings certain family members had been whispering privately.

One courtier had said Harry had been "very brave" with some who hadn't been as welcoming. Whether it was Meghan's humble background, her American roots, accusations she was a social climber, concerns about the speed of the relationship, or simply veiled racism in British society, not everyone—and not just the press—was altogether supportive of Harry's prospective bride.

For Meghan, it just meant she had to work that much harder to prove them wrong—beginning, shortly after their engagement, the lengthy process of becoming a UK citizen without skipping the line.

Citizenship was just the start. Knowing that his proposal had officially sealed Meghan's entry into his unique, hard-to-understand world, Harry insisted his fiancée have a dedicated team to assist her in learning all the ins and outs of royal life. "Harry wanted staff that Meghan could truly trust in all situations," a source said, "people that, no matter what, would have both their backs."

This team—who referred to Harry and Meghan as "PH" and "M"—included Amy Pickerill, who would become Meghan's assistant private secretary; Heather Wong, Harry's deputy private secretary and a former political appointee in the Obama administration, serving as Secretary of Public Affairs at the US Department of Homeland Security; Ed Lane Fox; and Jason Knauf.

Shortly after the engagement announcement, aides at Kensington Palace and the Cambridges joined Harry and Meghan at the Hurlingham Club in Fulham, London. The quintessentially English country house was the perfect place to toast to a new working relationship together and discuss Meghan's upcoming role within the Royal Foundation, including what type of projects she would like to explore within the charitable organization. "There were several meetings to make sure she was supported in carving out the right role for herself in the family, on empowerment, other issues she cared about, so she had the right resource support," a courtier shared. And that was just the beginning of her introduction to the family business.

Set to undergo the same informal training Kate had embarked upon following her engagement to William—a series of instructions that covered everything from how to most gracefully exit your chauffeured sedan while wearing a pencil skirt to when to curtsy to members of the family several rungs up the hierarchy from you— Meghan was connected to a team of experts. She had hoped to take etiquette lessons, too, but curiously they were never on offer.

Meghan's training wasn't just in niceties such as how to curtsy. She also underwent an intense two-day security course with the SAS, the British Army's most elite regiment. The training—which all senior members of the royal family except the Queen have completed at SAS headquarters in Hereford—is preparation for all high-risk security scenarios, including kidnapping, hostage situations, and terrorist attacks. Meghan took part in a staged kidnapping, where she was bundled into the back of a car by a "terrorist," taken to a different location, and then "saved" by officers firing fake guns (the kind used in Hollywood filming) for realism.

During the mock kidnapping, Meghan was even taught to develop a relationship with the enemy. She was also instructed on how to drive a car while in pursuit. A source said it was an "extremely intense and scary" experience for Meghan, but one that she was grateful to have gone through.

Kate didn't undergo her training until after her wedding to William, but Meghan's took place earlier, as the couple had received an unusually high number of threats. "There have been some absolutely terrifying and stomach-churning threats made to Meghan since she started dating Harry," an aide said. "Unfortunately, they continued for some time."

The level of threats wasn't the only difference between Meghan's and Kate's experiences as royal fiancées. A former senior courtier said of Kate, "She was lovely and smart and shy and modest, and beautifully gorgeous. And very watchful. She always used to say, whenever she rang me . . . when she was the girlfriend, 'I'm really sorry. I don't want to bother you with these facts.' I'd say, 'Of course you should bother me with them.'"

On the other hand, Meghan, said the courtier, "arrived in this job a fully formed adult, having lived already a third of her life. She is a Californian who believes she can change the world. She creates her own brand, she creates her own website, she does deals. She talks about life and how we should live.

"Good for her," the courtier, who admits to being "rather fond" of the former actress, continued. "That's the way in America. In Britain, people look at that and go, 'Who do you think you are?'"

Fair or not, it was going take Meghan extra effort to avoid ruffling feathers.

Jason and Ed had been filling in as Meghan's advisors in an informal capacity for months. But now that she was officially embarking on life in the Firm, royal watchers would be observing her that much more closely. Any curtsy deemed too shallow or any skirt believed to be too short would be noted and commented upon and, as such, Meghan would need someone to help her in a full-time capacity, both guiding her through the potential landmines and comforting her when the public criticism grew to be too much.

Amy Pickerill, or "Pickles" to friends, was appointed as Meghan's right-hand woman. The University of Nottingham graduate and former media relations manager was just a few years younger than Meghan and would become known to the public as the woman who collected the countless bouquets of flowers, cards, and gifts thrust in Meghan's direction during walkabouts. Behind the scenes, however, her job involved everything from managing Meghan's schedule to whispering advice on how to handle individual situations. Should Meghan be unsure of a topic of conversation or the name of someone she was meeting at an engagement, it was Amy's job to discreetly bring her up to speed. And should she simply need a comforting word after a long day, well, the aide offered those as well.

In regard to her dress, Meghan didn't want to be seen as too fashion forward. She had a "mindful vision," hoping that the press would focus more on her humanitarian work and less on whether she landed on best-dressed lists. Her "work wardrobe," as she called it, needed to consist of polished pieces in neutral hues that didn't detract from the people she was going to be meeting or appear too showy. Each outfit must also include at least one piece or accessory by a local designer, a show of her solidarity to whatever area she might be visiting. "She really does put a lot of thought into those details," said George Northwood, the British hairstylist who worked with Meghan for two years after her wedding. "I always remember wherever we went, she would always try to hero small businesses and local jewelry designers."

For that all-important first royal engagement—a December 1 trip to Nottingham to attend a World AIDS Day event and meet with Full Effect, a group of positive role models for kids—Meghan chose a khaki-hued midi skirt from the London-based brand Joseph, a basic black turtleneck, and a pair of black, suede over-the-knee boots crafted by British designer Kurt Geiger. Her look, which she put together herself, got the stamp of approval from Kensington Palace.

Meghan's decorum was on point as well. She didn't need any coaching in how to charm fans. When she turned up at 11:05 a.m. to greet the crowds, who had been standing in the thirty-six-degree weather outside the National Justice Museum since 6:00 a.m., Meghan spent nearly a half hour chatting with well-wishers and delighting in the flowers, homemade cards, and Haribo sweets (well-known to be the prince's favorite). Careful to not come off as pretentious, she extended her hand to each person along the route, introducing herself with a cheery "Hi, I'm Meghan," as if they weren't already familiar with her broad smile.

The move was a winner. As she shifted to the next person in line, she left a trail of compliments in her wake. One woman marveled at how eagerly Meghan stooped down to speak with her three-year-old, praising him for waiting in the chilly weather. Another was impressed that Meghan had noted her familiar California accent and inquired about her reason for being in the UK. If there were nerves about how she would come off on her first day of royal duty (and there were, as she confessed to a senior aide the night before), she didn't show them. She appeared genuine as she accepted sticker-laden cards from children, compliments on her shiny new ring, and questions about her recently wrapped role on *Suits*.

When one local and her husband bravely asked if she would indulge them in a selfie, Meghan was polite in her refusal. "Oh, I'm so sorry," she said with a smile, remembering the advice she had been given earlier by an aide. While she would have absolutely loved to pose with the pair, she was to be an official member of the royal family soon, and selfies were frowned upon. And Meghan was nothing if not a quick study.

While Meghan was learning the proper protocol for becoming a royal, some aspects of royal life were changing. Even the Queen understood that fact when she made the decision to invite Meghan to the Christmas church service at St. Mary Magdalene and family celebrations at Sandringham. Significant others had not typically been welcome at this gathering until the union was made official by the Church through marriage. Kate hadn't been invited to Christmas in 2010 after her engagement to William, but then again, it had been easier for Kate to spend the holiday with her parents at their nearby home in Bucklebury.

The Queen hadn't made an exception for Meghan because she preferred her to Kate. The monarch adored her ginger-haired grandson and wanted Meghan to feel welcomed by the family by inviting her to the royal holiday celebrations at Sandringham and the pre-Christmas lunch she held for extended family members at

Buckingham Palace. This was the steadfastness that the Queen was admired for in action.

The pre-Christmas lunch was an opportunity for the Queen to celebrate with many lower-ranking family members, who wouldn't get an invitation to Sandringham. It was also the first family event for Meghan, who wore a black-and-white lace midi Self-Portrait dress and diamond earrings.

Unfortunately, the Queen's gesture of support for Meghan was nearly eclipsed when Princess Michael of Kent, the wife of King George V's grandson Prince Michael of Kent, wore a blackamoor brooch to the celebration. Blackamoor, a style of Italian decorative art dating back to around the end of the Middle Ages, typically portrayed highly stylized images of African or other non-European men wearing head covering such as turbans and rich jewels to contrast with their very dark skin. Often depicted as servants, the blackamoor symbolized the subjugation of the Moors, a loose term to describe the Muslims of medieval Spain or anyone of Arab or African descent.

Royal family members, including the Queen and the Duchess of Cambridge, often wore brooches at official engagements to offer a symbolic message. Kate picked the Queen Mother's diamond maple leaf brooch for her first tour to Canada with William, and in 2013, the Queen wore a colorful flower basket brooch, gifted by her parents to mark Charles's birth in 1948, to Prince George's christening.

The blackamoor brooch has a complex history. Both Elizabeth Taylor and Grace Kelly once had the Venetian glass brooches in their jewelry collections. But in today's world, the image is culturally offensive and racist. The fashion house Dolce & Gabbana had been roundly criticized in 2012 when they used the exoticized European art style on the runway when debuting their Spring collection.

When it comes to royal fashion, much thought goes into every detail. Princess Michael's choice of brooch could have simply been a mistake, but in the back of Meghan's mind, she wondered if there wasn't a message being sent in the pin of the torso of an African man wearing a gold turban and ornate clothing. At the bare minimum, it showed insensitivity to Meghan's African American roots and the racism she had encountered since pairing up with Harry.

It was not Princess Michael's first time being accused of racism. In 2004, she was overheard telling African American patrons of a New York restaurant to "go back to the colonies."

Princess Michael, who lived nearby Harry and Meghan at Kensington Palace's Apartment 10, later apologized for wearing the brooch, in a statement saying she was "very sorry and distressed that it has caused offence." Some aides questioned the sincerity of the princess's apology. Regardless, the damage had been done, particularly since the Queen's purpose had been to make Meghan, who had just moved to England, feel at home during the holidays.

Harry and Meghan spent some of the holiday with William and Kate at Anmer Hall, as the Queen's Sandringham invitation to Harry's future bride did not include staying under her roof, which would not happen until the marriage was formalized.

The ten-bedroom Georgian country house—on the grounds of the Sandringham estate, two miles from the Queen's home—had been the Queen's gift to the Cambridges. Originally intended as a country place, William and Kate had taken up full-time residence in Norfolk shortly after Princess Charlotte's birth, because William was serving as an East Anglian Air Ambulance pilot nearby. There, the couple often entertained out of their huge kitchen with its glass-roofed dining area. Friends and family from nearby gathered informally in the inviting space for laid-back meals—a stark departure from lunch at Buckingham Palace or Sandringham, where guests were served by a full staff.

Christmas at Sandringham was as regimented as Sunday roasts were casual at Anmer Hall. The schedule began with members of

A one-year-old Meghan Markle giggled with mother Doria Ragland during a family picnic in Los Angeles, California, in the summer of 1982.
@meghanmarkle/Instagram

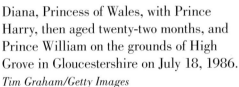

Diana, Princess of Wales, with Prince Harry, then aged twenty-two months, and Prince William on the grounds of High Grove in Gloucestershire on July 18, 1986.
Tim Graham/Getty Images

Harry, aged ten, joined his mother and family for a parade to commemorate the 50th anniversary of Victory over Japan Day on The Mall in London on August 19, 1995. *Antony Jones/Julian Parker/ Getty Images*

In 2011 Meghan attended the graduation ceremony at which her mother received a Master of Social Work from the University of Southern California in Los Angeles.
@meghanmarkle/Instagram

After announcing their engagement, Harry and Meghan posed for a series of stylish portraits (ABOVE AND OPPOSITE, TOP LEFT) with fashion photographer Alexi Lubomirski in December 2017 on the grounds of Frogmore House in Windsor.
Handout/Getty Images

It's official! Harry and Meghan proudly shared the news of their engagement at a photo call in Kensington Palace's Sunken Garden on November 27, 2017. *Chris Jackson/Getty Images*

On the same Botswana trip during which Harry proposed, the prince introduced Meghan to friends from conservation group Elephants Without Borders on August 12, 2017, and they helped fit satellite tracking collars.
@SussexRoyal/Instagram

Prince Harry and President Barack Obama bonded while watching a wheelchair basketball event at the Invictus Games Toronto on September 29, 2017. *Samir Hussein/Getty Images*

During their "engagement tour" of the UK, Harry introduced Meghan to a number of charitable organizations, representatives of which were present during a visit to Cardiff Castle in Wales on January 18, 2018. *Ben Birchall/Getty Images*

The newly minted Duchess of Sussex with Prince Harry in ceremonial uniform traveled down The Mall for her first Trooping the Colour—the Queen's official birthday parade—in a horse-drawn Ascot Landau carriage on June 9, 2018. *Max Mumby/Getty Images*

Meghan paid several private visits to the women of Hubb Community Kitchen at west London's Al Manner Muslim Cultural Heritage Centre in 2017, and a year later helped them launch *Together: Our Community Cookbook*. *Chris Jackson/Getty Images*

They do! The Duke and Duchess of Sussex shared their first kiss as husband and wife on the steps of St. George's Chapel at Windsor Castle following their May 19, 2018, wedding ceremony. *Ben Stansall/Getty Images* After the service, the couple took to an open carriage for a procession through the streets of Windsor (OPPOSITE). *Yui Mok/Getty Images*

The Duke and Duchess of Sussex joined the Queen to watch a Royal Air Force fly-over above Buckingham Palace to mark the centenary of the RAF alongside the Duke of York, the Prince of Wales and Camilla, Duchess of Cornwall, and the Duke and Duchess of Cambridge as well as other senior family members on July 10, 2018. *Max Mumby/Getty Images*

Harry and Meghan took in the sights of Australia's Sydney Harbor as they cheered on contestants during a sailing event on day two of the 2018 Invictus Games. *Chris Jackson/Getty Images*

As Captain General of the Royal Marines, Harry visited the base of 42 Commando Royal Marines in Devon for a Green Beret presentation on February 20, 2019. *Finnbarr Webster/Getty Images*

Shortly after announcing their pregnancy, Harry and Meghan went barefoot to meet members of mental health awareness group OneWave during an October 19, 2018, visit to South Bondi Beach on their sixteen-day Oceania tour. *Chris Jackson/Getty Images*

William and Harry went head to head at the King Power Royal Charity Polo Day at Billingbear Polo Club in Wokingham on July 10, 2019. *Max Mumby/Getty Images*

Harry and Meghan smiled as they watched local secondary school students play soccer while visiting the town of Asni in Morocco on February 24, 2019. *Samir Hussein/Getty Images*

After a night on the royal train, Meghan joined grandmother-in-law the Queen for a day of engagements, including the opening ceremony of the Mersey Gateway Bridge, in Cheshire on June 14, 2018. *Max Mumby/Getty Images*

Archie's first royal visit! Harry and Meghan's five-month-old son (pictured in Cape Town on September 25, 2019) joined the couple on their tour of southern Africa. *Samir Hussein/Getty Images*

Proud parents Harry and Meghan carried Archie out into Windsor Castle's Rose Garden for christening portraits on July 6, 2019, after a baptism in front of close family and friends by Archbishop of Canterbury Justin Welby. *Chris Allerton/ SussexRoyal*

A historic moment. Harry and Meghan introduced the Queen to her eighth great-grandchild, Archie Harrison Mountbatten-Windsor, at Windsor Castle on May 8, 2019, alongside Prince Philip and Doria Ragland. *Chris Allerton/SussexRoyal*

William, Kate, Meghan, and Harry, then dubbed the Fab Four, walked
together to the Christmas Day service at the Church of St. Mary Magdalene
on Norfolk's Sandringham Estate on December 25, 2018.
Samir Hussein/Getty Images

Harry and Meghan walked the yellow
carpet at the European premiere of
Disney's *The Lion King* in London on
July 14, 2019.

Max Mumby/Getty Images

Meghan wore a headscarf while visiting
the Auwal Mosque with Harry on day
two of their royal tour of South Africa, on
September 24, 2019.

Samir Hussein/Getty Images

Arch meets Archie. Harry and Meghan introduced their son to Archbishop Desmond Tutu and his daughter Thandeka Tutu-Gxashe at the Desmond & Leah Tutu Legacy Foundation in Cape Town on September 25, 2019. *Samir Hussein/Getty Images*

During a September 27, 2019, visit to Dirico, Angola, Harry walked through a minefield being cleared by the Halo Trust. *Tim Graham/Getty Images* During the same visit, the prince toured an area of Huambo that Diana famously walked in 1997 and found it now a thriving town. *Dominic Lipinski/Getty Images*

(ABOVE) For their final royal engagement, Harry and Meghan joined senior members of the Royal Family at the Commonwealth Day Service at London's Westminster Abbey on March 9, 2020.
Gareth Cattermole/Getty Images

(TOP RIGHT) Harry took a bundled-up Archie out for a walk by the Saanich Inlet in November 2019 during their four-month stay on Vancouver Island, Canada.
@SussexRoyal/Instagram

(RIGHT) Wearing his Captain General of the Royal Marines uniform for the last time, Harry attended the Mountbatten Festival of Music with Meghan at London's Royal Albert Hall on March 7, 2020.
Karwai Tang/Getty Images

the royal family arriving in order of seniority (after the Queen had settled in earlier in the week), with Prince Charles and Camilla arriving last, on December 24.

As with every aspect of the event, arrivals are carefully orchestrated. Family members are dropped off at the front entrance, where chauffeurs and valets are waiting to ferry luggage and gifts through the side entrance. While luggage is carried upstairs, Christmas presents are placed in the red drawing room, on a big trestle table marked off into sections for the Queen, Prince Philip, and every other family member. Then guests are assigned bedrooms in the 270-room "Big House," as it is called, and handed a timetable for meals and events. Shortly after 4:00 p.m. of Christmas Eve, the family gathers for afternoon tea.

The chefs had spent days preparing the many elaborate meals to be enjoyed by Sandringham's guests. There was Christmas lunch of turkey; sage, onion, and chestnut stuffing; roasted potatoes; mashed potatoes; parsnips and Brussels sprouts; and flaming Christmas pudding with brandy for dessert. The head chef himself carved the two turkeys in the royal dining room. It was the one time of the year when the head chef was invited into the dining room and rewarded by the Queen with a glass of whiskey to toast the holiday. (The second chef went upstairs to the nursery to carve a third turkey there. Children weren't allowed to join the adults until they could conduct themselves properly.) The evening buffet on Christmas Day was even more elaborate, according to the former royal chef Darren McGrady, whose spread of lamb chops with mint, cold poached salmon, foie gras en croute, oxtail, a side of pork, roast chicken, smoked turkey and roast York ham, mixed salads, new potatoes, and borscht is still on the menu today. Sweets were also plentiful, with traditional mince pies, brandy butter, and vanilla ice cream.

Following teatime on Christmas Eve—where the family was served freshly baked scones, two types of sandwiches, pastries like chocolate éclairs and raspberry tartlets, and a big cut cake—everyone would gather in the red drawing room to exchange gifts.

The family followed the German tradition of giving gifts on December 24. The children received typical Christmas presents, such as the huge fire engine set George received one year, a tricycle for Charlotte, and wooden toys for Louis. (When William and Harry were children, Prince Edward bought them pump-action water guns, which the boys, who came racing into the kitchen, used to spray all the chefs soaking wet.) But the adults all frowned upon lavish presents for one another. Instead, Christmas was an occasion for inexpensive and sometimes humorous gifts.

One year, Harry reportedly gave the Queen a shower cap emblazoned with the phrase "Ain't Life a Bitch," which she loved. Another time he gifted his grandmother a Big Mouth Billy Bass singing toy that was said to sit proudly in Balmoral, her Scottish retreat, and provide the Queen with great laughs. Kate, rumored to have made her grandmother's chutney her first year at Sandringham, once gave Harry a "Grow Your Own Girlfriend" kit. More recently, goodies from the perfumier Jo Malone have reportedly been a favorite gift of the Duchess of Cambridge.

Prince William once gave his grandmother a pair of slippers emblazoned with her face. Princess Anne bought her brother Prince Charles a white leather toilet seat, supposedly because he collected them. For her father, Prince Philip, who loved to barbecue, she got a pepper mill with a light on the end, to easily see the meat grilling as it grew dark.

The overwhelming seven outfit changes in twenty-four hours that Sarah Ferguson described of her Sandringham experience was the least of Meghan's concerns. Although Meghan was a trained actress, this was an audition like no other, and she wanted to impress her future royal relatives. To that end, Meghan's biggest challenge was finding the perfect novelty gifts to amuse her new extended family. At least one of her gifts was a huge hit—a spoon for William that had "cereal killer" embossed on the shallow bowl end of the utensil.

Christmas Eve dinner was a decidedly more formal affair. The attire was black tie and dinner consisted of dishes such as shrimp and Sandringham lamb, with tarte tatin for dessert.

Perhaps the most high-pressured event of all for Meghan was the Christmas Day church service. The day started with the full English breakfast served to the men at 8:00 a.m. (The women traditionally took breakfast on trays in their room.) Then the family walked en masse a few hundred yards down the well-worn path to the tiny stone church St. Mary Magdalene, which the Queen attended every Sunday while at Sandringham. (The Queen arrived not on foot but in her maroon Bentley.) Hundreds of fans lined up along the path, many who had been waiting since three in the morning to catch a glimpse of the royal family.

In a collared Sentaler camel coat with a chestnut Philip Treacy hat and chocolate suede Stuart Weitzman boots, Meghan could be seen quietly conferring with William, Harry, and Kate. They wanted to make sure she knew exactly what was going on and in what order.

The crowds couldn't have been more excited to see Harry with his new fiancée. Cameras braced and people cheered as William, Kate, Harry, and Meghan walked side by side. The "Fab Four" had arrived.

William, Kate, Harry, and Meghan were a hit, and not only at Christmas. On February 28, 2018, the four reunited to make their first official joint engagement. The occasion on that snowy morning in London was the first Royal Foundation Forum, an opportunity to showcase William's, Kate's, and Harry's goals across their core interests of mental health, underserved youth, the armed forces, and wildlife conservation. Upon marriage, Meghan was to become the fourth patron of the foundation, an umbrella organization for the young royals' charitable initiatives started by William and Harry in 2009 to use as the main vehicle for their charitable giving.

Growing up Windsor meant a life marked by two principal themes: duty and service. William and Harry's grandmother had famously told the world on her twenty-first birthday, "I declare before you all that my whole life, whether it be long or short, shall be devoted to your service and the service of our great imperial family to which we all belong." Her commitment to the monarchy and the commonwealth has always been unwavering.

From the time both of the princes were little boys, William and Harry had learned, not just from their grandmother but from their parents as well, that there was no higher calling than service. Both young heirs realized the value of their birthright in harnessing change. The Royal Foundation provided the means to do that.

"We are part of a respected institution with the timeless values of family, service, duty, and integrity," Harry said at the forum in London, where all four sat together on a stage, taking questions from a moderator. "We feel a tremendous responsibility to play our part to effect societal change for the better. I'm incredibly proud my soon-to-be wife will be joining us. We're pretty tied up with planning a wedding at the moment, but we're really looking forward to working as a pair and as a four going forward, hoping to make as much of a difference where we can."

The Royal Foundation event gave Meghan an opportunity to forecast, for the first time, what her life as the newest member of the royal family might look like.

When the conversation turned to her, she made an impassioned plea for female empowerment. "You'll often hear people say, 'Well you are helping people find their voices,' and I fundamentally disagree with that, because women don't need to find a voice," she said. "They have a voice; they need to feel empowered to use it, and people need to be encouraged to listen."

This was a bold statement for the royal family, but not for this younger generation.

Meghan envisioned a life on the front line, not on the sidelines, hoping to use her influence to make a difference. Almost three months after her public introduction at the Royal Foundation Forum, Harry and Meghan attended a Commonwealth Youth Forum event at the Commonwealth Heads of Government Meetings and pledged their support to young people in the LGBTQ community, something that would have been unthinkable fifty years earlier. Harry was also appointed as Commonwealth Youth Ambassador by the Queen. With Meghan at Harry's side, the couple hoped to highlight the work of young people and always champion those without a voice.

In fact, over thirty Commonwealth nations still had anti-gay laws on their books. If anyone thought Meghan was prepared to set her values aside, they would be sorely mistaken. Her first days as a royal fiancée were already evidence that while she intended to respect tradition, she wouldn't suppress her voice.

The new generation of royals were all full steam ahead, but just like with all family businesses, the road was not always smooth. When asked during the Royal Foundation Forum if there were family disagreements living and working in such close proximity with one another, William, normally guarded about life behind palace walls, replied with surprising candor. "Oh yes."

"Have they been resolved?"

"We don't know!" Prince William laughed.

Harry jumped in to say it was good to have "four different personalities" who "all have that same passion to make a difference.

"Working as family does have its challenges; of course it does. The fact that everybody is laughing shows they know exactly what's it like," he said, joking that he couldn't remember if all their arguments had been resolved, as they come "thick and fast."

"But," Harry said, "we are stuck together for the rest of our lives."

12

A Problem Like Samantha

The trouble began with Samantha Markle. Meghan's romance with Harry had hardly been public a full twenty-four hours when her half sister sensed an opportunity. Never mind that she hadn't seen her estranged half sister in more than a decade.

Samantha—who had changed her name from Yvonne and dyed her hair a fresh shade of blond—was Thomas's eldest child from his first marriage to Roslyn Loveless. Thomas had met Roslyn in Chicago when he was working at the local news station as a nineteen-year-old; she had been just eighteen. The two were pregnant and married within the year. Thomas Jr. followed two years later. After splitting up in 1975, Roslyn headed off to New Mexico with Yvonne and Thomas Jr. As teenagers, the children had briefly moved back to California to be with their father. They had not stayed.

Partly due to their seventeen-year age difference, Meghan had crossed paths with her half sister only twice since growing up, the most recent time being when Thomas asked her to travel with him to New Mexico for twenty-four hours to attend Samantha's college graduation in 2008. That was the occasion of the one picture of the two sisters that would be shared across countless news outlets.

A trusted confidant shared, "The reason why the press keeps running the exact same picture is because that's all that exists. If there were more, Samantha would have sold them."

With the handful of snaps she had from Meghan's youth, Samantha reached out to *The Sun* with her story about how snagging a royal had been the actress's lifelong ambition.

"It was something she dreamed of as a girl when we watched the royals on TV," Samantha said. Though the sisters had scarcely interacted since Doria decided to leave Thomas when Meghan was just two, in Samantha's version, the sisters were close enough to share their crushes with each other. Meghan apparently confessed to having one on the younger prince. "She always preferred Harry," Samantha claimed. "She has a soft spot for gingers."

That was harmless enough, but Samantha went on to paint Meghan as a manipulative climber, carefully plotting each move from TV star to dedicated philanthropist to Harry's girlfriend. Worst of all, she accused Meghan of keeping her out of the picture because of Samantha's 2008 multiple sclerosis diagnosis, which had left her confined to a wheelchair.

"Her ambition is to become a princess," said Samantha, who was paid handsomely by *The Sun*. "Her behavior is certainly not befitting a royal family member."

As Harry and Meghan's relationship ramped up, so, too, did Samantha's press. When Meghan embarked on her weeklong humanitarian trip to India in early 2017, taking part in talks about women's healthcare and feminine hygiene on behalf of World Vision, Samantha slammed her for not doing more. When Meghan wrote an essay for *Time* about the stigma surrounding menstruation, Samantha made her own publishing announcement. "Excited about my book," she tweeted, 'The Diary of Princess Pushy's Sister.' "(Three years on and the book, has yet to see the light of day.)

While Samantha's media blitz didn't transform her into a household name, the notoriety was accompanied by cash. Samantha knew that to maintain a steady supply of the latter, she needed to keep the stories coming. So, as Harry and Meghan's relationship blossomed, so, too, did Samantha's presence in Meghan's narrative. A confidant explained, "In the beginning, what Samantha was trying to create was this Kate and Pippa dynamic, like close siblings, but that's not the case. Meg didn't grow up with Samantha. She barely saw her."

The actual truth was a lot less salacious and not uncommon for blended families. With an almost-twenty-year age difference between them, the half sisters had simply never been close.

Samantha's brother, Thomas Markle Jr., was largely positive about his half sister in an initial January 2017 interview sold to *The Sun*, where he explained his arrest for waving around an unloaded gun during a drunken fight with his girlfriend, Darlene Blount. The window fitter said he hoped he hadn't brought shame to Meghan and that his actions wouldn't have him excised from the royal wedding guest list.

But a year or so later, when a gold-imprinted wedding invite hadn't made its way to his Oregon home, he picked up on his sister's narrative that Meghan was nothing but an opportunistic social climber desperate to raise her station in life.

"Meghan Markle is obviously not the right woman for you," he wrote in an open letter to Harry published in *In Touch*. "I'm confused why you don't see the real Meghan that the whole world now sees, Meghan's attempt to act the part of a princess like a below C average Hollywood actress is getting old."

Like Samantha, who accused Meghan of shunning her because of her illness, Thomas Jr. leveled an even more hurtful accusation that she had used "her own father," leaving him forgotten, alone, and bankrupt.

That couldn't have been further from the truth. Thomas, an

Emmy winner, had been plagued by money troubles from the time Meghan was a small child, and this had contributed to his breakup with Doria, who herself juggled a variety of jobs, including designing clothes, and running a small gift shop before obtaining a Master of Social Work from the University of Southern California in 2011 and earning her social work license in 2015. Thomas declared bankruptcy once in 1991 and then again in 1993. But what made that unusual was that in 1990, he won $750,000 from the California State Lottery. (According to family, he used Meghan's birthday as part of the winning number combination.) With his winnings, he bought Samantha a car and helped finance a flower shop opened by Thomas Jr. According to his son, however, the bulk of his father's earnings went into a jewelry business, which a friend convinced him was a good investment but later failed. A year on, when he filed for bankruptcy, Thomas's total personal property was valued at $3,931. Bighearted Thomas wasn't a bad person—just bad with money.

Very early on, Meghan had the ambitious goal of getting to the point where she could provide financially for herself and her parents—taking on that heavy psychological burden at an age when most kids are more concerned with Abercrombie & Fitch than living on a budget.

She kept true to her ambitions and started sending her father money as soon as she landed a job on *Deal or No Deal*, earning $5,000 for seven episodes—a steady paycheck she gladly shared with Thomas to cover bills and other living expenses. She loved him and had faith that he just needed a little help to get back on his feet, even if he would often make the same financial mistakes over and over.

Meghan and her inner circle were furious with Samantha's and Thomas Jr.'s absurd claims. As one confidant pointed out, neither her half sister nor her half brother cared when they hadn't been invited to Meghan's first wedding to Trevor. "They probably didn't even know she got married, because they were never in contact," the friend said. "It's such a joke. Of course, they care now that she's marrying a prince."

More than once Meghan asked her father to intervene with Samantha and make her stop selling stories to the media—which Thomas once tried to do.

"You know what you're doing is hurting your sister?" he told Samantha, or "Babe" as he mostly calls her.

"All Meghan needs to do is contact me herself to put an end to it," she replied.

Thomas relayed this back to Meghan, but she never reached out to her half sister, convinced she would probably tape the call and sell it to a tabloid. Meanwhile, their father felt caught between his daughters. A family source said, "He loves them equally, and he didn't want to push either away." And yet, that was exactly what Samantha felt her father was doing. "Sam has always felt he picks Meghan over her, despite how hard she tries," the source said. "Thomas doesn't have to spend holidays alone, but he chooses to, despite getting invites from Sam and Tom Jr."

Meanwhile, Harry couldn't believe how badly Meghan's family members were behaving. It was hard for him to watch the effects on his fiancée. She was frustrated and angry at the things Samantha and Thomas Jr. were selling to the papers. Even more frustrating was the fact that she couldn't just throw out a statement or jump on Twitter to defend herself. She had to stay quiet while they attacked her. Members of the royal family have long been expected to live by the mantra, "never complain, never explain." As a longtime Buckingham Palace aide candidly put explained, "You shut up and ride it out." Meghan would try not to read the press, but often aides brought items to her attention when they needed to ask her if something was fact or fiction. Sometimes those aides themselves were the focus of her half siblings' attacks. At one point, Thomas Jr. started sending demanding emails to Katrina McKeever, the

Kensington Palace deputy communications secretary, in which he detailed the need for financial aid because, he claimed, the press attention prevented him from getting work. Jason and his team found the situation "surreal," but they also felt great responsibility to guide Meghan through the chaos.

While her siblings' falsehoods were upsetting, even more disheartening was the press that willingly published them without checking the facts. The usual negativity was to have been expected when she began dating Harry, but now that they were engaged, the couple hoped the media would be more diligent. And yet, the criticism continued, with stories published based on preconceived notions, erroneous assumptions, and overblown claims from estranged family members.

A classic example was what happened with the royal family pheasant shoot that took place on Boxing Day, a British holiday on December 26.

Although Harry and his brother grew up shooting, the younger prince missed the annual Boxing Day shoot on his first Christmas at Sandringham with Meghan. Some newspapers criticized Meghan, suggesting she had prohibited Harry from the longtime family tradition. The papers describe her as a vegan and an animal rights activist who put down her foot by refusing to let him go. In fact, none of that was true; Meghan was not a vegan, nor had she banned Harry from the hunt.

Meghan, who had wooed Harry with a Sunday roast and received her marriage proposal while cooking a chicken, was frustrated by the absurdity. "These ridiculous stories about family traditions are such bull," a trusted source said. "She does every single thing that everyone else does. She loves tradition."

The truth was that Harry and Meghan had returned to London early, because Harry had agreed to serve as a guest host and editor of the BBC Radio's flagship *Today* program, for which he had already recorded an interview with Barack Obama, the president's first since leaving office.

In the piece, Harry and Obama covered serious and heartfelt topics, such as the excessive use of social media and the power that people in positions of authority in government wield—for good or for bad.

While Harry loathed large portions of the media, he understood that certain outlets could be useful when one of the issues he cared about passionately needed a boost. The prince had conducted the interview with President Obama during the Invictus Games at the tail end of his presidency but had decided to hold it. But the conversation remained topical and on point, and Harry proved that all those years on the other side of the camera made him an adept interviewer, breaking news with his exclusive. The president made a veiled reference to Donald Trump without mentioning him by name, cautioning that excessive use of social media could be harmful by people holding positions of authority in government. He shared how he missed the work but felt serene despite the unfinished business and enjoyed being able to spend more time with his wife and family and set his own schedule.

There was also a funnier side to the interview, when Harry introduced a lightning round during which listeners learned Barack Obama preferred Aretha Franklin over Tina Turner and *the* Queen to the band Queen.

"Great answer," Harry said, laughing.

President Obama came ready to play. After declining to answer the question "Boxers or briefs?" when Harry followed with, "William or Harry?" the president had a quick comeback: "William right now!"

For the December 27 radio show, the prince also featured another important guest: the Prince of Wales, his father.

Listeners were treated to a rare insight into the more tender side of Harry's relationship with his father, which had been prerecorded.

"What I've tried to do all these years is to make sure that I can ensure that you and that your children, my grandchildren, also everyone else's grandchildren, have a world fit to live in," the future king said.

"I totally see it and I totally understand it because of all these years of conversations that we've been having. I do end up picking your brains more now than I ever have done," Harry replied.

"Well, darling boy, it makes me very proud to think that you understand," he said.

"That I'm listening?" Harry joked.

"Well, that's even more amazing," Charles said.

In addition to interviewing President Obama and his father, Harry offered his analysis on Meghan's first royal Christmas, which he called "fantastic."

"We've got one of the biggest families I know, and every family is complex," he said. "She has done an absolutely amazing job, just getting in there. And it's the family, I suppose, that she's never had."

With his statement about the family "she's never had," the prince added fuel to the extended Markle clan's anger and feeling of insignificance now that Meghan had entered a totally different realm of society. Harry's comment only heightened the already tenuous family dynamic and foreshadowed what was to come.

If Meghan was concerned about the controversy Harry sparked with his comment, she didn't have much time to worry, since the tabloids soon moved on to her alleged missteps in protocol during the couple's first joint visit to Wales on January 18. Rather than focus on the way she encouraged an especially shy little girl to join the others in their dance routine at the Star Hub community center in Cardiff or how eagerly the children rushed to envelop her in a group hug or even the boon she gave to Welsh brand Hiut Denim by wearing their black, high-waisted skinny Dina style jeans, a number of articles noted that the couple arrived to the event at Cardiff Castle more than an hour late. Missing from numerous of the reports was the fact that the Great Western Railway train from London's Paddington Station to Cardiff Central, also used by members of the public, had been delayed through no fault of their own.

Among her other "wrongdoings," according to reports, were that she walked ahead of Harry at one point, high-fived a fan, and gave one little girl a personalized autograph complete with both a heart and a smiley face. (The "autograph" was actually a tactful Meghan dodging the favor by writing the young girl's name instead, since signing one's name as a royal was a no-no.)

"Why let facts get in the way of a story," a Kensington Palace aide complained that night.

That same day, Harry took Meghan an hour outside of Cardiff to meet Tiggy Pettifer at her Glanusk Estate home, a six-thousand-acre spread on the River Usk. Tiggy had been Harry's childhood nanny starting in 1993 and a rock for the brothers when Diana died in 1997—she once called the boys "my babies." A strong character, she ruffled feathers at the Palace by letting the boys live as normal a childhood as possible after their mother's death. For example, she once let the young princes rappel down a fifty-meter dam without helmets. Staff at St. James's Palace were so horrified at her carefree attitude that they launched an inquiry, but because the boys adored their nanny so deeply, nothing ever came of it. She resigned in 1999 but had remained in close contact with William and Harry ever since. "Harry was excited to introduce Meghan to Tiggy," a source said. "She's one of the most important women from his childhood, so to bring Meghan, the most important woman in his adult life, to meet her was important to him. He knew they would get along splendidly—and they did."

Publicly, though, Meghan continued to get pummeled with criticism. On February 1, she was lambasted for wearing pants to the

Endeavour Fund Awards, an evening recognizing the achievements of injured veterans and a cause close to former soldier Harry's heart. Never mind that Princess Diana famously wore a similar tuxedo-style look or that the Duchess of Cambridge wore trousers and a blazer to greet families at a pre-holiday engagement in Cyprus. In her sophisticated Alexander McQueen separates, Meghan deftly handled a mix-up when she and her co-presenter were left holding the wrong notes. The crowd laughed along with her. It was a moment that would have flummoxed a less-seasoned public figure.

As much as Meghan tried to ignore the constant barrage, a source close to her said, "It's hard to balance being yourself and overthinking every move in order not to be criticized."

It wasn't just the attacks in the press that Harry and Meghan had to worry about. Once the pair went public, hate mail aimed at Meghan arrived almost daily to the Palace where officials were overwhelmed by threats made from multiple sources, via post, through the Palace's official email, and social media.

On February 12, one day before Harry and Meghan departed for an official trip to Scotland, Kensington Palace security specialists intercepted a letter addressed to the couple. While on the outset it seemed to be much like any other piece of mail received by the busy mailroom based at Clarence House, this one was filled with racist musings and an unidentified white powder. The material, feared to be anthrax, turned out to be harmless. At least physically. The night of the incident, though, Meghan barely slept, later admitting to a friend that she worried the incident was her "new normal."

A good friend of Meghan's called her Grace Under Fire, because despite whatever pressure she was under, she didn't fall apart.

"She knows how to work hard," the close confidant said. "That's not something that scares her off or intimidates her." And, the source added, "No subject is too upsetting or uncomfortable for her when you are her friend."

Which was why Meghan was so wounded when her oldest, life-long friend, Ninaki Priddy, joined the chorus of critics and those willing to cash in on their relationship. The two had known each other since elementary school, when they did everything together— sleepovers, birthday parties—and then attended the same Catholic middle school, Immaculate Heart, as eleven-year-olds. Both children of divorced parents, they established a trust so deep that they thought of each other as sisters. They confided all their secrets in each other and celebrated important milestones—such as Meghan's first wedding to Trevor, where Ninaki served as Meghan's maid of honor.

In the *Daily Mail*, Ninaki not only sold many very personal photos of childhood memories (including birthday parties, vacations, and prom) but also leveled a series of harsh accusations at the woman she had known since they were both five years old.

Describing Meghan's first husband, Trevor, as having "the rug pulled out from under him," Ninaki, who still remains in contact with the director, said, "Once she decides you're not a part of her life, she can be very cold. It's this shutdown mechanism she has. There's nothing to negotiate, she's made her decision and that's it."

While it's true that at the time of their divorce Trevor told pals he was blindsided, many of Meghan's close friends had been anticipating the split for some time, because she told them about the problems she had been having in her marriage. Ninaki was accurate that Meghan was not an arguer. She avoided confrontation. "With Meghan, if you've done her wrong, she'll probably decide to quietly move on without saying a word," a friend said. Instead of fighting with people, she's more likely to ice them out.

But the tabloid article went much further than pointing out Meghan's aversion to conflict, maliciously painting her as a conniving social climber who had had her sights on snagging a prince ever since she was in high school. Having provided a photo of a fifteen-year-old Meghan in front of Buckingham Palace from a trip they took together to Europe, Ninaki said she wasn't "shocked at all" by the news of her old classmate's royal engagement. "It's like she has been planning this all her life," she said. "She was always fascinated by the royal family. She wants to be Princess Diana 2.0."

It was a type of betrayal Palace aides had seen over and over to any woman that marries into royalty. "When money is on the table, people will say *anything* to get more of it," a close aide commented. "I've seen it happen over and over for years."

The mother of another school friend gave a similarly outlandish story to a tabloid, claiming Meghan was "obsessed" with Princess Diana, William, and Harry from an early age. Sonia Ardakani said she gave a copy of Andrew Morton's biography *Diana: Her True Story* to a teenage Meghan, who also supposedly watched videos of Diana's 1981 wedding with her daughter Suzy. Sonia, who called Meghan "a beautiful person with a big heart," also told the *Daily Mail* that her daughter's friend "had sharp elbows. The thing I really admired about her is that she would fight, tooth and nail for the things she wanted in life . . . and Meghan always got what she wanted."

For those who followed these things closely, the comments by old friends and acquaintances appeared to purposefully contradict those made by Meghan in her BBC engagement interview.

"While I now understand very clearly there is a global interest there, I didn't know much about him," Meghan said about Harry before the two were fixed up. "I think for both of us, though, it was really refreshing because given that I didn't know a lot about him, everything that I have learned about him, I learned through him as opposed to having grown up around different news stories or tabloids, whatever else. Anything I learned about him and his family was what he would share with me, and vice versa. So for both of us it was a very authentic and organic way to get to know each other."

It had been Meghan's choice to take on the good and the bad of marrying a prince. Behind the scenes, though, she admitted to being "hurt and disappointed" by her old friend's betrayal. Even though she and Ninaki had drifted apart following her divorce from Trevor, she never expected to see her childhood friend raking her over the coals in a tabloid. When the Palace began advising her, a senior aide did warn her. "If there is anyone who has a story on you or is mad at you, expect them to be exploited by the press, which will buy their story," he said, telling Meghan, "If there is anything, please tell me so I can be one step ahead."

Part of what helped Meghan get through this difficult time was her faith. "Her relationship with God and with her church is extremely important to her," a close friend said. "That's something most people do not know about her. It plays a central role in her life, as an individual, as a woman."

While Meghan was raised with an awareness of God, her family wasn't particularly religious. She attended Catholic school, but that was for educational, not religious, reasons. Her mother, who had been brought up Protestant, was spiritual, picking and choosing elements of different religions, including Buddhism, that she found inspiring. Thomas had been an altar boy at the age of twelve and a confirmed member of the Episcopal Church at fourteen. Although he regularly attended services as a child at the Church of the Nativity in his hometown of Newport, Pennsylvania, as an adult he didn't go to church often. According to her father, Meghan was not christened as a child because he and Doria did not share the same beliefs. They agreed to let her discover her faith for herself. While Meghan was growing up, religion "was not pushed on her," a family friend said.

"Her relationship with God, her spirituality, is born out of her own individual experience," said the friend, who has often prayed with Meghan. "When I talk about her faith being a big part of her life, it's her faith in God. It's her faith in her family. Her faith in the people closest to her."

At Northwestern, one of her best friends came from a Christian family. The two would often pray together while at school. After she graduated, Meghan spent many holidays with her friend's family.

Prayer turned out to be an important tool for Meghan as she faced life's challenges. She used to gather the cast and crew of *Suits* for a prayer circle before starting work. Her invocations on set were never about a specific theology. Instead, she wanted to bring everyone together during moments of transition or difficulty.

"It's prayer and conversations with God that have gotten her through the darkest moments," a source said. "That's something that plays a significant role in her life and her relationship with Harry. The two have been on a journey of faith together."

Before marrying Harry, Meghan chose to be baptized into the Church of England, though she did not need to become an Anglican before marrying him. "This was her choice and a step forward on her own spiritual journey," a friend said. "There was no pressure on her to do this. While she could have done it after the wedding in her own time, Meghan wanted to be baptized before marrying Harry at St. George's Chapel 'out of respect to the Queen.'"

The intimate forty-five-minute service took place on March 6 at St. James's Palace's Chapel Royal—the private chapel where King Charles I received the Holy Sacrament before his execution in 1649, Princess Diana's body laid for a week before her funeral, and Prince George was christened. Prince Louis would also be baptized there four months later, a ceremony both Harry and Meghan attended.

Prior to the baptism, Meghan had regular meetings with the Archbishop of Canterbury, Justin Welby, with whom she formed a "close bond," according to an aide. They discussed many personal matters, including her previous marriage to Trevor. The archbishop asked her what she had learned from her divorce. "The Church of England has a very clear statement on the nature of when people who have been divorced and a previous partner still living can get married, and we went through that," Welby said in February. "It's clearly not a problem."

In front of Prince Charles; Camilla, the Duchess of Cornwall; Harry; and several of Meghan's friends, including Jessica, Lindsay, and Markus, Meghan was baptized from a silver-gilt Lily Font with holy water from the Jordan River poured onto her head using a solid-silver ewer brought by Crown Jeweller Mark Appleby. Before the service, all the silverware was brought to the chapel from its normal home in the Tower of London with the Crown Jewels, as well as the ornate flask that held the holy oil used for her anointment.

During the service—which the Queen, William, and Kate did not attend—the Chapel Royal choir of six Gentlemen-in-Ordinary and ten Children of the Chapel performed. "It was sincere and very moving," the archbishop said. "It was a great privilege."

"It was uplifting," said one of the eighteen guests, who, after the baptism, attended a dinner party at Clarence House hosted by Charles and Camilla in honor of the holy event.

Meghan was fully in the process of embracing her life as a future royal. The same month as her baptism, Harry and Meghan took out a lease on the Great Tew Estate in Oxfordshire—a four-thousand-square-foot converted barn originally built in 1708. Although Harry and Meghan kept Nottingham Cottage as their London base, Nott Cott was becoming too cramped for the couple.

Harry had been looking at homes in the country before he had even met Meghan. In early 2016, the prince considered purchasing with some of the money he inherited from his mother a Norfolk property he had viewed. In 2017, he put out feelers for places in Oxfordshire.

Great Tew, in Chipping Norton, Oxfordshire ("Chippy" to locals), is home to a number of high-profile figures who enjoy the countryside about an hour and a half's drive from London. Kate Winslet and the Beckhams had homes in the area, and other celebrities, such as Eddie Redmayne and Stella McCartney, were regulars at Soho Farmhouse, which was located on the same four-thousand-acre estate Harry and Meghan rented their plot on. While they didn't often visit Farmhouse itself, the royal couple made the most of the amenities offered by the establishment, such as fresh croissants the main kitchen sent over and products from the Cow Shed spa. One of the Farmhouse chefs had even come over and cooked when they hosted guests one evening. If Harry and Meghan didn't want to leave their home, one could hardly blame them. The four-bedroom house featured a tiered shaker-style kitchen with doors that opened out onto the landscaped gardens.

The Oxfordshire house gave the couple an opportunity to host comfortably. Even when they had guests, they rarely used the large dining room—preferring casual gatherings where the food was served straight from the oven to the kitchen table. But their favorite spot to entertain was the garden patio with its brick barbecue.

The lush green grounds around the property were also the perfect environment for their two dogs to thrive. That summer the couple welcomed a new addition to the family, a black Labrador rescue they named after Botswana's currency: Pula. The word means "rain" in the Bantu language of Setswana—and for very good reason. With its semi-arid terrains, the country considers rain valuable and a blessing. Just like the high-energy pooch.

Many family and friends (including Redmayne and his wife, Hannah Bagshawe, who had become part of Harry and Meghan's wider circle) spent time in the couple's comfortable home that was decorated with a few items Meghan had shipped over from her time in Toronto.

Jessica visited a couple of times, including just before the wedding. The two spent the weekend letting their hair down, wearing face masks, drinking "copious amounts of wine," calling Jessica's husband, Ben, to say hi and giggling because they were both tipsy.

Doria visited two times, and not only did she have her own room and bathroom, she had an arrival free of intrusion from the press.

Meghan's mother was collected directly from the tarmac at Heathrow, checked out through the VIP arrival area, and then driven straight to the countryside. It was a much-needed respite from the onslaught of paparazzi that had shaken up her life ever since it was revealed that her daughter was dating a prince.

The Palace had been on hand to give Doria advice on how to deal with the new, unwelcome interest in her life that she felt was so odd. Jason told her to avoid speaking with journalists and to call him immediately with details of anyone who left notes at her house, of which there were many. Reporters frequently dropped letters through her door that offered her a chance to "tell her side of the story." He also said to alert him as well as the authorities if anyone followed her. Harry made it clear that if Doria was harassed, he would personally pay for her to get the necessary protection.

In LA, paparazzi camped outside her house and followed her as she drove to the homes of her hospice clients. They raced alongside her, snapping pictures with their large cameras, as she made her way up the walkways to her clients' front doors. It was an alarming scene not just for her but also for the people already in a vulnerable state.

Doria found an unlikely ally in—of all people—Oprah Winfrey. The former talk show host, who had been introduced to Meghan by a friend, reached out to Doria to offer her support when she was first swept up in the media storm. It turned out that on occasion they went to the same church, the Agape International Spiritual Center in Los Angeles. "Oprah has been a friend and a help to someone who's been in a pretty extraordinary situation," a source close to Meghan said. "There are not many people who can understand the situations that Doria's found herself in, so it's great to be supported by someone who understands the pressure of being in the public eye."

Doria was able to spend time with Oprah when she needed to

get away from her house without worrying that she would use their friendship to get an interview. (A senior palace aide had an honest conversation with Oprah before the wedding, where she assured them that "that's not what any of this is about.") "Meghan will always be so grateful to Oprah for being someone her mother can turn to," a source said. "Doria has plenty of friends, but there's a comfort you can take in knowing that someone like Oprah is close by and supportive."

Still, there was nothing Oprah could do to stop photographers from hassling Doria on her way to work. While Palace officials kept in regular contact with Meghan's mother, they were also powerless.

The attention paid to Meghan's father turned out to be just as harmful but in an entirely different way.

Back in December, as Harry and Meghan were reveling in their engagement, a newspaper published an article about Thomas that they'd been piecing together for months, sharing pictures of his home atop a 120-foot bluff in Rosarito Beach, a quiet Mexican resort town that overlooked the Pacific Ocean, and details of his life, such as the red Ford Escape or silver Volvo he drove to his local Walmart to stock up on groceries or to the storage unit where he had bragged to the owner about his daughter who was on television. But there were no quotes, as anytime a reporter approached him, he responded with the line prepared for him by Palace officials: "I can't speak out of respect for my family."

Once the *Mail on Sunday* article came out with his home's location, he had to deal with constant intrusions from reporters and photographers. One paparazzo even shelled out the cash to rent the unit right next to his. "At this point Meghan was just worried for her father," a source close to Meghan said. "They were coming at him from every angle and she was concerned for his well-being and safety more than anything."

Thomas, who put up plywood to cover the windows of his house

that faced the street, hated that by staying silent he was allowing the media to control his image. Some of the entertainment TV
shows in the US and a number of British newspapers were relentless, offering big money for any distant relative of Meghan's to spill
family secrets. (*Good Morning Britain* flew in the estranged wife of
Meghan's half brother, whom she barely knew and hadn't seen for
years, as well as her sons—one who had a legal marijuana business.) Whether they were honest or not was beside the point. The
public was hungry for any snippet of information about Meghan's
life no matter the tone or motivation of the comment.

All the public knew about Thomas was what had been captured on camera: pictures of him taking out the trash, washing his
clothes at a local laundromat, buying beers for the security guards
in his community, and heading out of Home Depot with a new toilet
(which some tabloids called his "throne"). But without him filling
in the gaps, sections of the press crafted the image of an unhealthy
recluse with little more to keep him company than Heineken and a
pack of smokes.

Jason, Thomas's point person at the Palace, made it clear to
Meghan's father from the very start that he was on hand night or
day to help him navigate the press situation. It was a strange situation to be in and everyone, especially Harry and Meghan, wanted
to make sure he felt supported. Although he gave Thomas his private cell phone number, email, and also that of his deputy, Jason
never heard from him. He would check in from time to time, but
Thomas always said he was just fine. "Thomas is a proud man," a
source said. "Stubborn."

Enter Jeff Rayner. By this point the photographer and co-owner
of the Coleman-Rayner news agency was a familiar face, having
staked out Thomas's home for months. He made Thomas an offer
that seemed mutually beneficial. They could set up a few candid-
seeming shots around town that would shift his image from over-
weight hermit to devoted father eagerly preparing for his daughter's

big day. By the time he took his place at the end of the aisle at St. George's Chapel, everyone would know him as a devoted dad who studied up on the monarchy before his face-to-face meeting with the Queen.

Over the course of several calls, Harry and Meghan told Thomas directly that he should do his best to ignore *all* press. But ultimately, he didn't listen. With some encouragement from his other daughter, Samantha, who managed to get a cut of the deal in the process, Thomas took up the photographer on his proposition. He and Jeff went around town, putting together a few setups, including Thomas reading a book about British history at a coffee shop and visiting an Internet café to read the latest news stories on his daughter and future son-in-law. The plan was to spread the sales of the photos out for maximum profit and maximum exposure.

The photos ran in multiple outlets around the world but did little to help his public image. In fact, the person they did seem to help was Rayner, who banked at least $130,000 for the photo agency from their sales. Thomas took thirty percent.

Just one week before Thomas was set to take center stage at Windsor Castle, in a suit crafted far from the Mexico beach town, the Palace got word that the *Mail on Sunday* intended to run information that would expose the "candid" frames as fakes, including the one of Meghan's father flipping through *Images of Great Britain: A Pictorial Tour Through History.*

At Harry's instruction, the Palace communications team, in consultation with their legal team at Harbottle & Lewis, began working on a strategy to stop the publication of the embarrassing story.

First, though, Meghan needed to hear straight from her dad what happened. According to a trusted confidant who was with Meghan as events unfolded, she told her father, "Dad, we need to know if this is true or not, because my team is going to try and stop this story from running—if you are telling me it's fake.

"If they do that, they're going out of their way to protect you,

Dad," Meghan said over the phone. "You're telling me you're being victimized, right?"

Once again, he lied to Meghan. "Of course," he promised, failing to admit he had participated in the staging of the photos.

"Every single time she was calling him, she was like, 'Dad, I love you. I just want you to know I love you. Everything is fine. Just get here. We'll have the wedding. We'll celebrate. Don't worry about any of this stuff. Let's just put it behind us,'" the source shared.

"You want to believe the best, right?" the source continued. "I've heard her say, 'My dad never sought this out. I really believe that he's the victim, and now I feel sad because I believe he's been fully corrupted.'"

Before Meghan got off the phone with her father, she reminded him that a car would be arriving outside his door the next day to drive him to Los Angeles. From there, he was to make the transatlantic trip to London, where all the arrangements had been handled. He'd be accompanied door to door with chauffeured cars, personal security, and a guide to answer any question. He wouldn't have to worry about a thing.

Meanwhile, the communications staff at Kensington Palace did all they could to keep Thomas's ill-conceived plan from exploding, collaborating with her father to issue a report with the Independent Press Standards Organisation and a notice to UK newspaper editors about the situation. But to no avail: the morning after Meghan phoned her father, the *Mail on Sunday*'s front page hit: "MEGHAN'S DAD STAGED PHOTOS WITH THE PAPARAZZI." Screen shots from closed-circuit cameras made it painfully clear he had staged each and every one.

Meghan was devastated by her father's deception, but she was also concerned for his welfare. Thomas hadn't demonstrated the best judgment, to be sure. But the wedding was only one week away. She was desperate to get him to London, where he would be protected from the press by palace escorts and protection officers.

She called her father right away, but he didn't answer. She called again. And again, and again. She left some version of the same message each time: "Dad, I still love you. Nothing has changed. We're going to get you out of Mexico and safely to London. I'm sending a car to come and get you."

If only he had gotten in the car.

13

The Thomas Markle Situation

On her last night as a commoner, Meghan Markle was treated like a queen.

At 6:15 p.m. the night before her May 19 vows to Harry, she and Doria pulled up to their accommodations for the evening: the stately 350-year-old, five-star Cliveden House.

The estate has long been at the center of politics and high society. However, it was during the first half of the twentieth century, when Nancy and Waldorf Astor took residence at the property, that the Cliveden became most famous for its lavish hospitality and glamorous guests. The Astors entertained a diverse mix of marquee names, from Winston Churchill to George Bernard Shaw, Gandhi to Henry Ford.

Now it was host to the future Duchess of Sussex. Swiftly whisked from their chauffeured Range Rover to the East Wing of the property, the mother and daughter were shown around their set of suites, including the $1,900-a-night Inchiquin Suite. As Meghan and her mom looked around the room's stately mix of heavy, upholstered drapery, antique furniture, and original works of art, they were both handed cold flutes of Taittinger champagne.

After months of preparations, everything was ready. Instead of relying on a traditional wedding planner, the couple turned to someone known to the royal household: Thea Garwood, who worked with Harry and William's former private secretary, Jamie Lowther-Pinkerton, for several years in 2007 when she was an engagement secretary for the brothers. She had been heavily involved in the planning for their Diana memorial concert and became a much-trusted and impeccably organized figure in their lives. Thea, known for her calm in even the most stressful of situations, coordinated discussions between all parties involved, from the Lord Chamberlain's office (the main channel of communication between the Queen and House of Lords) to the baker and florist—which Meghan chose herself.

No detail was forgotten, including armed police protection officers patrolling the hallways of Cliveden House. A ring of about two dozen additional guards encircled the home's 376-acre grounds. Harry's orderly and former paratrooper Tifare Alexander (Tif to those closest) was also on hand if Meghan needed anything.

The wing—where staff members ferried pitchers of sparkling water, cups of green tea, and Arnold Palmers (one of Meghan's and her father's favorite drinks) to the suites—had been reserved exclusively for the duchess-to-be and any of her visitors. While she and her mother would be the only ones to stay the night, friends who stopped by included pals Lindsay and Jessica, as well as her beloved rescue beagle Guy, who'd hitched a ride out to Windsor the day before with none other than the Queen.

Michelin-starred in-house chef André Garrett prepared a sit-down dinner in the private dining room, offering the group their choice of autumn squash ravioli (a nod to Meghan's love of pasta) or grilled Dover sole.

And should Meghan's guests wish, the spa was at their disposal, masseuses at the ready and the rose- and lavender-scented hot tubs and pools open and waiting.

Meghan was feeling especially in need of a spot of stress relief. While some brides fill the weeks ahead of their wedding with worries about floral arrangements, seating assignments, and appearing their absolute best in their dress, Meghan had been dealing with a deeply personal crisis playing out in the press both in the UK and abroad.

Despite Meghan's barrage of voicemails and texts, Thomas had not only refused to get in the waiting car to the airport, he hadn't responded to a single message from his daughter.

"My God, my phone," Meghan told a friend, explaining that she'd called her father at least twenty times.

"I'm assuming he's getting my messages," she added, worried.

Rather than know anything for certain, she and Harry were updated on her father's plans (whether or not he was going to attend her wedding) through the tabloids and gossip websites.

After the embarrassing *Mail on Sunday* article appeared, Thomas reached out to *TMZ* to plead his case, explaining he was trying to "recast" his image after being "ambushed" by other photographers. But to spare his daughter and the royal family any further embarrassment, he would no longer attend the wedding.

While in public the Palace maintained a stoic silent facade, behind closed doors there were recriminations and anger that Meghan's father had turned what was supposed to be a time of celebration and dignified proceedings into a circus. Having cut himself off from aides and his daughter, Thomas was feeding the press a seemingly never-ending stream of nonsensical statements. The news cycle around the nuptials was now drip-fed with scurrilous statements being released by *TMZ*, the same outlet that had broken the story of Prince Harry's escapades in Las Vegas. Palace courtiers were waiting minute by minute for the next bombshell to drop. No one knew what to expect next.

"It was very, very tough," another aide said about the Palace's response to the Thomas Markle situation. "There were no easy solutions, and they handled it about as best they could even though to the outside world it looked like a total mess. It's very easy to blame the Palace, but, my God, I've not seen any situation quite like it—where you've got a woman marrying a prince and the father of the beautiful young woman is five thousand miles away, and just not playing ball, and not only not playing ball, but he's up to silly games."

In one of his many interviews, Thomas claimed a furious Harry called him up and hissed, "If you had listened to me, this would never have happened." But no such conversation occurred. In another dramatic turn of events, just the day after saying he was not attending the wedding, Thomas told reporters that he couldn't imagine missing such a historical event.

A wounded Meghan directed Kensington Palace officials to release a statement she wrote herself about the incident, calling it "a deeply personal matter" and requesting her privacy as they sorted it out. While she in no way wanted her family drama to play out so publicly, she felt forced to take some sort of action.

Despite her father's behavior, she was nonetheless crushed at the thought of his not being there for the wedding. From the time she was a little girl, her father had doted on her, from creating an interracial Barbie family for Christmas to helping out with set design for all of Meghan's school plays to flying in from LA with a toolkit to help her move into her Toronto townhouse with the simple request of being paid in coffee.

"As much as she was hurt and humiliated, she wanted him to be there and was willing to move on," a close friend said. "Plus, she was worried about him; she honestly wasn't sure if he was actually okay. His behavior was bizarre."

His bespoke suit and custom shoes were waiting at the Oliver Brown tailors in Chelsea, as was the military veteran Harry had asked to help accompany Meghan's father for his journey from London to Windsor. "The treatment that Doria received when she arrived here is exactly what was planned for Thomas," a senior aide added, noting that he would have been put up in a hotel and given a protection officer and assistant during his stay.

With only four days left before her wedding day, though, Meghan received more devastating news from her father—again through a celebrity gossip website.

Laying the blame firmly at the feet of the prying press, Thomas claimed the stress had caused him to have a heart attack. His doctors advised him that he needed surgery the upcoming Thursday, just two days before his daughter's vows, to clear a blockage, repair damage, and implant several stents into his blood vessels. Short of some sort of miraculous recovery, he said, he would be in no shape to fly across the Atlantic and thus would not be attending the royal wedding.

Troubled, Meghan reached out to Thomas via text message, "I've been reaching out to you all weekend but you're not taking any of our calls or replying to any texts . . . Very concerned about your health and safety and have taken every measure to protect you but not sure what more we can do if you don't respond . . . Do you need help? Can we send the security team down again? I'm very sorry to hear you're in the hospital but need you to please get in touch with us . . . What hospital are you at?"

Ten minutes later she followed up with another. "Harry and I made a decision earlier today and are dispatching the same security guys you turned away this weekend to be a presence on the ground to make sure you're safe. . . . they will be there at your disposal as soon as you need them. Please please call as soon as you can . . . all of this is incredibly concerning but your health is most important," she wrote.

That evening Thomas sent a short response to say that he appreciated the offer of security but didn't feel in any danger. Instead, he wrote, he would recover at a motel. Meghan asked for details but he didn't reply.

With confirmation that Thomas was unable to travel, Meghan asked the Palace to release another statement on her behalf: "Sadly, my father will not be attending our wedding. I have always cared for my father and hope he can be given the space he needs to focus on his health."

Not a word about the subject had been spoken when Meghan brought Doria to meet the Queen and Prince Philip earlier in the day, but the situation still caused her to quietly feel embarrassed about the public drama during their afternoon tea at Windsor Castle.

Questions were raised about the validity of Thomas's claims, but Meghan told Kensington Palace staff that no one was to discredit her father. "Meghan is very clear that despite everything that happened, people on her behalf are not to criticize him," a Palace source said. "The week of the wedding there were lots of things that could have been said, but she quite rightly took the long point of view that correcting the record wasn't worth trashing her father."

Meghan placed some of the blame on herself. Having spent the past year and a half in the glaring spotlight, she understood what the pressure from the media was like.

"He's vulnerable," she told a friend. "He's been baited. A lot of the tabloid journalists have been coaxing him and paying him. I don't know if he really even had a chance."

Harry also blamed the media for the whole situation. "The pressure he was put under for six months before he finally cracked and started to participate," a senior courtier said of Meghan's father, "that's what Harry's angry about."

One individual close to the couple summed it up this way: "There is a sort of aggressive intrusiveness, and a reckless, irresponsible, almost hostility to the media's actions that's deeply harmful. I don't think the paparazzi are the same. I think that has changed. But the sort of ruthless malevolence of some sections of the media, and it is malevolent, is genuinely bad. What they've done to her father, drawn him out from his private life and forced him out into the open, and then waving checks at him, it's just absolutely terrible. He wanted to live privately. He would have continued to live privately. He would have been at the wedding if the media had left him alone as they were asked to. And there's no public interest argument to excuse intruding into the private life of Thomas Markle."

In an effort to make things better for his bride, Harry reached out to the man he thought to be the most suitable replacement: his father. Prince Charles had some experience, having escorted down the aisle not two years earlier a family friend, Alexandra Knatchbull, whose father, Lord Brabourne, had fallen ill at the last minute. "I asked him, and I think he knew it was coming," Harry said in a BBC documentary. "He immediately said, 'Yes, of course. I'll do whatever Meghan needs, and I'm here to support you.'" (The future king now keeps a framed black-and-white photograph of himself escorting his daughter-in-law at his Clarence House residence.)

After a week of will-he-or-won't-he, with Meghan's father stealing the spotlight and overshadowing what should have been the happiest time of her life, Kensington Palace announced shortly before her big day that Prince Charles would give away the bride. The Kensington Palace statement was brief: "Ms. Meghan Markle has asked His Royal Highness The Prince of Wales to accompany her down the aisle of the Quire of St. George's Chapel on her Wedding Day. The Prince of Wales is pleased to be able to welcome Ms. Markle to The Royal Family in this way."

Harry and Meghan spent part of the day before their wedding traveling in their navy blue Range Rover up the Long Walk toward Windsor Castle for one final look at the venue they had fallen in love with. Crowds had already gathered in the small English market town ahead of the grand spectacle, and hundreds of broadcasters from around the world were already set up to capture what were sure to be magical moments.

The final rehearsal—which also served as an opportunity for Doria to meet William, Kate, George, and Charlotte for the first time—went a long way to soothe Meghan's jangled nerves, which had been keeping her awake. "In those final days she knew she had to let everything be as it was; she couldn't change what had happened," a close friend said.

Everyone, including William, felt sorry for Meghan. To witness her have her wedding day potentially ruined by her own father was heartbreaking. Doria was devastated for Meghan but not surprised. To her mind, her ex had rarely been a reliable person.

Thankfully Meghan had her friends and mom by her side to lean on. "If it wasn't for Harry, Doria, and her friends, Meghan herself says that she wouldn't have mentally got through it," a friend said.

The night before the wedding, following last-minute media preparation sessions, Meghan got a facial and energy-healing session at Cliveden House from the skincare guru Sarah Chapman, who had become a close friend in the months running up to the wedding. Meghan enjoyed her calming energy and felt that a session with Sarah was more than just a facial treatment—it served as therapy, too.

Still, despite the relaxing appointment, she had one piece of unfinished business. She sent her father one last text. He did not reply.

Sitting in a bath later that night, FaceTiming with a friend, the bride-to-be said she had left her dad a final message. "I can't sit up all night just pressing send."

Maintaining her calm, Meghan reminded her worried friends that the next day was about the fact that she had found true love. "I'm getting married," she said. "I want to be happy about that."

14

Stand by Me

Thanks to a 6:00 a.m. wake-up call, Meghan was practically up with the sun.

Soon, trays of cereal, fresh fruit, juices, and tea were being wheeled into her suite, where she had breakfast with her mom.

"It was just like old friends catching up, having breakfast together," her makeup artist and close friend Daniel Martin said. "We were playing around with her beagle, Guy. It was a very chill morning."

Other than what had happened with Thomas, the entire wedding process was running smoothly (perhaps because there was no room for any other drama).

If Meghan radiated calm, Daniel, tasked with preparing the bride of the biggest wedding of the year, definitely had some nerves. The makeup artist—who had become a good friend of Meghan's after they met during New York Fashion Week not long after *Suits* was picked up—had been planning for this day since December, when he received a text from her asking what his plans were for May 19.

The Met Gala was around then, he texted back. Then probably to Cannes for the film festival. But for her he could shift things around. Why?

Her response was an emoji of a bride and a groom.

Immediately he began to think about how he would achieve the right look: natural but effervescent, almost "lit from within." The biggest challenge had been their conflicting schedules, which meant they were never able to do a proper run-through. Daniel had to work from the images of her early May hair trial as inspiration. But because of their years working together, he knew what Meghan wanted; she was a woman confident enough to let her own beauty, and a hint of freckles, shine through.

Due to the secrecy surrounding the whole event, however, Daniel wasn't sure who else was involved in the process. Two competing beauty pros can make for a very uncomfortable situation. But when he spotted Julia Roberts's longtime hairstylist, Serge Normant, coming down the stairs, he said, "Thank goodness."

While Serge twisted Meghan's locks into one of her signature looks, the most perfectly tousled of chignons, Daniel went to work on her mother's makeup, blending peach shadows to sharpen her eye. Then the men swapped, and Daniel gave Meghan a dewy glow with a mix of toner, moisturizer, a sunscreen primer, and just a spot treatment of foundation on her T-zone. He finished up by smudging chestnut, cocoa, and rust shadows onto her lids, lining her eyes, and applying lashes to their corners. Skipping lipstick, he went with a balm to enhance her natural color and, lastly, added a swipe of cream coral blush on her cheeks for a slight flush.

Meghan streamed a playlist from her Spotify on her phone. Billie Holiday, Ella Fitzgerald, Buddy Holly, and Ben E. King played as they gossiped while preparing. "It was just very easy, like old friends getting her ready for a press junket like we used to," Daniel said.

When Meghan caught a glimpse of herself in the tall antique mirror—her classic gown framed by a sixteen-and-a-half-foot veil hand-embroidered with fifty-three flowers that represented the commonwealth countries, the winter sweet that grew in front of the cottage where she and Harry lived, and a California poppy to represent her home state—she was radiant. The fabric of her gown, a specially woven, double-bonded silk cady served as a light-reflecting mirror to make her glow. The hem at the front was three-quarters of an inch shorter than she was, so she looked as though she were floating.

Meghan was hustled past the oversize white canopy tent that had been installed to prevent anyone from getting even the slightest peek of her dress and into the Queen's maroon-and-gold 1950 Rolls-Royce Phantom IV, which had been parked outside her suite for nearly three hours, and it was only then that the enormity of the moment sunk in. Two billion pairs of eyes would be watching her get married. Trailing Meghan's Rolls in his own town car, Daniel gaped at the enormous crowds dotting the countryside's rolling hills. "People had camped out for days just to catch a glimpse," he marveled.

Many who had never before seen themselves represented in royal celebrations—such as Brits with Caribbean roots in Brixton—reveled in Meghan's big day.

Meghan had gone to the district in South London in January to meet with the talented DJs and producers who made up the youth-led radio station Reprezent, a program developed in response to growing knife crime in the area. The official visit offered a chance to win over the community, which was largely of Afro-Caribbean descent, one not previously on the royal family's radar.

Still new to such engagements, Meghan had been the one to

reach out to the training program. With its focus on mental health support for youth, it lined up with the goals she and Harry shared. Three days before Christmas, Reprezent's founder and CEO, Shane Carey, received a call from a Palace aide that the pair would like to stop in for a visit, sending him into a tailspin of long nights as he anxiously prepared to show off the work he'd been "slogging at" for the past fifteen years.

It was well worth the effort. Following an afternoon meeting with Carey, Harry and Meghan took a spin through the studios. While they both gamely donned headphones to listen to a track by the St. Lucian–born house artist Poté, it was Meghan who impressed the seventeen-year-old DJ Gloria Beyi with knowledge of her work. And she stunned YV Shells, a twenty-four-year-old medical student who worked at the station while pursuing his degree, when she revealed she had heard about his work promoting gender equality.

Following fist bumps instead of handshakes, the couple left on such a high that they chose to make an impromptu detour to greet the fans who had gathered outside. Meghan knelt to greet each child in the line, which snaked around the studio. When one gentleman told her that he would be making the trek to Windsor that May to join the mobs of fans lining the roadway to their vows, she thanked him for his kindness. "That means so much to me," Meghan chirped. "It's going to be a very special day for all of us."

And indeed, Brixton locals took to the streets to celebrate the couple's nuptials. Above a stretch of roadway generally reserved for the flags of Caribbean islands and African nations that represent the neighborhood, someone had strung up from one side of the street to the other the Union Jack and American flags. Antoney Waugh, a native of Jamaica who met Harry and his bride in January, said, "She's changing the norm."

Meanwhile, at Windsor Castle's Round Tower, wedding guests in their finery and fascinators stepped into a scene out of an old-fashioned fairy tale. Passing under the archway of tumbling foliage the florist Philippa Craddock and her team of thirty had spent four days assembling, they were enveloped by the sweet peas and jasmine lightly scenting the fourteenth-century Gothic church.

George and Amal Clooney, David and Victoria Beckham, Elton John, Priyanka Chopra, Idris Elba, Serena Williams, Oprah Winfrey, and Meghan's former *Suits* castmates, including Abigail Spencer and Rick Hoffman, found their famous names printed out on cards set in the English oak pews of St. George's Chapel, or, if they were lucky enough to be seated in the quire at the front, decorated with silver birch, foxgloves, and cow parsley harvested from the grounds of the Windsor estate. Craddock, in fact, had spied the cow parsley's delicate white flowers scattered throughout the English countryside just days earlier and asked John Anderson, the Crown Estate's Keeper of Gardens, if there was any on hand they could use, working it into the arrangements of garden roses and Meghan's favorite peonies.

The Rolls-Royce stopped at the chapel first to drop off Meghan's mother, who wore Oscar de la Renta. She had been fitted for the outfit in Los Angeles, two months prior to the ceremony. Of the initial fitting, co-creative lead Fernando Garcia said Doria "brought us snacks. They were healthy snacks because she's a runner." The hatmaker Stephen Jones created Doria's mint beret and also made hats for a few of Meghan's friends.

Then the Rolls-Royce picked up Jessica and Ben's seven-year-old twins, Brian and John, whose closeness to their "Auntie Meg" had earned them roles as pageboys. In only ten minutes, the California girl, who left behind the sunshine and unfettered existence of her home, would make her official transition to Duchess.

Absent a maid of honor to help Meghan with her gown, it was Clare Waight Keller, the designer of her dress, who stepped in. The then-artistic director for Givenchy rode ahead of the bride so she would be waiting on the castle's West Steps when Meghan arrived.

It was the culmination of a process that had begun not long after Harry and Meghan had announced their engagement. From a list of the many designers who had submitted sketches to Meghan, she decided to meet with the Birmingham-born Keller, who not only had the requisite British roots but was also the first female artistic director of a brand Meghan had loved for years.

Aides arranged for Clare to sit down with Meghan at Kensington Palace, during which time they spent thirty minutes poring over sketches and discussing Meghan's wish for something modern yet timeless. By their second meeting in January 2018, Meghan decided to task Clare with making the gown. "It was an extraordinary moment when she told me," Clare recalled. "It was an incredible thing to be part of such an historic moment."

Through a series of texts, phone calls, and sketches sent back and forth, the women settled into an easy relationship. In February, Meghan arrived in a discreet town car to the South West London property where Clare stored archives of her designs and finished pieces. There, they discussed the final design, before two small teams began creating the gown, which included a small piece of blue fabric snipped from the dress she had worn on her first blind date with Harry sewn inside. On March 27, when Meghan took a commercial flight to LA to spend a few days with Doria ahead of the big day, she brought sketches of the dress among other details about the wedding to show her mom.

In the run-up to the wedding, Clare said that she and Meghan met many times, in a way that never felt official or stately. "We talked about the ceremony, the implications of her coming into the family and what her role was going to be in the future, and what she wanted to represent, what emotions she wanted to portray, how she wanted to carve out a new idea of a way to dress for a royal, and also the magnitude of it. She was so excited about the whole thing."

Right before the wedding, the dress—which took several fittings all done by Clare herself to ensure secrecy—was moved to a secure room at Cliveden House in the early hours in a cloak-and-dagger operation, devised by Meghan's personal assistant, Melissa Toubati, and Jason, that involved several protection officers and a man-made tunnel. The pair laughed at the insanity of their scurrying around with the world's most wanted dress.

Everything about the dress had been shrouded in secrecy—including its designer. Clare's appearance on the church steps was the first confirmation to the public, and even to her husband and three children, that she had been given the all-important role of dress designer. "Like a doctor's law in that you don't talk about your patients, so I just stuck to that principle," the designer said.

In view of the cameras, Clare took pains to arrange the veil, the tulle-and-silk creation so delicate and of such pure white that workers had to wash their hands every thirty minutes over the five hundred hours it took to complete. "I knew that the dress, as she went up the steps, would make this beautiful line," the designer said. "With the veil being so long, I wanted to make it absolutely spectacular."

Meghan looked back at Clare to see if the veil was ready before she moved, stopping to admire the crowd for a brief moment. Clara Loughran, Harry's trusted Palace aide who had overseen all floral logistics for the special day, waited at the top of the steps in order to hand Meghan her bridal bouquet of lily of the valley, myrtle, astilbe, jasmine, astrantia, and Diana's favorite forget-me-nots.

Clare handed the veil to the pageboys, who had carefully rehearsed the night before at the church with a stand-in veil of polyester lace. Jessica and Ben's sons, with their broad, gap-toothed grins, were "just loving the moment" as the trumpets began to play, Clare said. "He'd never heard a trumpet before," Ben said of Brian's wide-eyed reaction to the fanfare of their arrival. "And I'm so glad we gave them good haircuts beforehand!"

Glittering in Queen Mary's diamond bandeau tiara and a pair of custom Givenchy silk duchess satin pumps completing her look,

Meghan began the 255-foot walk toward her awestruck, teary-eyed groom, dapper himself in the Household Cavalry Blues and Royals uniform crafted on London's Savile Row.

Doria also cried a bit as she watched her daughter walk down the aisle. While the public thought the mother of the bride looked alone, Meghan had made sure she was seated with two of her closest friends—Benita and Genevieve—who both know her mom very well. Doria was particularly close with Benita, whose daughters, Rylan and Remi, were not only Meghan's godchildren but also her bridesmaids.

By the time the bride and groom were eye-to-eye, Harry sending off his father with a grateful "Thank you, Pa," it was impossible to take in anything but the overwhelming love between them. "You look amazing. I missed you," Harry told Meghan. "Thank you," she replied shyly.

Though the hour-long ceremony was filled with requisite pomp and circumstance, the couple managed to make it personal.

"It was a somewhat global wedding, but being able to try and make everybody feel inclusive, it was really, really important to us," Harry said in recordings he and Meghan made for the Windsor Castle exhibit *A Royal Wedding: The Duke and Duchess of Sussex*. "In making choices that were really personal and meaningful, it could make the whole experience feel intimate, even though it was a very big wedding."

To that end, the couple filled the sunlit medieval chapel, a resplendent mix of stained glass and vaulted ceilings, with those who had shaped their lives. Representatives from many of the charities they had worked with over the years were present. Harry's former girlfriends Cressida Bonas and Chelsy Davy were also among the witnesses for the moment when the Archbishop of Canterbury, Justin Welby, asked if there was any reason Harry and Meghan could not be wed.

Bishop Michael Curry, the first African American to serve as presiding bishop in the Episcopal Church, delivered the sermon. The bishop, who had never met the couple, was very surprised when he received a call from the Archbishop of Canterbury's office. And he was floored when he learned he was to preach at Harry and Meghan's service. "Get out!" was his shocked response.

As soon as he met Harry and Meghan for the first time at the altar, Bishop Curry said their love was palpable. "You could see it in how they looked at each other," he said. "I became really aware that, you know what, the love that they had for each other, is what brought all the various worlds together, that crossed all the boundaries of our differences. That love did it."

A mixed-race member of the British royal family meant more than just a new chapter—it was a societal shift, kicked off by an African American bishop proclaiming how the couple's love had the power to change the world.

"The late Dr. Martin Luther King once said, and I quote, 'We must discover the power of love, the redemptive power of love. And when we do that, we will make of this old world a new world. But love, love is the only way,'" Bishop Curry preached.

His choice to weave in quotes from the legendary civil rights activist alongside psalms from the New Testament symbolized that Meghan was to be a different type of duchess. Bishop Curry didn't expect his speech to be accompanied by responsive shouts, but he said he "could see the 'Amens!'" in the crowd's eyes.

Following Bishop Curry's sermon, the twenty-member Kingdom Choir launched into the classic "Stand by Me." (Like Bishop Curry, the Kingdom Choir was also Prince Charles's suggestion.) A lot of behind-the-scenes work had gone into the three-part harmony gospel arrangement of Ben E. King's song, which had been used as a rallying cry during the civil rights movement. The couple shot down almost a dozen previous versions of the song that the choir leader, Karen Gibson, had prepared. Then Prince Charles, who recommended much of the musical accompaniment to Harry and

Meghan, arranged for Gibson, five choir members, and a keyboard-ist to play in person at Kensington Palace.

"The version everyone heard was the twelfth version, and even now I don't know if it was exactly what they wanted since we had simply run out of time," Karen said after the wedding. "At the time I didn't understand why they kept saying no, but of course they were right. The version they got was pure. And it absolutely suited the style of the wedding."

Still, Karen wasn't sure the performance on the wedding day had inspired excitement. Used to demonstrative audiences, the only response they got that day "was the rustling of people turning their heads around," she said with a laugh. But when they left the church "we were literally mobbed." The actor Tom Hardy—a close friend of Harry's who had flown in from a film set in New Orleans for just twenty-four hours to be at the wedding—gave her a hug. Within days, their performance had been watched several million times on YouTube, the British media was calling Gibson the "godmother of gospel," and the Queen had invited the choir to a Buckingham Palace garden party the following month.

The emotion of their music continued to fill the room as both Harry and Meghan vowed to have and to hold—but not to obey. The bride chose to omit the outdated term just as Kate did in her 2011 wedding to William. Once they had exchanged rings (his made of platinum and hers created with rare Welsh gold featuring a Welsh dragon stamp), they were proclaimed, to the glee of the crowd, husband and wife. They were now Their Royal Highnesses The Duke and Duchess of Sussex.

As the nineteen-year-old cellist Sheku Kanneh-Mason (the first black musician to win the BBC Young Musician of the Year in the award's thirty-eight-year history) played three pieces, includ-ing Schubert's "Ave Maria," Harry and Meghan moved to a private room in the chapel with their parents in tow for the Signing of the Register. Charles made sure that a solo Doria was looked after, offering his hand as they walked into the small space to witness Harry and Meghan sign their names. "It was a lovely gesture," Camilla, who was by Charles's side, said in the BBC documentary *Prince, Son and Heir: Charles at 70*. "A lot of people seeing my husband actually take the bride's mother by the hand to sign the registry, it's something that moved everybody . . . It's the things he does behind the scenes that people don't know about. I don't think people realize quite how kind he is."

After the ceremony, the newly wedded couple paused at the top of the chapel steps just after 1:00 p.m. to, at long last, engage in the time-honored tradition of sharing their first kiss as husband and wife. Then, with the voices of the Kingdom Choir singing "This Little Light of Mine" ringing out from inside the church, they climbed into their horse-drawn, open-top Ascot Landau carriage for a twenty-five-minute celebratory ride through the streets of Windsor.

Lifting her hand to her chest, Meghan had just one word when she saw the huge crowds gathered on the grounds of the castle: "Wow!"

Sitting down in the carriage beside his bride, Harry laughed that his trousers were "too tight."

And just like that, the wedding of the year, or at least the portion they were willing to put on display for the world, had come to an end, the couple literally riding off into their happily ever after as they alternately waved to the cheering fans and stared at each other, marveling at the momentous step they had just taken.

15

Presenting the Sussexes

Though the public's glimpse into the spectacular event had ended, for Harry and Meghan, their wedding day was just getting started.

Having wound through the streets of Windsor and back to the castle grounds, the newlyweds' carriage brought them to the State Apartments. Their guests were beginning to mingle through St. George's Hall, peering up at the ceiling, which was studded with the coats of arms and the armored *King's Champion* statue on horseback at the hall's east end and admiring the Californian baker Claire Ptak's multi-tiered, peony-covered Amalfi lemon and elderflower syrup cake. Harry and Meghan were ferried into the gilded Green Drawing Room, where the photographer Alexi Lubomirski had precisely twenty-five minutes to capture six different portrait setups, including one featuring all four page boys in their miniature uniforms and six bridesmaids in their tiny Givenchy gowns. Alexi was already on first-name terms with the couple, having taken their engagement portraits in December 2017.

Harry had some key business to attend to first. The prince moved from his bride's side to lavish praise on Clare. "He came straight up to me," recalled the designer, who was on hand to adjust Meghan's train and veil so everything would look perfect for their photos.

"Oh my god, thank you," he told Clare. "She looks absolutely stunning."

As Daniel, there to touch up Meghan's makeup, chatted with Doria, who was noticeably relieved to be out of the spotlight, Alexi and his crew set about arranging Harry on the silk damask Morel & Seddon couch he had once shared with his late mom, Princess Diana, after his 1984 christening. Meghan was situated below him on the Axminster carpet, with the pageboys and bridesmaids filling in all around.

Alexi was able to elicit genuine smiles from his small subjects with just one sentence. "Who likes Smarties?" he shouted, as a roomful of hands shot up.

He used the same joke on Doria, William, Kate, Charles, Camilla, the Queen, and Prince Philip, after he carefully arranged the family on the silky side chairs. "I wanted it to feel like a family picture," he explained. "I didn't want it to feel too much like a sports team photo or an army photo." It helped that his Smarties line worked on the adults, too. Even the Queen smirked.

With only a few more minutes to capture the portraits of the couple alone, the photographer quickly made the decision to walk out onto the lawns of the Queen's rose garden. As the trio strode around the hedges and clusters of flower beds, the sun was starting to dip behind the castle's turrets. He suggested one last setup on a small staircase. Harry lowered himself on the concrete while Meghan, finally free from her beautiful but encumbering veil, slumped against him, resting comfortably against his chest. It was the snap of the day. They laughed about making it through the gauntlet of their morning, joking about how worn out they were from the emotion. "It was just one of those magical moments," Alexi said, "when you're a photographer and everything falls into place."

The photographer immediately drove to his mother's home, which happened to be nearby and was a safe place to work without the threat of prying eyes. During the car ride, he scanned through the digital files that he hadn't had time to look at while working. Instead, he had relied on his assistant to review the images in the moment. So, when he saw the picture he'd taken in a rush during the last three minutes of their session, he breathed a sigh of relief. They were "amazing" and "emotional."

"Emotional" might as well have been the word of the day. And no one was more skilled at evoking it than the groom when the wedding reception began. As the guests (many having slipped out of their heels in favor of the white cushioned slippers provided for comfort) mingled through the neo-Gothic hall, restored to its full glory following a 1992 fire, Harry stepped up to speak. When he first uttered the words "my wife and I," he was rewarded with a round of applause from the crowd. For Harry, he had been looking forward to saying that as much as everyone else enjoyed hearing it.

Everyone was in a good mood, aided by the Pol Roger Brut Réserve non-vintage champagne being passed around. For the underage set, including Harry's cousins Lady Louise Mountbatten-Windsor and Viscount Severn, there were mocktails made with Sandringham Cox's apple juice and elderflower. Also making the rounds were exquisitely presented canapés of Scottish langoustines wrapped in smoked salmon with citrus crème fraiche, grilled English asparagus wrapped in Cumbrian ham, garden pea panna cotta with quail eggs and lemon verbena, and poached free-range chicken bound with a lightly spiced yogurt with roasted apricot. For lunch, there was fricassee of free-range chicken with morel mushrooms and young leeks; pea and mint risotto with pea shoots, truffle oil, and Parmesan crisps; and ten-hour slow-roasted Windsor pork belly with apple compote and crackling.

The Queen was the official host of the afternoon event, but it was Harry's best man, William, who introduced the new husband and wife and announced his dad's toast.

Charles's dry humor was on full display as he spoke about feeding baby Harry and changing his diapers, before allowing that he turned out all right. Then, in a move that elicited tears from the crowd, he opened up about how moving it was to see his younger son become a husband. "My darling old Harry," he closed, "I'm so happy for you."

No one was happier for Harry than Harry, who delivered an off-the-cuff speech about how excited he was to be part of this new team and acknowledging how his bride had navigated the challenge of putting together this event while facing some unwelcome outside hindrances "with such grace." He also offered some good-natured ribbing like his dear old dad, joking that he hoped the American half of the room wouldn't make off with the hall's swords and pleading with everyone to be quiet when they left so as not to disturb the neighbors.

Then, before the duo could slice into their sponge cake, which was laced with syrup sourced from the elderflower trees at the Queen's estate in Sandringham, Harry took the microphone once more and slyly inquired if anyone in the crowd knew their way around a piano. Elton John—in his signature pink glasses—picked up the cue. Having long ago agreed to a mini concert, he sat down at the piano.

"What is going on here?" an astonished friend of Meghan's murmured.

Then Sir Elton launched in.

"My gift is my song, and this one's for you," he sang.

After "Your Song," he performed "Circle of Life" (*The Lion King* being one of Harry's favorite movies) and "I'm Still Standing," which left guests, including Oprah, dabbing at their eyes.

He also belted out "Tiny Dancer" in a nod to Meghan with the opening lyrics, "Blue jean baby, LA lady." It was the perfect performance for the boy he had watched grow into a man and the son of one of his closest friends. In fact, it was at that very same venue, for Prince Andrew's twenty-first birthday party, that Elton had first met Diana in 1981.

To support Harry in his mother's absence were Diana's two sisters, Lady Sarah McCorquodale and Lady Jane Fellowes; her brother Charles Spencer; her old roommate and Harry's godmother Carolyn Bartholomew; and Julia Samuel, Prince George's godmother and the head of the charity Child Bereavement UK, for which William served as patron. (The charity supported children and families who had lost a loved one and those caring for sick family members with terminal diagnoses.) Lady Jane had read from the Song of Solomon during the service to honor her late sister's memory.

Buoyed by Diana's spirit, Harry and Meghan made their way to their temporary Windsor Castle accommodations for a bit of relaxation before prepping for the private evening reception. Harry planned to have a quick nap, but, filled with so much energy and excitement from the day, he couldn't keep still for a moment.

During the three-hour gap between receptions, Meghan changed looks. The London salon owner George Northwood tied her strands into a higher, tighter chignon with curled, face-framing tendrils. For the lower light of the evening, Daniel was after a slightly dreamer, sexier look, adding darker shadows to Meghan's eyes. Her second dress—a high-neck, silk crepe Stella McCartney design—was sultrier, too. It was time for Meghan to party.

"The role that she's taken on is very austere, it's very sort of serious, and I think there's a great weight that she's acquired through that and she takes it very seriously," Stella told the BBC. "It was the last moment that she could reflect, sort of the other side to her."

For an item that covered both borrowed *and* blue, Harry loaned Meghan his late mother's emerald-cut aquamarine and twenty-four-carat yellow gold Asprey ring.

"I just want to get on with this and get going," Meghan said to Daniel, who dabbed a touch of organic oil onto her skin, handed her a stack of blotting papers and lipstick, and sent her off to the 1968 silver blue Jaguar E-Type Concept Zero that a tuxedoed Harry navigated down the Long Path to their reception at Frogmore House.

Two hundred friends and family, who had received the hand-drawn invitations for the evening reception, arrived at Frogmore House close to 7:00 p.m. in double-decker buses. Some chose to take their own transportation, including Doria, who napped in the back of a Range Rover. Harry's cousins Princess Beatrice and Princess Eugenie skipped the more pedestrian rides in favor of a black Bentley. George and Amal Clooney pulled up in a silver Audi.

(Notably absent were Skippy, Harry's old friend, who had questioned the prince's relationship with Meghan, and his wife, Lara. They were invited to the wedding ceremony and lunchtime reception but didn't make the cut for the evening bash. At a brunch the day after the wedding, Skippy told friends, "Meghan had changed Harry too much." His Eton pal said the prince was awed by the likes of the Clooneys and Oprah. "We've lost him," Skippy concluded. Many of Harry's old friends said that the evening guest list was the prince and his bride's way of saying, "These are the people we want in our lives moving forward.")

After switching off their cell phones (the bride and groom had made it clear that this part of the celebration was to be resolutely private), the guests at the evening party spilled out from two white marquees onto the wide expanse of lawn that had served as the backdrop for Harry and Meghan's engagement photos months earlier. They, too, had made their own midday wardrobe swaps. Serena Williams, previously in head-to-toe pink Versace, wore a floral Valentino gown accessorized with the designer's sneakers for maximum comfort. Meghan's close friend Priyanka Chopra traded her lavender Vivienne Westwood suit and coordinating fascinator for a sparkly gold tulle Dior gown and Lorraine Schwartz jewels.

Famously not fond of stiff affairs, Harry had fantasized of a celebration to rival the heady nights out of his youth, when he and his pals would down the signature champagne-topped treasure chest cocktails at the tiki-themed nightclub Mahiki or spend long evenings dancing at Boujis. And though the Frogmore House setting—a stately 336–40 year-old home once inhabited by King George III—was undeniably staid, the reception itself was anything but.

At precisely 7:30 p.m., the group, in their black-tie finery, was ushered into the custom-built marquee erected in front of the seventeenth-century mansion, finding their spots at one of twenty tables named for various foods with different British and American pronunciations. While one group of pals set down their cocktail glasses at a table labeled with "tomato," others were assigned to "basil," "oregano," "potato," or "arugula." In describing the event to *Vanity Fair*, the *True Blood* actress and close friend Janina Gavankar said, "There were so many nods to the beautiful mashup of two cultures."

Despite the large number of guests at the evening reception, the dinner was a truly intimate affair—especially when compared to the pomp and circumstance of the afternoon witnessed by millions.

"The ceremony was just incredible to be a part of, and such an honor to even witness, but then in the evening, you really felt that you were at your friend's wedding. It was a small safe group. Many of us know each other or have gotten acquainted over the last year and a half. It was just different," said a close friend and guest. "It felt just like them. You could see every single thing that they had lovingly selected. We girls were going, 'Oh That's so Meg.'"

However, the locally sourced, organic menu—prepared by the Michelin-starred chef Clare Smyth (who herself quickly struck up a friendship with Meghan) and featuring such dishes as sage and on-ion roast chicken, aged for sixty-four days at Devon's Creedy Carver farm—that was Prince Charles's doing.

As waiters circulated the first of three courses, William started his speech. Recalling the embarrassing reenactment Harry did of the gushy phone conversations between Kate and him while they were dating, he vowed that revenge would be sweet now that he was his brother's best man.

To ensure his little brother's embarrassment, William handed the microphone off to "God's gift, Charlesworth," the princes' nick-name for their boarding school chum Charlie van Straubenzee.

An investment management firm executive and longtime mem-ber of Harry's inner circle of friends, Charlie chose the elegant occasion to bring up old boarding school memories.

"All I wanted was a cuddle from my mummy," Von Straubenzee said as reported in the UK newspaper *The Times* of first meeting Harry at Berkshire's Ludgrove School, where the royal had been assigned the role of dormitory monitor. "Instead, Harry nicked my teddy bear and chucked it out onto the roof. Ladies and gentlemen, I ask you, how can you put someone in charge of a dorm when that someone is worse behaved than the whole dorm combined?"

Poking fun at "our strawberry blond prince's" longtime denial of his red-hued locks, Charlie described how Harry often hated other gingers as a kid without recognizing that he was a member of their tribe. Then he covered Harry's penchant for falling off horses while playing polo—generally due to his nursing a hangover dur-ing the match. Having gotten his digs in (including a mention of the well-reported antics of Harry's youth), Charlie turned emotional when talking about not just the prince's struggles from losing his mother as a boy but the impressive way he had come through the other side of anger and depression.

Diana would be so proud and so happy to see that Harry had found love with such an amazing woman, Charlie shared, and she

would be thrilled at the prospect of them starting their lives together. Meghan, he concluded, was a phenomenal match for his
dear friend, and he was so grateful to her for how happy she made
Harry.

Overcome with emotion as well, Harry stepped up to the mic to
once again offer his gratitude to everyone who had made this day
possible. He thanked his dad for his unending love and his help
in putting together the event. Charles, who footed much of the bill
for the evening bash, would later make a crack that the budget had
"long gone out the window." He also extended his thanks to his
mother-in-law for her role in raising such "an amazing daughter,
my wife," words that elicited a huge cheer from the group. Finally,
he turned to his bride: "Words can't express how incredibly lucky I
am to have such an amazing wife by my side."

Then, as had been rumored, Meghan made a speech of her own.

A first for a royal bride, the move reinforced the idea that this
American was no typical duchess.

"You could literally hear a pin drop," said a close confidant,
who described the speech as a momentous occasion even for the
Americans.

"For her to have been quiet for as long as she had, and then
have this really safe space where she could give these heartfelt remarks, it was a really special moment," the source said. "She spent
so many years, whether on campus, on TV, or advocating for women
to be empowered, speaking out. And she's respected that. She does
have a lot of respect for tradition, a lot of respect for the family and
the institution that she has joined. But it's just a different way of
living. We'd missed hearing her speak."

And apparently Meghan felt the same way, because she laughed,
"I know it's been a while."

The bride took her moment at the mic to express her appreciation to the Queen for warmly welcoming her into the fold from
the start. Charles got his own thank-you for stepping in to fill the

role of her father in escorting her down the aisle and for his courtesy in helping her mother through unfamiliar territory. Doria, too, was thanked for her support and wisdom. The bulk of her praise, though, went to Harry, the prince she had been fixed up with by chance and who continued to shatter her every expectation.

All her American pals whistled and clapped.

"That's our Meg," the confidant said. "She just connects."

After all the heartfelt remarks, the comic relief arrived in the form of the *Late Late Show* host, James Corden, who strode to the center of the tent dressed as Henry VIII. His wife, Julia, a friend of Meghan's, recoiled in mock-horror.

"Your Royal Highnesses, ladies and gentlemen, I had no idea what to wear to a royal wedding," joked the late-night talk show host, who had donned full Tudor regalia from tunic to tights, "so I looked it up in the royal etiquette manual and found this outfit. I hope I've come in the right gear."

After James wrapped up his act—including a bit about what the use of a tent said about the size of Windsor Castle—the guests followed Harry's orders to have a serious party.

For their first dance, the couple chose "I'm in Love" by the sixties soul singer Wilson Pickett. The wedding staple gave way to more soul classics, such as the Temptations' "My Girl" and Sam and Dave's "Soul Man," performed by a twelve-piece American Southern band. Then "DJ to the Stars" Sam Totolee took to the turntables. Having cut his teeth in the thumping clubs of Ibiza and played at private events for the likes of Diddy, Elon Musk, and Pippa Middleton's 2017 vows, Sam played track after track of club music—as instructed by Harry.

Sam stopped spinning only to allow Idris Elba to take over for a one-hour spell. As the actor, who had bonded with the prince when he lent a hand during the Invictus Games one year, said on *Ellen*, "One day he said, you know, 'What are you doing on the [wedding] day?' And I was like 'Hmmm, nothing' and he goes 'Would you like to, a, come to the wedding and, b, would you like to DJ at the reception?' And I was like 'No . . . yes! Of course, I would!'"

If the same thumping hip-hop and house beats Harry once went wild for at the nightclubs of his twenties (the loud music carrying well across Windsor's thirteen acres) or the cocktails from the "drinks of the world" themed bar didn't get the wedding guests into the party spirit, George Clooney was also on hand to help. Coaxing people to the bar, he had partygoers laughing as he started free-pouring shots of Casamigos tequila, the liquor brand the movie star co-founded. "I wanted to make sure everyone had the best time," Clooney said.

At 11:00 p.m., it was time for the grand finale. While staff members inside brought out small canapés to soak up the ginger-and-rum-based signature "When Harry Met Meghan" cocktails, other staff outside rushed to find rope to shoo the swans off the lake where the show was about to take place. Then guests were encouraged to step outside for a spectacular fireworks display.

Holding hands with her new husband, Meghan kept her focus on the sky. Her future was directly in front of her, as bright and brilliant as the dramatic display lighting up the air. The wedding saw the culmination of a unique journey for a couple, who overcame significant odds to be in that moment. Yet the start of their marriage presented fresh obstacles.

16

Mum's the Word

Harry and Meghan were fresh off their secret honeymoon, which they had flown to on a private jet loaned by a friend. They spent the majority of the weeklong trip in the sun at a location so private, most of their friends still don't know where they went.

They were still basking in the glow of their newlywed status on June 18, 2018, when Thomas Markle conducted an explosive interview with *Good Morning Britain*. A live feed from a hotel room in San Diego carried Meghan's father as he touched on a range of topics. He apologized for taking part in the staged photographs before the wedding, even though he was reportedly getting paid $10,000 for the TV interview. "I realized it was a serious mistake," he said. "It's hard to take it back."

It was hard to imagine how he expected his daughter and Harry to forgive him. Advisors and friends close to Harry and Meghan were at a loss as to what to do with a man who had once again gone rogue. The Palace valued discretion and privacy above all else. "I think he's not well, and I think he's vulnerable," a source close to the couple shared. "Those newspapers and broadcasters who pay regularly for another interview, I think that's just beyond disgraceful."

Thomas's latest humiliation was particularly disappointing for the couple, who had actually postponed their honeymoon so they could attend a garden party at Buckingham Palace to celebrate the Prince of Wales's seventieth birthday. Six thousand people—among them representatives from 386 of Charles patronages, twenty military affiliations, and members from the country's emergency services—paid tribute to the prince's half century of humanitarian work. Although Prince Charles's actual birthday wasn't until November, Harry and Meghan's presence at the May 22 event reflected the growing bond between Charles and the Sussexes.

"His enthusiasm and energy are truly infectious," Harry said that afternoon, paying tribute to his father. "It has certainly inspired William and I to get involved in issues we care passionately about and to do whatever we can to make a difference. In fact, many of the issues William and I now work on are subjects we were introduced to by our father growing up.

"So, Pa, while I know that you've asked that today not be about you, you must forgive me if I don't listen to you—much like when I was younger—and instead, I ask everyone here to say a huge thank-you to you, for your incredible work over nearly fifty years. Work that has given self-confidence and opportunity to thousands of young people who might not have had the best start in life, or to champion causes like climate change long before almost anyone else was talking about it; and above all, for your vision and ability to bring people together to make change happen. You have inspired William and I, and looking out here today, it is clear to see that we are not alone."

Meghan had her own reasons for admiring her father-in-law, who had poignantly walked her down the aisle when her own father let her down. At the time, a trusted confidant said Meghan "found such a supportive and loving father in Charles, which has really changed her life for the better." Not a father-in-law but a "second father," according to the source.

A friend of Charles's said that the Prince of Wales had "taken a real shine to Meghan. She's a sassy, confident, beautiful American. He likes very strong, confident women. She's bright, and she's self-aware, and I can see why they've struck up a very quick friendship."

Charles liked Meghan's energy. "The Prince of Wales has always been fond of people from the Arts, like Emma Thompson, who he's been mates with for years," another source said. "Meghan ticks the boxes. Most of all she's married to his beloved youngest son and made him whole. Charles takes enormous delight and pleasure in that."

Perhaps Camilla understood her husband's need for family connection, because in the early days she and Charles made sure Meghan was supported as she navigated the ups and downs of life in the public eye. Both had been reassuring and sympathetic in those difficult moments before the wedding. The couple had spent a private weekend at Castle of Mey that summer, the Scottish retreat once owned by the Queen Mother, who had been especially close to Prince Charles. Harry and Meghan had quietly jetted off for five days to Caithness on the northern Scottish coast. At the sixteenth-century castle tucked away from the public, Meghan was able to spend quality time with Charles and Camilla.

Before her father appeared again in the media, Meghan was adjusting nicely to her role as the newest member of the royal family. Not only had she developed a rapport with Charles and Camilla, but she had accompanied the Queen on a June 14 "away day" to

Chester—without Harry. Just the two of them (and several aides) traveled together overnight on the Royal Train.

It was a daunting journey for the new wife, despite the amenities of Her Majesty's personal train, which had private bedrooms (Prince Philip's pillows are plain; the Queen's, with a small royal cipher in one corner, are trimmed with lace); a sitting room with a sofa of hand-stitched velvet cushions; a dining table for six; a desk where the Queen worked on her papers; and secondary air suspension for a smoother-than-average ride. (The train conductor drives extra slowly around 7:30 a.m. to make sure the water stays in the tub while the Queen has her bath.)

Meghan was extremely grateful for the Queen's generosity. It was an honor to be taken under the Queen's wing so soon after her marriage. Kate's first engagement, despite knowing the Queen for years, was a full ten months after her wedding to Prince William.

The Queen had a level of confidence in Meghan, because as a Palace source shared, "she handles these situations flawlessly because she's always well prepared and respectful. She's very clever and good at understanding what's required."

Sure enough, Meghan, in an elegant cream cape Givenchy sheath dress from her wedding gown designer, Clare Waight Keller, gave a near-flawless performance on the train trip. (Although she was criticized by the tabloids for not wearing a hat, despite the fact it was not required.)

"The Queen was wonderful, warm, and generous toward the new Duchess," a source close to Her Majesty said. "She made sure Meghan knew what was going on and made her feel very much at home because it was her first trip."

Indeed, before the two stepped off the train, the Queen gifted Meghan with a delicate pair of pearl-and-diamond earrings.

Meghan, an avid learner studying all she could on royal protocol, was often seen carrying binders full of research so she didn't put a foot wrong. She took her new role incredibly seriously. That day was different, though; she was getting a royal master class in training from the Queen herself.

"They had a very warm happy day out and introduction to royal life—because the Queen has so much knowledge to pass on and Meghan is a keen student," a source close to Meghan shared.

The two spent the day about two hundred miles north of Buckingham Palace, opening a bridge, visiting an entertainment complex, and having lunch at the town hall with local politicians and other civic dignitaries.

Despite all her careful preparation, Meghan was unsure about how to proceed when she and the Queen had to get into Her Majesty's Bentley. She politely asked the Queen, "What is your preference?"

"You go first," the Queen answered.

"Oh, okay," said Meghan, who tried her hardest to get everything right—which made her father's public display on national TV in England all the more dispiriting.

Unfortunately, Thomas's appearance on *Good Morning Britain* was just the start of a new media blitz.

In July, he talked to *The Sun* on a wide range of topics. He said he thought his daughter looked terrified during public engagements and that the clothes chosen for her were way too conservative. He also claimed that Meghan cut ties with him so completely he had no way of getting in touch with her—when she had held on to the same cell phone she had used to barrage him with texts ahead of the wedding. In fact, on June 10, three weeks after he had failed to attend her wedding because of his heart angioplasty, Thomas claimed to have texted his daughter. "My surgery was successful," he wrote. "I will be on blood thinners and the diet for the rest of my life, but I will live. Just thought you might want to know." No such text was sent.

Two days later, *The Sun* ran another interview with Thomas, who this time threatened that he might show up unannounced if he didn't hear from Meghan. "I want to see my daughter. I'm thinking about it," he said. "I don't care whether she is pissed off at me.

"It's sad that it's got to this point," he continued. "I'm sorry it's come to this. Yes, some of it is my fault. But I've already made it clear that I'm paying for this for the rest of my life."

Anyone else spreading falsehoods would have been easier to discredit. But this was Meghan's father. Thomas had cut himself off from the Palace completely and was consulting only with Samantha by this point. Meanwhile, writers began penning editorials about the many ways in which the Palace had mismanaged the whole affair with the Markle family. Thomas put the Palace and Meghan in a no-win situation.

Unlike Harry, who often scoured the press and checked out some of the royal correspondents' Twitter accounts, Meghan tried to avoid her press. Still, diligent communications staffers and friends contacted her when anything came out that was especially heated or litigious, so she was apprised of most of the hurtful commentary.

One of her closest friends said a heartbroken Meghan "wanted to repair the relationship." Despite the many humiliations she had suffered, as summer came to a close, Meghan made one final effort to communicate with her father in the form of a five-page letter.

"Daddy, it is with a heavy heart that I write this, not understanding why you have chosen to take this path, turning a blind eye to the pain you're causing," she wrote. "Your actions have broken my heart into a million pieces, not simply because you have manufactured such unnecessary and unwarranted pain, but by making the choice to not tell the truth as you are puppeteered in this. Something I will never understand."

Meghan pleaded with her father in writing: "If you love me, as you tell the press you do, please stop. Please allow us to live our lives in peace. Please stop lying, please stop creating so much pain, please stop exploiting my relationship with my husband."

Thomas carried his daughter's handwritten letter in its FedEx envelope in his briefcase for months, not sharing it with the media because it showed the many discrepancies in his tabloid revelations. He replied with his own four-page letter, in which he suggested a path forward, toward a reconciliation.

The best way they were going to get past everything, he wrote in a reply letter, would be to stage a photo op for the press where himself, Meghan, and Harry are together and happy.

Meghan couldn't believe it. "I'm devastated," she confessed to a friend. "My father's clearly been fully corrupted."

"It is so painful for her because she was so dutiful. Giving him money. Trying to give him whatever help he needed," a confidant said. "She will always feel devastated by what he's done. Always, but at the same time, she has a lot of sympathy for him. Because he never went knocking on the press's door. He was silent for almost two years. Then they just sort of whittled him down. Bombarding him every day. Moving in next door to his house. He couldn't escape it. So now, it's just like he's so far gone."

She didn't reach out again. Instead, Meghan put up what her father described in one of the many interviews he gave following their written exchange as a "wall of silence."

Later that year, Samantha tried to deliver a letter to Kensington Palace, requesting a face-to-face meeting with Meghan. Samantha, in London for another round of media interviews, shared the entire moment with a Splash News photographer, who had been tipped off about the unannounced visit. However, she dropped off the letter at the wrong security gate, instead taking it to the entrance of a private road that ran *behind* Kensington Palace. Nonetheless, Meghan told friends she was "weirded out" by her half sister's behavior.

It wasn't easy losing family members. Giving up on her relation-ship with her father—a man she once raved about in interviews, crediting him for her working knowledge of TV sets, her work ethic, and her appreciation for handwritten thank-you notes—was a hard sacrifice to make for her new life, no matter how wonderful.

And, by all measures, it *was* pretty wonderful. A few months after the drama with her father, George Clooney arranged for Harry and Meghan to fly from London to Lake Como on his own private jet. In the early evening of August 16, the newlyweds arrived into Milan's airport, and from there were driven in an unmarked motor-cade to George and Amal's Villa Oleandra.

The Clooneys, who had been staying at their twenty-five-room mansion for the past month, had already hosted a series of high-profile friends, including Cindy Crawford and Rande Gerber and Stella McCartney and her husband. The previous summer, David and Victoria Beckham visited with their children.

Located in the village of Laglio, the retreat George purchased in 2002 had an outdoor theater, a swimming pool, and a garage to house the movie star's five vintage motorbikes. It also included a tennis court, a full gym, huge bathrooms, and a "pizza parlor" com-plete with pizza oven. The ornately carved ceilings in each room were a talking point alone.

During the three-day visit, a source said, "Meghan and Amal spent a lot of time relaxing by the pool and playing with the twins while George and Harry checked out George's motorbike collec-tion. Harry took one of them out with one of his protection of-ficers. George recently had an accident, so he wasn't back on his bike yet."

The duke and duchess weren't the only guests that weekend. Eugenie and her fiancé, Jack Brooksbank, were already at the villa when Harry and Meghan arrived, their visits overlapping briefly. To maximize security, the group stayed in every night, well fed by rotating chefs. On the final night of Harry and Meghan's stay, George hired the chef from Il Gatto Nero, one of his favorite local restaurants, to prepare an Italian feast for fifteen. The party, including neighbors and their houseguests, dined at long trestle tables in the landscaped gardens. As live music echoed over the estate, guests enjoyed the gathering until the early hours.

Harry and George had been friends long before the prince met Meghan. After connecting at a charity event, the two men discovered that despite their age difference, they had a lot in common, including their love of motorbikes. George had collections of bikes in Lake Como, LA, and Sonning.

On at least two occasions, George and Amal hosted Harry and Meghan in Sonning, which was about an hour from the Great Tew Estate the royals rented in Oxfordshire. Harry and Meghan brought their dogs with them to the house, where the Clooneys loved to take friends out by the lake. There, they had a secluded decked area and inside was a lounge decorated with traditional club wood paneling, heavy drapes, dark velvets, plush chairs, and a bar.

Back in Oxfordshire, Harry and Meghan fell into new routines as a married couple. Sipping coffee or tea together in the kitchen every morning became a ritual. Then they took turns making breakfast from the organic seasonal produce they ordered from nearby Daylesford Farm or the groceries they had delivered by Waitrose.

They also did their fair share of hosting themselves. In early July, Serena, in town to play Wimbledon, and her husband, Alexis Ohanian, stopped by for a little time in the countryside. Some days later, Meghan, along with Kate, went to watch the tennis champ play against Angelique Kerber in the Women's Final. Although now a duchess alongside Kate, who has been a royal patron of Wimbledon since 2016, when she took over from the Queen, Meghan still dropped into the VIP area to hug Serena and her mother, Oracene Price. "Meghan is an amazing woman and a great friend of the family," Oracene said. "We're very proud of everything she has achieved."

The unseasonably warm fall of 2018 meant they could enjoy the garden patio almost up until the start of their official sixteen-day royal tour of Australia, Fiji, Tonga, and New Zealand. This wasn't Harry and Meghan's first official overseas tour, which had been a two-day trip in July to Dublin. Short and not too far from England, they made sure that the private jet they chartered to travel to Ireland got them home in time to watch the second half of the Croatia vs. England soccer match from the comfort of their Oxfordshire living room.

There was another big difference between the two tours. This time Meghan was pregnant—and the couple were thrilled, since they had wanted to start a family right away.

On October 15, the day before Harry and Meghan were set to fly to Australia, the Palace took the small group of press gathered in Sydney for a pre-tour briefing completely by surprise. The reporters thought they were going to get the typical logistical information they needed to cover the tour—times and places the bus would be leaving, etc. Instead, huddled around an iPhone 6 sitting atop a teacup and saucer in a makeshift low-fi loudspeaker, they received very big news from the couple's communications secretary, Jason: "The Duke and Duchess are expecting a baby . . . We'll be sending out a statement in about 15 minutes."

Meghan, expecting in the spring of 2019, was just under twelve weeks pregnant when the tour began. But a Palace aide said Harry and Meghan were comfortable with the decision to announce the news early to avoid an entire trip of speculation around whether Meghan was pregnant. "She was already showing, and hiding it would not have been possible," the aide said. "The rumors would have dominated the coverage and taken away from the entire purpose of the tour. Meghan didn't want that."

(The timing of the announcement might have worked with the tour, but it conflicted with another happy royal event: Princess Eugenie's wedding. Family members had found out about the pregnancy just days prior, at the wedding of Harry's closest cousin. It did not go down particularly well with Eugenie, who a source said told friends she felt the couple should have waited to share the news.)

Being pregnant didn't slow Meghan down at all—not even as she faced fourteen flights and seventy-six engagements over the next sixteen days. The first stop was Sydney, where the couple landed with their custom blue luggage bearing their names and matching Rimowa carry-on cases, containing toiletry bags, spare clothes, notes, and other essentials that an assistant made sure was on each flight. Also in tow was a ten-person entourage, including their private secretary and chief of staff, Samantha Cohen; private secretaries Amy Pickerill and Heather Wong; senior Buckingham Palace aide Marnie Gaffney; and hairstylist George Northwood.

In Sydney to take on engagements and host the fourth Invictus Games, Harry and Meghan managed to sneak out for an evening off with Jessica and Ben Mulroney, the latter of whom was covering the Games for Canada's CTV network. A real estate billionaire loaned them his home for an intimate and completely secret evening with a five-course meal prepared by a private chef.

The couple arrived to Beatlemania-size crowds wherever they went. Local press claimed they had the "magic touch" when their small Royal Australian Air Force plane touched down in Dubbo, one of the biggest farming states in New South Wales, which had been severely affected by the country's worst drought in over half a century. As they walked out onto the tarmac, dark clouds rolled in and the heavens opened, soaking the bone-dry terrain with more rain in one day than it had had the past six months. It was an answered prayer for the 38,943 locals whose farming community has seriously suffered from failing crops. Almost half the population celebrated the miraculous change in weather at a picnic with the royal couple. Everyone, including Harry and Meghan, was soaking wet but utterly thrilled. While royals pulling in big crowds is no new feat, there was something different about the Sussexes' oceanic visit. Young people who never had interest in the British monarchy had suddenly become engaged with the royals. Teenage girls and boys, many of them Indigenous Australians, spoke about how they saw Meghan as a symbol of female empowerment or a face that represented them in a way other members of the royal family hadn't before. "It's cool to think there are young girls who look at the Duchess of Sussex and think, 'Hey, she kind of looks like me,'" said Sherry-Rose Bih, an African Australian social enterprise entrepreneur who spent time chatting with the duchess at a reception for young leaders in Melbourne.

After Australia, Harry and Meghan were off to Fiji and Tonga, two stops that raised concerns over exposure to Zika, which can cause serious birth defects if a pregnant woman is exposed to the virus. Although the two countries were labeled by the World Health Organization and the Centers for Disease Control as "areas with risk of Zika infection," and so not recommended for pregnant women to visit, Harry and Meghan were adamant in not altering the tour schedule.

Having sought out medical advice before they left England, Meghan adhered to the precautions recommended by health professionals. She wore long-sleeved, light-colored clothing, which made it harder for mosquitoes to bite, and every time she stepped outside, she was "drenched" in DEET, according to an aide. Both Harry and Meghan had their own personal hand sanitizer pumps and DEET repellent lotion bottles in the seat pockets of their car. In Tonga, health authorities sprayed chemicals twice in the area two days before the couple made their appearance.

If Meghan was concerned about Zika, she didn't show it. In front of hundreds of students and faculty at Fiji's University of the South Pacific, she confidently delivered an impassioned speech on the necessity of universal education—one of three formal addresses she delivered on tour, which was more than any other royal consort. Meghan wrote the entire three-minute speech herself, which helped to explain why she hardly needed to refer to her printout, which was covered in handwritten notes.

Meghan proved herself a formidable force in the royal family, appearing unfazed by the overwhelming number of engagements, hysterical crowds on walkabouts, and major jet lag she said took her over a week to conquer. In fact, she put her sleepless nights at Admiralty House in Sydney to good use. Before visiting Dubbo, she baked banana bread with her own recipe, which featured chocolate chips and ginger, and brought it to a home visit to a local farming family with a box of Fortnum & Mason "Royal Blend" tea (her personal favorite). "My mom always taught me if you go to someone's house you always bring something," she said on arrival. The Australian media quickly dubbed the Duchess of Sussex "Queen of Hearts."

Harry also did more than his fair share to challenge the perception of the once-stuffy British establishment. Shirts unbuttoned, ties banished (he brought only two for the entire four-country tour), and candidness when it came to speaking about his own struggles made him a relatable royal family member. The tour also showed just how seriously he was taking his April 2018 appointment as Commonwealth Youth Ambassador, with a heavy focus on empowering young people from all walks of life. This theme drove the tour from start to end.

During their last stop in New Zealand, Meghan continued to show enthusiasm and energy. At a meeting with mental health advocates at a beachside café in Wellington, Harry had a candid discussion with teenagers dealing with mental health struggles about his own history. Meanwhile, Meghan tackled an area she was expert in: social media. More specifically she talked about the negative side of online life for young people. "You see beautiful photos on social media and you don't know whether she's born with it or maybe it's a filter," Meghan said. "Your sense of self-worth becomes really skewed when it's all based on likes."

Harry backed up his wife by adding, "Issues stemming from social media and gaming are a major problem for young people in the UK—and globally." But perhaps thinking of his own impending fatherhood, he advised that they shouldn't be too quick to blame parents for kids' problems. "Fingers are often pointed at the parents," he said, "but that's not always fair, as they, too, need to be educated about these things."

Up until the very last minutes of the tour, Meghan was indefatigable. Whether writing her own speeches, seeing that the leftover pastries from an event were brought out to share with children from a local school waiting outside the venue to meet the royal couple, or ditching Palace aides and security to walk the last stretch of Rotorua's Whakarewarewa Forest alone with Harry so he could take pictures of her against the redwood trees, Meghan proved that her pregnancy didn't change her strong work ethic.

Despite scaling back on a few engagements (at the request of Prince Harry and Kensington Palace aides, who felt she should pace herself), the four-months pregnant duchess showed no signs of faltering. "Pregnancy is an often-tiring time," said the New Zealand prime minister, Jacinda Ardern, who spent three days with the duke and duchess during the tour. "But the way she gave everything her all was incredible. She's an amazing woman and I'm so glad to have gotten to know her." (The couple have stayed in regular contact ever since, exchanging emails and even meeting up again at Kensington Palace on January 21, 2019. Meghan regularly wears the earrings Ardern gifted her in New Zealand—a pair of simple gold studs with a feather engraving on each by the kiwi musician and jeweler designer Boh Runga.)

Unfortunately, life was not going to get any more relaxing when Meghan returned from tour.

17

Duchess Different

Between her pregnancy announcement and flawless engagements on her first major royal tour, Meghan finally enjoyed a few weeks of very good press. But that streak came to a crashing halt on November 10, when the *Mail on Sunday* issued the first in a stream of damning stories. Harry and Meghan's assistant, Melissa Toubati, had reportedly quit after just six months on the job. The paper quoted a senior aide, who stated that Melissa, hired by Kensington Palace in March, was a "hugely talented person [who] played a pivotal role in the success of the Royal Wedding and will be missed by everyone in the Royal Household," and alleged that Meghan was a bad boss.

One week later, the *Mirror* followed up with its own story on Melissa's abrupt departure, reporting that Meghan had reduced the assistant to tears on several occasions. "She put up with quite a lot. Meghan put a lot of demands on her, and it ended up with her in tears," an unnamed source claimed. "Melissa is a total professional and fantastic at her job, but things came to a head and it was easier for them both to go their separate ways."

The tabloids' name-calling ("Hurricane Meghan" and "Me-Gain") and unflattering descriptions of her behavior ("Getting up at 5 am, bombarding aides with texts, and her eyebrow-raising fashion") didn't show any signs of letting up.

Meanwhile, Harry and Meghan were concerned why nothing was being done by the Palace to counter the misleading negative stories about Melissa leaving. According to multiple sources familiar with her sudden departure, despite the glowing press accounts, the couple had grown dissatisfied with Melissa's work and were not disappointed when she left. Meghan wondered if someone at Kensington Palace, where Melissa had some good friends, was more interested in protecting one of their own than her.

At their lowest moments, Harry and Meghan appreciated the support of the #SussexSquad, their global fandom who support the couple online. The passionate supporters, men and women from all backgrounds, regularly defended them from negativity in the press and pushed the Sussexes' activities into the top Twitter trends. Inspired by Harry and Meghan's charity work, the "Squad" has even gone on to launch initiatives of their own, such as the #GlobalSussexBabyShower to raise $50,000 for children's charities and planting 100,000 trees around the world in the couple's names. "To see that support and positivity means a lot," Harry told a friend.

Despite the swell of grassroots support for the couple, Harry and Meghan continued to fuel controversy. When the Palace announced on November 24 that despite the ongoing renovations on Apartment 1 at Kensington Palace, the newlyweds were going to relocate to Windsor, it launched a whole new round of criticism in the media.

After months of press speculation that Harry and Meghan would move out of Nottingham Cottage and into the Duke and Duchess of Gloucester's home adjacent to William and Kate's Apartment 1A, royal watchers were surprised to learn that the couple were moving miles away. Twenty-two, to be precise.

"The Duke and Duchess of Sussex will move to Frogmore Cottage on the Windsor Estate early next year as they prepare for the arrival of their first child," the Palace announced of their new home, located a stone's throw from Windsor Castle and just yards from Frogmore House, where they had held their wedding reception and engagement photoshoot. "Windsor is a very special place for Their Royal Highnesses and they are grateful that their official residence will be on the estate."

The Queen took great pleasure in gifting homes to her family members, a senior aide said. Her Majesty gave Sunninghill Park to Prince Andrew; Bagshot Park to Prince Edward and Sophie, Countess of Wessex; and Anmer Hall to William and Kate. "It's her thing!" the aide added.

Frogmore was perfect for Harry and Meghan, given its connection to Windsor—except it wasn't next door to William and Kate and their children. That was enough to set off a narrative of "Dueling Duchesses" that launched two days later. On November 26, *The Telegraph* reported that before the wedding, Meghan had left Kate in tears following a bridesmaid fitting for Princess Charlotte. "Kate had only just given birth to Prince Louis and was feeling quite emotional," a source said. On November 28, *The Sun* added to the vague story by claiming Meghan's "strict demands" caused Kate to cry.

A source, who was at the mid-May fitting and has never discussed what really happened until this book, said that stories about tears have been "puzzling" to those who were present. "Some of the children weren't cooperating, and there was a lot going on. Everyone tried to help where they could, but it's never easy with kids at fittings. There were no tears from anyone. And in the end, the fitting was fine. Kate and Meghan were both a little stressed but professionals in the room, and there were other people there, including Clare [Waight Keller], Melissa, and two Givenchy assistants."

Those close to Meghan questioned whether it could have been someone from the Palace or a former employee behind the story and wondered out loud why aides refused to just set the record straight there and then. "There are people, whether they work with the family or are members of the family, that know that a lot of this stuff isn't true, and aren't allowed to say anything, like that ridiculous story about Meg and Catherine, about the bridesmaids dresses," a trusted confidant shared. "That story was ridiculous and so false." At the time, though, a Kensington aide said only that the women, who were both hurt by the accusations, were "very different people." (Several aides across the Royal Households now confirm to the authors of this book that there was no fitting that left the Duchess of Cambridge in tears.)

Meghan would agree with that assessment. Their relationship hadn't progressed much since she was Harry's girlfriend. Although Meghan might have understood Kate's wariness to strike up a meaningful friendship at that point, she was now a fellow senior working member of the royal family and the wife of William's brother—and still they were no closer. Flowers for her birthday were nice, but Meghan would far rather have had Kate check in on her during the most difficult times with the press.

Refusing to address incorrect rumors only helped to reinforce them. Traditionally, the Palace had no comment when it came to rumors, but the Sussexes felt they weren't afraid to bend the rules if it was to correct a story about higher ranking family members. (Case in point, a spokesperson went on the record in July 2019 to deny the claims of a cosmetic clinic that Kate has had "baby Botox.") Harry and Meghan were frustrated by this approach, since it didn't seem they enjoyed the same support.

In this case, the duchesses were not the best of friends. But they also were not at war with each other either. There were awkward moments, such as the day the women happened to cross paths at Kensington Palace (in early 2017, when Harry and Meghan were still only dating), and although both were headed out to go shopping—on the same street—Kate went in her own Range Rover. The truth was that Meghan and Kate just didn't know each other that well. Although some aides claimed at the time that they "talked and texted regularly," by the time of Harry and Meghan's wedding, the sisters-in-law had spent only a handful of occasions together.

No workplace is perfect. In the rarefied world of the monarchy, the pressure could be insane. So were the internal politics between the three different households, which often seemed in competition with one another. Such were the interests between Buckingham Palace, Clarence House, and Kensington Palace that even royal watchers on social media started snickering when it appeared the households were scheduling events and social media posts on the same day to outdo one another. "There has always been competitiveness between the households," admits a senior aide. "That will never change."

Palace staff admitted frustration over the negative or untrue stories appearing day after day in the British tabloids. Yet it could hardly have come as a surprise that leaks were happening internally. One courtier privately bragged to friends at their ability to place a story, positive or negative, in any publication at the click of a finger, and another told a respected newspaper editor that he could "handle anything after putting up with one of Meghan's temper tantrums." Several staff described to the authors of this book the atmosphere inside the three households as "competitive," "miserable," and "full on."

The root of the problem didn't rest completely with the household staff—some of it came from the princes themselves. The rift that had begun when the Duke of Cambridge first questioned the pace at which his brother's relationship was moving had only widened now that Harry was married.

William and Kate's feelings seemed obvious to the Sussexes that summer and beyond. Among all the friends and family Harry and Meghan hosted at their house in Oxfordshire, the Cambridges failed to visit during their time living at the house. "The invite was there," a source said.

It was a far cry from how Harry had envisioned his future. The younger prince once told a friend he had an image of getting married and spending time with William and Kate, the two couples together, their children best friends.

The friction between the brothers was one of several reasons Harry wanted to base his family in Windsor. "He wanted to get away from the goldfish bowl that was Kensington Palace," a source said. "Everywhere you turn you're surrounded by staff and family. He was at a point in his life where he was working with his brother, doing the foundation with his brother, and living by his brother. It was too much."

But the press continued to save its harshest criticism for Meghan. One story had her demanding spray-bottle air fresheners for her wedding day to spritz around "musty" St. George's Chapel (the Queen's regular place of worship, which contains the Royal Vault), horrifying Buckingham Palace officials. The truth was that the discreet Baies scented air diffusers for the chapel provided by Diptyque—much like the candles from the same brand that Kate chose to scent Westminster Abbey for her 2011 nuptials—had been okayed by all parties involved.

Another story in December had a "furious" Kate intervening after Meghan "bollocked" a member of her staff. The Kensington Palace staff member was rumored to be deputy communications secretary Katrina McKeever, who had left the Palace after five years to explore new opportunities. Even Kensington Palace didn't understand the bizarre story. Katrina left on a good note with the Sussexes, who sent her a handwritten letter and huge floral arrangement when she left.

A week later, *The Express* reported that Palace staff called Meghan "Duchess Difficult," a title she has been unable to shake off to this day. No sign was too small to be considered an act of defiance—even her black nail polish and the one-shoulder gown she wore to the British Fashion Awards in December, where she presented Clare Waight Keller with the prize of British Designer of the Year. A photo booth snap of Meghan, Clare, and the actress Rosamund Pike posted to the British Fashion Council's Instagram account was taken down within two hours. A Palace source said, "It was a private memento that was never meant to be shared." A British Fashion Council source, however, said the organization took down the photo because of the deluge of racist comments posted underneath.

The columnist Richard Kay (once Princess Diana's favorite reporter) quoted a source, who sniped, "There was something ostentatious in the way she posed holding her bump, plus she was wearing dark nail varnish that the Queen hates."

Princess Diana had worn red nail polish and off-the-shoulder gowns. Princess Eugenie painted her nails in a Union Jack flag manicure to celebrate the Queen's Jubilee in 2012 and wore a similar plum shade to Meghan's at a Serpentine Galleries party. Even Kate, who normally toes the line, had a pedicure in red at one event. While most of the time the Windsor women, including Meghan, stuck to neutral tones, they made exceptions if the occasion was appropriate. There was no nail polish protocol.

The indignation over Meghan's nail polish was indicative of a bigger issue. It was open season on Meghan, with many looking for anything and everything to criticize. "Duchess *Different*," a close friend of Meghan's said, "*that's* what people have a problem with. She's the easiest person in the world to work with. Certain people just don't like the fact she stands out."

A number of courtiers believe there were some working in the institution who were biased against Meghan because she was an

American and a former actress. There are inherently different working styles between Americans and Brits. Americans can be much more direct, and that doesn't often sit well in the much more refined institution of the monarchy. Sometimes the American matter-of-fact tone in British society could be viewed as abrasive.

"This is a script that wrote itself as soon as you knew that an American actress was coming into the royal family," another aide added.

Meghan felt like some of the commentary and tabloid stories were more than a culture clash; they were sexist and prejudiced. If a man got up before dawn to work, he was applauded for his work ethic. If a woman did it, she was deemed difficult or a bitch. The double standard was only exacerbated when it came to successful women of color, often labeled as demanding or aggressive.

On December 3, Meghan was in the audience at London's Southbank Centre when Michelle Obama, in town to promote her memoir, *Becoming*, said, "What happens to black women is that we become a caricature . . . People will take the things from us that they like. Our style, our swag becomes co-opted, but then we're demonized. We are angry, we are too loud, we are too everything. And I experienced that. How dare I have a voice and use it."

Case in point: in February 2019, Meghan came under attack by the press and commentators again when she wrote encouraging messages on bananas to Bristol's street sex workers during a royal engagement. Standing in the kitchen of the One25 charity, an organization that helped vulnerable women break free from street sex work, addiction, poverty, and violence, the duchess had just watched a volunteer prepare food parcels to be handed out the same day to vulnerable women working on the streets. Sharpie in hand, Meghan picked up a banana from each meal bag and started carefully writing messages of support: "You are strong." "You are amazing." "You are loved."

It was an unexpected move that touched the hearts of staff at the nonprofit charity, whose mobile outreach van provided support to around 240 local sex workers in the city's red-light district each year. "I saw this project this woman had started somewhere in the States on a school lunch program," Meghan said, recalling the story of a cafeteria manager who worked at Kingston Elementary School in Virginia. "On each of the bananas she wrote an affirmation, to make the kids feel really empowered. It was the most incredible idea—this small gesture."

For the sex workers, it was a kind gesture. Said one speaking anonymously, "We feel invisible out here, and although it seems silly, to be acknowledged and to see words I don't hear very often, it meant a lot."

The message wasn't heard the same way by everyone. One tabloid sent an undercover reporter to try to obtain one of the bananas from One25's van, and *The Sun* called the gesture "offensive." Piers Morgan—who regularly attacked the duchess in over 100 opinion pieces and interviews after not receiving an invite to the wedding—said she was making a "mockery" of the monarchy and prostitutes. A *Daily Mail* columnist printed this sentiment about the sex workers: "They are not special: they know this every time they have sex with a man for money."

Meghan was disgusted by the coverage. "These people are animals," she told a friend.

"They're nothing but trolls," added Harry.

Royal protocol required Meghan to stay silent and resist defending herself no matter how much she might have been offended. So, when *The Sun* reported a front-page story in April 2019 about the Queen "banning" her from wearing jewelry that once belonged to Diana, she had to remain silent. Again.

"Aspects of Meghan's behavior, including before the Royal Wedding, caused resentment with forces within Buckingham Palace," the tabloid alleged, referring to inaccurate reports of Meghan's tyrannical style, including refusing to use the Queen's staff for most aspects of her wedding, like the flowers or cake. Meanwhile, according to the article, Kate was allowed to wear whatever she wanted: "It is at the discretion of the Queen and trusted advisors which items in the Royal Collection she chooses to loan out and to whom." But what the source clearly got confused, however, is the fact that the Royal Collection doesn't own any of Diana's collection.

Both Meghan and Kate had worn a number of the iconic pieces associated with Diana, which after her death had been passed on to her sons or the Queen, depending on whether they had been privately owned or gifts in a royal capacity. Kate wore to state dinners the Cambridge Lover's Knot tiara, which Diana had worn many times in her life. Meghan was seen on the royal tour to Australia, New Zealand, Fiji, and Tonga wearing Diana's butterfly diamond earrings and a sapphire bangle bracelet.

This wasn't the first time that supposed squabbles over the jewelry had emerged in the press. *The Sun* reported Meghan had her heart set on "a tiara with emeralds," believed to be the Grand Duchess Vladimir tiara for her wedding and not the tiara Queen Mary wore on her wedding day. Smuggled out of Russia after the 1917 Revolution and purchased by Queen Mary in 1921, the tiara is one of the most elaborate in the collection. Worn by both Princess Diana and Queen Elizabeth, it was refurbished to include interlocking circular rings of diamonds with large emerald and pearl drops hanging from each circlet.

Due to the hanging jewels, the tiara is sometimes confused with the Cambridge Lover's Knot. Made by the House of Garrard for Queen Mary in 1914 from pearls and diamonds already owned by her family, the Lover's Knot tiara was modeled after a headpiece owned by her grandmother Princess Augusta of Hesse. After Queen Mary died in 1953, the crown was passed down to her granddaughter Queen Elizabeth II.

The Vladimir tiara, however, might have appealed to Meghan because the color green was incorporated into several aspects of the wedding (the couple took their engagement photos in the Green Drawing Room, and for the wedding, the Queen wore a green dress and Doria a mint suit). A source involved with elements of the wedding planning said, "At some point during early planning there could have been talk about the ideal tiara having emeralds in it."

However it's not true that Meghan demanded another tiara after her selection with the Queen—a rite of passage for royal brides. Since she became the monarch, Queen Elizabeth II has loaned statement pieces to all royal wives, including Camilla and Kate. According to a high-ranking aide, "Her Majesty takes great joy in being able to offer a little something" for important events and enjoys being part of the process, which usually involves the sovereign picking out designs for special occasions like state dinners and other formal engagements. "She will often have something in mind," the source said.

What was different with Meghan's selection was that Harry tagged along. The couple, who had been engaged and living together in Kensington Palace for almost four months, arrived at the reception room in Buckingham Palace, where they were then escorted down a secure elevator, forty feet below the palace, to the large vault where five tiaras had been assembled for display ahead of the couple's appointment in February 2018.

While typically self-assured even in the most intimidating of situations, Meghan was nervous about trying on priceless pieces of jewelry, some of which have rarely seen the light of day. There was nothing in her Southern California childhood, acting career, or evolution as a feminist advocating for women across the globe to suggest comfort with diamond-encrusted diadems. That was unlike the Queen, who, in the words of her late sister, Princess Margaret, "is the only person who can put on a tiara with one hand, while walking down stairs."

Before the meeting, Meghan had spoken to Clare Waight Keller, who had already started designing her sculpted wedding dress. "They had an idea of what would work," a source said of the designer and bride's tiara choice, "but weren't sure of what the final options would be. It was a case of waiting to see what they were presented with."

They looked through archival images of different tiaras they liked from photo archives, but ultimately none of that mattered since they knew the choice was not theirs to make. To borrow one of these tiaras was a privilege and gift, and like most gifts, you took what you were given.

Each tiara is stored in its own safety box within the vault, a basement room about 150 feet long that is split into sections. The large space—its size, proof of the extent of Her Majesty's collection of hundreds of tiaras, brooches, necklaces, earrings, and other jewels—is not sparse or cold, like a bank's vault. Instead, it's well-lit, like a showroom.

Crown Jeweller Mark Appleby—the one to lay out the tiaras for display (attaching jewels that had been stored separately in little pouches and attaching the center stone of Queen Mary's diamond tiara)—was not present in the room for the meeting, because it was an extremely personal and intimate moment. But he was on standby if any assistance was required or there were any complications. All the workstations for the crown jeweler's staff were empty, as no one other than the curator of the Queen's jewelry, Angela Kelly, was on hand to present the tiaras to the Queen and Meghan, as she had done with the Duchess of Cambridge and went on to do with Princess Eugenie.

With the official title of Personal Assistant, Advisor, and Curator to Her Majesty the Queen (Jewellery, Insignias, and Wardrobe), Angela was the only person other than the crown jeweler who had access to Her Majesty's personal jewelry collection. From the way

each stone was polished to the placement of the matching bracelet, rings, necklace, and tiara upon the pink fabric–lined tray with
a lace-trimmed cover, hand-sewn by the monarch's grandmother
Queen Mary—it was clear how much care Angela put into their
maintenance.

While gloves were normally worn when handling tiaras,
Angela—who was also responsible for the basic cleaning of the
Queen's jewelry before and after it was removed from the vault—
chose to go without so she could have a better grip on the often-
priceless pieces.

With the Queen and Prince Harry looking on, Angela presented five different tiaras for Meghan to consider. Although the
Queen was a great conversationalist, as was Meghan, who became
particularly talkative when she was nervous, everyone was quiet as
they focused on the task at hand.

Angela had presented various options to the Queen before the
meeting. Her Majesty then offered her own thoughts until she and
Angela had whittled down the choices to five. With Meghan seated
in front of a full-length mirror, each tiara was carefully placed upon
her head, until a decision was made.

While the headpieces were usually held in place by a satin
band or hair clip, they didn't do a proper fitting that day since
bringing in a hairstylist would have detracted from the intimacy
of the personal moment. There was plenty of time later to do a full
hair trial, Angela explained, which included trying different ways
to hold the tiara with pins and making Meghan nod her head to see
if it moved. That day was all about the tiara, and one outshone all
the others as it rested on her dark hair.

It was Queen Mary's diamond bandeau tiara. Crafted for the
late Queen Consort in 1932, the tiara centers on a brooch of ten
diamonds given to her as a wedding gift by the County of Lincoln
in 1893. The large detachable brooch sits within a sparkling plati-

num band of eleven flexible sections pierced with interlaced ovals and pavé set with large and small brilliant diamonds. While it was not a favorite of Queen Mary's, who wore it for less formal events, Meghan said it "stood out."

The Queen agreed with Meghan upon her choice of tiara for the wedding. Meghan tried on all five but knew right away which one she liked best. "It was a special moment for both of them," a Palace aide shared.

When more than a year later the story broke about Meghan demanding a different tiara to wear on her wedding day, she called a friend and said, "How sad, I love my tiara."

While the papers got it wrong about its source, they weren't wrong about the fact that there had been a conflict during Meghan's wedding preparations. There were no disagreements with Meghan and the Queen about the tiara. The dustup was between Angela Kelly and Harry.

It all began in late March, when Meghan's hairstylist Serge Normant flew from New York to London to do a hair trial using the tiara they had chosen for the wedding. The pair had hoped to visit Buckingham Palace to meet Angela, who would have handled the tiara just as she had done when they picked it out with the Queen.

Except no matter how many requests were sent by Kensington Palace, the Queen's personal dresser didn't respond. After several failed attempts, Angela's availability remained unknown. Harry was furious.

Angela—who started as one of the Queen's dressers in 1993 and quickly worked her way up the Master of the Household's department to senior dresser and then first personal assistant—had an especially close relationship with the Queen. One of the few people allowed to touch the monarch, Angela has been the Queen's right-hand woman or, as some say, her "gatekeeper," for more than a decade. Her Majesty has often visited Angela's "grace and favor" house in Windsor, and when the two are alone, Buckingham Palace staff can hear their laughter from all the way down the hallway.

Like most senior staff at Buckingham Palace, Angela is on call should Her Majesty require her service—and at the time of the first hair trial requests, she had apparently been busy at Windsor Castle, where the Queen was based for Easter Court. But as the weeks went by, and the requests from aides working for Harry continued, a time for Meghan to try the tiara had yet to be scheduled.

Harry, while obviously familiar with Palace protocol, didn't believe that Angela was truly unavailable. Instead, he thought she was purposefully ignoring Meghan. What followed between the prince and Angela was a heated exchange that was far from the typical restraint expected. According to a source, Harry had no problem confronting the issue head on. "He was fed up," said the aide.

With the wedding just a few weeks away, the lack of tiara hair trial continued to be an issue of contention. Members of staff at Kensington Palace just weren't able to get in touch with Angela to make it happen. People were frustrated—and confused. Why was it so hard to set up a time for Meghan to try the tiara with her hairdresser? In the end, Harry had to speak to his grandmother about the situation. And she got her trial.

A senior Buckingham Palace aide insisted that Harry was simply being "oversensitive" when he accused Angela of trying to make things difficult for his fiancée. But a source close to the prince said nothing could convince Harry that some of the old guard at the Palace simply didn't like Meghan and would stop at nothing to make her life difficult.

18

Brothers Divided

High-ranking aides across all three royal households were so alarmed at the press coverage and speculation on social media about a rift between the brothers and their wives that they began openly discussing the impact it could have on the monarchy if things weren't righted. For months headlines had focused on the fractured relationships between the two couples. And the chatter on social media was just as loud. The whole situation was so out of control, a source said, "even the Queen was concerned."

Courtiers attended a retreat in the spring of 2019 where the concerns were openly discussed. "We need to design a system to protect the monarchy full stop," one said. "It's no secret, the future of this monarchy relies solely on the four people currently in Kensington Palace. The public popularity only lies with them . . . When he [the Prince of Wales] becomes King, the only way it lasts is if the four of them are not at war. We cannot have them at war."

"Harry was upset that it was playing out so publicly and that so much of the information being reported was wrong," a source said.

"There had been moments where he felt people working with his brother had put things out there to make William look good, even if it meant throwing Harry under the bus. It was a confusing time, and his head was all over the place—he didn't know who or what to believe, and he and William weren't talking enough either, which made everything a lot worse."

This was by far the most damaging development because it echoed the period in the mid-1990s, during the breakdown of Charles and Diana's marriage, when the press and the public began to openly question the longevity of the monarchy. Despite protests from courtiers that the brothers were on solid footing, the rumors wouldn't subside

On March 14, 2019, Buckingham Palace announced that William and Harry were going their separate ways by separating their offices.

"The Queen has agreed to the creation of a new Household for The Duke and Duchess of Sussex, following their marriage in May last year. The Household, which will be created with the support of The Queen and The Prince of Wales, will be established in the spring."

Harry and Meghan's household had been an open secret since November. Aides were quick to insist it was a natural progression. The princes were no longer "the boys," as Diana had called them; they were men with very different personalities, personal styles, and future constitutional roles. As a spokesperson put it, they were on "divergent paths."

Everyone believed that the brothers getting much-needed space from each other would go some way to repairing their relationship. "It is very hard that they share work together," a courtier said. "That's not normal in a family. That will at points, of course, create some tension."

Prince Charles, who funds many of his own public, charitable and private activities through the revenues of his private estate, the Duchy of Cornwall, "controlled the purse strings," which also caused some of the issues between William and Harry. The brothers sometimes had to vie for additional funds for projects from their father, who also helped cover expenses related to Camilla and some of those for his sons (including Kate and Meghan's wardrobes). "They actually genuinely have to debate who gets what amount of money from their father to fund their projects," an aide said. "Add in the fact that there is an inherent hierarchy and that is really tricky."

"While Charles may be a father to Harry, he's also their boss, and that makes their relationship complex for a number of reasons," a source added. "Charles is extremely focused on his public image, and there have been times Harry has felt that has taken precedence over everything else."

Harry wasn't the only one who had a complicated relationship with the Prince of Wales. "The boys can be hot and cold with their father," disclosed a source, who gave the example of planning the photo session for Charles's seventieth birthday, which they called "an absolute nightmare."

"Neither William nor Harry made much of an effort to make themselves available," the source said.

A second aide, who had been involved in meetings on the brothers' futures, explained, "Where you are born in this family dictates your position of power, and because of that, Harry has always come second to his brother, especially when it comes to funding. There were times in the past that Harry wanted to take on bigger projects and do more work, but he couldn't get the money to support it. William was always the priority. A lot of their quarrels have been over budgets. That's what happens when you are in business with your family."

Prince Andrew and Prince Edward didn't share a working arrangement with their older brother, Prince Charles, so they didn't experience the same tensions as William and Harry. It was understandable that Harry didn't want to be in his brother's shadow now that he was starting his life with Meghan, courtiers argued.

Harry and Meghan wanted to create their own individual household in Windsor, meaning their own office staffed with their own team, who would be separate from all others. But senior officials quickly ruled out that option.

The senior courtiers who Diana used to refer to as "men in gray suits" were concerned that the global interest in and popularity of the Sussexes needed to be reined in. In the short period of time since their fairy-tale wedding, Harry and Meghan were already propelling the monarchy to new heights around the world. The Sussexes had made the monarchy more relatable to those who had never before felt a connection. However, there were concerns that the couple should be brought into the fold; otherwise, if left as they were, the establishment feared their popularity might eclipse that of the royal family itself.

"To palace officials wondering how to handle the couple there was another figure who looms large when you think of young women using a royal platform for global charitable crusading: Harry's own mother," the political editor Tim Shipman wrote in the *Sunday Times*, quoting a source as saying, "The danger to them is that Meghan is going to be bigger than Diana."

Meghan did not enjoy universal support within the institution of the monarchy and some of the British tabloid media painted her as a threat, but she had been widely embraced by the public. For people of all different backgrounds, at home in the UK and abroad, Meghan was a trailblazer—a woman who confidently inhabited a realm that had once been considered off-limits.

Feminists praised her continued focus on women's empowerment through the power of her new royal patronage. On January 10, 2019, Meghan announced her commitment to Smart Works, a British organization dedicated to helping women improve their employment opportunities through mentoring and providing professional wardrobes. She had worked privately with the program as a volunteer, coaching clients on such things as their interview skills and suit choices. Its founder and former *British Vogue* fashion editor, Juliet Hughes-Hallett, spent several months getting to know the duchess before the announcement, and she was impressed by how hands-on Meghan was from her first visit in March 2018. "Meghan was excited and wanted to get involved from the very beginning," she said of the royal's involvement with the program, which has helped thousands of women find jobs since its 2013 launch. "What struck everyone the most was her empathy and how good she was at making the women feel safe. Plus, she's great fun to be around."

The announcement coincided with a public visit to the charity's West London base, where from the moment Meghan arrived, poking her head around the door of their back office to say hello to some of the staff she had gotten to know so well, it was clear she fit in. "It's not just donating your clothes and seeing where they land but really being part of each other's success stories as women," Meghan said while helping curate donated pieces for a mom of three, Patsy Wardally, a trained plumber looking to reenter the workforce after raising her autistic daughter. The interview coach Marina Novis, who spent time with the duchess during her many visits, said, "It's amazing seeing her talking to the candidates because she really listens and asks very pertinent questions. Last year [before her wedding] she was talking to us about confidence, and then we asked, 'How do you manage with confidence?' She said, 'I'm about to take on a big role, happening now. The most important thing to do is to just breathe and have that inner confidence about it.'"

Meghan brought that confidence to all four of her patronages, including the two handed down by Her Majesty: the National Theatre and the Association of Commonwealth Universities (ACU), which brings together universities and academics from over fifty countries to advance knowledge. "She is passionate about the impact the arts can have, whether it's social prescription to do with health or to do with community building," the National Theatre artistic director Rufus Norris said. "And what a lovely way to bring together her experience in a world she knows so well into her new world."

Meghan's philanthropic portfolio closely followed her interests and abilities. "She wanted it to be a reflection of who she is, what she is capable of, and a preview of the many things she would like to explore as a working member of the royal family," an aide said. "Female empowerment and gender diversity will always be a cornerstone of her work." Meghan shared her horror at the lack of both when visiting the ACU in February after being shown data revealing that UK professors were overwhelmingly white and male. "Oh my god," she exclaimed during a conversation with the University of Manchester's lead for equality, diversity, and inclusion, Dr. Rachel Cowan. "This is quite a shock to see and clear we have some way to go."

A longtime advocate of the "adopt, don't shop" animal movement, Meghan also became a patron of the Mayhew animal welfare center, where, on her second visit to their northwest London headquarters, she told CEO Caroline Yates, "Animals are such an important part of my life. There is such a big need for services like this—in London, the UK, and around the world—but I'm painfully aware of how important funding is. I want to help you grow in any way that I can."

Meghan's movements and fashion choices were followed not just in the UK but by America's most prominent publications as well. Anna Wintour called Meghan's style "fantastic" at the April 2019 Women in the World summit. "I've been thinking a lot about suits recently," the editor in chief of *Vogue* told the audience. "Thank you to the Duchess of Sussex!"

While the creation of separate courts allowed the brothers to pursue their own interests, it was also designed to make sure necessary resources were in place for the brothers' changing responsibilities. "The Cambridges and the Sussexes have different futures, and that means that you need to ready both of those households for reign change," a senior aide said, referring to when Prince Charles becomes king. "Trying to get as much of the structures in place to put them all onto a permanent footing is the end goal."

Harry realized he may have a finite period for he and Meghan to make the most impact on a global scale. Mindful that once George turns eighteen and becomes an active senior royal, the focus of the institution will be on the succession of Charles, William, and George—leaving Harry sidelined, just as his uncles Edward and Andrew were when Charles and his brothers came of age.

Despite the pitch, the Sussexes never received their own office to manage their affairs. A source said it was made clear they would not be receiving any preferential treatment. The news was a blow to the pair, but in a compromise of sorts, they got their own small team within Buckingham Palace. Although it wasn't all they asked for, it was more than what had originally been in the plan for them—an offer of sharing a staff with other royal family members under the larger Buckingham Palace umbrella.

Prince Charles wanted the split to be cost neutral. But according to aides, William fought to make sure that enough resources were allocated from the budget for the newly established Sussex household to have a proper working space and a suitable communications budget. The Duke of Cambridge knew that the Sussexes were important to the royal family and needed necessary support. And smaller roles for Harry and Meghan would have meant more work for the Cambridges. Over several weeks, William and his dedicated private secretary, Simon Case, attended meetings with senior Buckingham Palace aides to ensure that Harry and Meghan received the best deal possible.

With the extra funds the couple were able to hire Sara Latham, a highly regarded PR professional and ex–Clinton administration official, to manage the press strategy for the newly formed Sussex household.

A dual US and UK citizen, Sara had worked on Hillary Clinton's 2016 bid for the presidency and as chief of staff to the campaign's chairman, John Podesta. She also had experience in British government, as special advisor to Tony Blair's Secretary of State for Culture, Media, and Sport from 2005 to 2006. Her most recent post before joining the Firm was as a managing partner for Freud's, an international PR firm started by the ex-husband of Elisabeth Murdoch, who was the media titan Rupert Murdoch's daughter. Having worked alongside Nick Loughran, one of Harry's favorite former communications staffers and the husband of the Kensington Palace assistant Clara, Sara was also somewhat familiar with royal culture.

Smart, funny, and a great strategist, Sara told it like it was—and Harry and Meghan immediately took a liking to her.

When the household split was announced, so came the dividing up of staff who had previously worked with both brothers, as well as lots of rearranging. Jason Knauf, the Sussexes' longtime communications director, moved over to work for the Duke and Duchess of Cambridge in an expanded role involving the couple's charitable work and later becoming CEO of their foundation. Over the months ahead he would also oversee the split of the Royal Foundation and untangle many of the joint initiatives they once had. "There was an option for the four to keep going as they were, but the Cambridges were keen to get going on a clean break," a source said. "Both couples wanted to pursue their charities separately." While it wouldn't be the immediate end of all ventures as the "Fab Four" (their final group project, a crisis text service called Shout, was announced later in May), it did mean an end to doing anything together as a group under the umbrella, such as the Royal Foundation Forum, the event in February 2018 where they had showcased their programs, including Heads Together and United for Wildlife.

Christian Jones—the former press secretary for the Department for Exiting the European Union—was tapped to run the Cambridges' new communications operation. Both Harry and Meghan were upset to lose Christian, who had worked with the Sussexes when the two couples shared an office. Meghan had immediately hit it off with Christian after his hiring in December 2018. From their first lunch together at the Notting Hill Italian restaurant Chucs, Meghan was a fan. She adored that he spoke to her like a friend and wore sneakers to the office. She also loved his ideas. The two regularly brainstormed together with no airs or graces. However, the new opportunity spearheading the vision for the future king was a job Christian just couldn't turn down.

As to Meghan's reputation as a tough boss, aides described her as very determined but thoughtful, too. She often sent treats to the Palace offices, such as in early 2018, when she sent the communications team and private staff at Kensington Palace a large selection of sorbets to thank them for their help, and she often sent flowers and handwritten notes to key aides on their birthdays.

Still, Meghan will be the first to say she's "focused on implementing change."

"That's the reality," a source close to the duchess said. "That is what drives her and gets her up in the morning. And she has the platform to do it."

In a major show of support by the Queen, Meghan was made vice president of the Queen's Commonwealth Trust—a platform for young change-makers across the fifty-four member states that champions, funds, and connects young leaders. Harry joined her as president. In her first engagement as VP, Meghan joined a panel of female powerhouses—including the singer Annie Lennox and the former prime minister of Australia Julia Gillard—for an event to discuss the importance of International Women's Day at King's College London. At the event, Meghan was asked by Anne McElvoy, a senior editor at *The Economist*, how she responded to newspaper headlines describing her feminism as "trendy."

"The idea of making the word 'feminism' trendy, that doesn't make any sense to me," Meghan said. "This is something that is going to be part of the conversation forever."

Like his wife, Harry also didn't waste any time putting his office to work. In April 2019, Harry and Oprah announced a partnership to produce a mental health series for Apple TV+ in late 2020 or early 2021. Oprah, who flew to London in March to meet Harry and a very pregnant Meghan, said the idea came about after a conversation with the prince. "What do you think are the most important issues facing the world right now?" she asked him. To which he answered unequivocally, "Climate change and mental wellness, mental fitness, and mental health."

"I am incredibly proud to be working alongside Oprah," Harry said in a statement. "I truly believe that good mental health—mental fitness—is the key to powerful leadership, productive communities, and a purpose-driven self . . . Our hope is that this series will be positive, enlightening, and inclusive—sharing global stories of unparalleled human spirit fighting back from the darkest places, and the opportunity for us to understand ourselves and those around us better."

Harry's professional life was really taking off. Just as important, however, his private one seemed to be settling down. He hoped that William's advocacy on behalf of his household was the beginning of a fresh start for him and his brother. "At that moment, he decided to put the past behind him and appreciate the efforts his brother had made," a source close to the couple said.

Harry was willing to accept that he and his brother were two different people. William was married to the institution of the monarchy with a very set role, while Harry was on his own path. And

Harry had to admit that both princes had their noses put out of joint. In the end, though, they were a family, and that was not a bond worth breaking.

William was glad to be back on good terms with Harry. One Palace source shared that William told him in late March, "You know what? Me and my brother, for the first time in two months, have had a really lovely conversation together."

Over Easter that year, Prince Harry arrived solo to the family Easter Sunday church service at Windsor Castle, since a very pregnant Meghan was not up for a big public engagement. Inside the chapel, the two chatted and laughed with each other.

"To see them warm with each other," a Buckingham Palace aide said, "was delightful."

19

Nesting in Windsor

After the Easter service, Harry returned to Frogmore Cottage with William and Kate, who stopped by to see how Meghan was doing.

Meghan joined William, Kate, and other family members in their family room (instead of the formal reception room), where they chatted over a cup of tea. The visit was brief, just thirty-five minutes, but it was the beginning of the couples' coming together and putting things behind them—at least that was what Harry hoped after the show of support from his brother. Before William and Kate left, Harry excitedly showed them around the house, as it was their first time visiting Frogmore Cottage since the renovation.

Harry imagined his brother and sister-in-law coming regularly with their children to the cottage in Windsor, which "has a special place in their hearts," according to a source close to Harry and Meghan. While they were falling in love, they were able to enjoy long walks on the private grounds of Frogmore House without fear of paparazzi. Later, of course, it was the site of their engagement photos and wedding reception.

"As a place to raise a child, it's really lovely," a trusted confidant of Meghan's said. "They could open their door and have all of those private gardens. Both of them felt it would be a really positive thing for their child to be there, go on walks privately. While it wasn't something they had considered before, once it became an option, they were both really excited about it."

But first Frogmore had to be substantially renovated. Built in 1801, it was originally a country house for Queen Charlotte and her unmarried daughters. The cottage had many tenants (including Henry James Sr., the American theologian and the father of the philosopher William James and the novelist Henry James) until the early twenty-first century, when the ten-bedroom home was split into five separate units to house Windsor estate staff. Before Harry and Meghan moved into the cottage, which had been gifted to the couple by the Queen in the fall of 2018, it needed to be gutted and totally updated—complete with a family kitchen, nursery, and conservatory.

Plans for Harry and Meghan's Frogmore Cottage renovations included conservatory extensions, several new gas fireplaces, and an open-plan kitchen. Meghan's mother was expected to visit for extended periods in order to have plenty of time with her new grandchild; however, her work at home meant they could only be short stays. Despite reports of a "granny annex," Doria would stay in a guest room just a few doors up from Harry and Meghan's master.

All traditional floorboards, window frames, and doors were maintained. Also, part of the plans included extensive landscaping, since one of the attractions of Frogmore Cottage were the beautiful gardens where their baby could one day play freely.

While the £2.4 million price tag for the structural renovations was covered by the Sovereign Grant, the allowance provided annually by the government to support the Queen in her official duties and cover the family's travel, palace upkeep, and royal employee payroll, the couple paid for the interior work themselves. Both careful with their money, Harry and Meghan did not spend, as rumored, £1 million on art. "Couldn't be further from the truth," said a friend, who noted that most of the art in the home were prints or framed vintage posters, including a nude character study by the modern New York artist Inslee Fariss, which Meghan kept in storage after moving out of her Toronto home.

The house is big, but the building itself is shallow, with a lot of the rooms starting at the front and finishing at the back. "It's one of the things that Meghan and Harry love about it," a friend said. "All that beautiful light coming in on both sides. The energy is just so good there."

Being within the Windsor estate security zone provided the couple with the safety they desired for their new life outside of London, but extra provisions were made for the couple prior to their move. Mature trees were planted around Frogmore Cottage to keep out prying eyes (or lenses) that tried to catch a glimpse. Hi-tech laser fencing ensured that trespassers were kept at bay, too. It also helped that next door to their home was a separate building just for protection officers, hired from Scotland Yard's Royalty and Specialist Protection branch, to be permanently based.

It was a much-needed ring of steel to keep the Sussex family safe, particularly after they were forced to move out of their Oxfordshire house early when Splash News (the same agency that was caught in Jamaica) sent a helicopter to take aerial photos of the house. The photos were so clear it was possible to see inside their master bedroom and living areas. In mid-January 2019, *The Times of London* ran one of the pictures, and many outlets followed. Harry was furious and Meghan crushed.

A source close to the couple said they immediately felt vulnerable, especially with Meghan being heavily pregnant. While the area was safe and protected, "being out in the middle of the countryside, where you don't know who is out there at night or if someone has managed to sneak nearby" was enough for them to say goodbye to Oxfordshire. The original plan was to keep the house until the end of the lease and then potentially buy it. But they moved back to Nottingham Cottage, which felt even more cramped and uncomfortable, until Frogmore was ready. (Harry later sued Splash News, and on May 16, 2019, he received significant compensation, which he donated to charity, and an apology from the photo agency for the intrusion.)

In addition to the physical precautions at Frogmore, Harry and Meghan also began taking extra safety measures with digital information after they suffered a major data leak. On September 12, 2018, a computer programmer based in Russia managed to hack into an online cloud storage account that contained over two hundred unseen photos of Harry and Meghan that had been taken by the photographer Alexi Lubomirski.

Among the stolen images were pictures of the couple sharing personal moments during their engagement photo series as well as others from their wedding day reception (including some of the Queen). The large set also included outtakes with eyes half closed and other unflattering moments meant for the trash can. The hacker leaked a handful of the photos to Tumblr. Many fans assumed they were fake, photoshopped images, but behind the scenes there was concern at Kensington Palace when they received a tip about the security breach. Harry and Meghan "were alarmed to hear that it was so easy to get such personal files of theirs," a source close to the couple said. "The whole situation was a wake-up call."

According to a royal source, Frogmore also posed "logistical challenges" to the couple in their various initiatives. "They're going to be away from their [Buckingham Palace] office," the source said. "They're both really hands-on in their work, so that's difficult."

Because of this connection to their work, Harry and Meghan planned to retain a London base in the future. They no longer used Nott Cott, which remained unoccupied after they vacated it.

There was ample precedent for the Sussexes to maintain two residences. William and Kate were gifted Anmer Hall on the Sandringham estate in Norfolk by the Queen, but their primary residence was Apartment 1A at Kensington Palace. Prince Charles retained Clarence House as his official residence and Highgrove in Gloucestershire for weekends in the country. Similarly, Princess Anne retained a private Buckingham Palace apartment—as does Prince Andrew.

For the moment, though, the couple was firmly established in Frogmore, where for the final weeks of her pregnancy, starting in April, Meghan didn't leave once. Her final trimester had been nothing but busy, with her four royal patronage announcements and back-to-back engagements, including attending the premiere of Cirque du Soleil's *TOTEM* show at London's Royal Albert Hall to raise money for Sentebale. And then on February 15, she flew from London to New York on a commercial British Airways flight.

This would be her first time in New York since getting married, and Meghan looked forward to five nights of shopping and good food with some of her closest and most loyal friends. Despite being a duchess, she was happy to crash at Misha Nonoo's Greenwich Village duplex right next door to the celebrity hotspot Waverly Inn for the first three nights. Misha was now engaged to Hess oil heir, Michael Hess, whom she married in the fall.

Her first day in the city, Meghan met up with Jessica, who took her for macarons and tea in SoHo bakery Ladurée, which offered them a private space. The expectant mom also bought baby clothes at the fancy French children's store Bonpoint. But it was her first night walking around New York City's West Village that Meghan truly felt like her old self. Dressed all in black with her hair down, she went virtually unnoticed. One man pulled out his phone to take a photo before he was stopped by her protection officer, who was walking several steps behind Meghan. But that was nothing compared to the crowds she dealt with in the UK.

Four days later, however, after Meghan had moved to the Mark Hotel on the Upper East Side, the paparazzi were out in full force after news leaked that she was having a star-studded baby shower hosted by Serena Williams and Meghan's college friend Genevieve.

Serena had reserved the Grand Penthouse at the Mark, where approximately twenty of Meghan's closest friends from her teenage years to the present gathered for a party, described by one guest as "chill and relaxed." Meghan loved having nearly all of her friends in one place. Coordinated by Jennifer Zabinski of JZ Events, who had also planned Serena's 2017 wedding to Internet entrepreneur Alexis Ohanian, the event featured a color scheme of blues, pinks, yellows, and greens—with no hint to the gender of the baby. Not that the genderless creations were necessary, as Meghan quietly shared that she was expecting a boy with a number of friends at the fete, such as Amal Clooney, who hadn't already been told.

The guests—including Misha, Gayle King, Jessica, wellness guru Taryn Toomey, Lindsay, NBC cable entertainment chief Bonnie Hammer, actress and close pal Janina Gavankar, and her *Suits* costar Abigail Spencer—dined on a menu prepared by the Michelin-star chef Jean-Georges Vongerichten while the harpist Erin Hill played in the background. The shower was co-ed; makeup artist Daniel Martin, hairdresser Serge Normant, and Markus were on hand to celebrate as well.

The party had a flower-arranging lesson led by the New York florist Lewis Miller, who became famous for his "Flower Flashes," a series of random pop-up floral arrangements he designed throughout the city on everything from trash cans to landmarks. The guests' floral arrangements were donated to Repeat Roses, which supplies floral arrangements from events to hospitals, nursing homes, home-less shelters, and other facilities rather than throwing them out.

Then it was dessert, displayed alongside gold-embellished con-tainers filled with sugar crystals, into which stork-shaped cookies had been arranged. The cake was a two-tier white-fondant confec-tion decorated with paper figures of Meghan, Harry, and a stroller. But there were also Ladurée macaron towers, key lime and cherry tarts, red velvet and carrot cakes, cotton candy pompoms, and a jar of multicolored gluten-free doughnut holes.

Meghan left for the UK on a high. As she boarded the Cloo-neys' private jet with Amal, who was traveling with her twins, Ella and Alexander, Daniel, her makeup artist and friend, sent her a text that Beyoncé and Jay-Z had just paid tribute to Meghan at the BRIT Awards. "I think all I wrote was 'Girl,'" said Daniel, who at-tached the video of the Carters in front of a regal portrait of Meghan in a crown by illustrator Tim O'Brien. "She wrote me back, like, the big-eye emoji."

But while the trip had been a hit with Meghan, senior courtiers back in the UK were spitting out their morning tea when they saw her lavish baby shower thrown by friends turn into a media circus with what looked like carefully stage-managed paparazzi walks of the duchess in big black sunglasses from her hotel to her car and a laundry list of insider party details reported by US press.

"It's fair to say that the optics of the somewhat flashy shower did not go down well with certain individuals at the Palace," a se-nior aide revealed. Meghan was often criticized for being too Holly-wood, meaning too flashy. Especially for the reserved aesthetic of the monarchy. "I think a few people that had defended her over the months felt a little disappointed. But sometimes in this role you're damned if you do and damned if you don't. Ultimately, the trip was just Meghan's friends celebrating a really exciting moment in her life."

Meghan didn't have much time to absorb any backlash, as just forty-eight hours after returning to London, she was on another plane with Harry, bound for Morocco, at the request of the British government. In her final trimester she was full of energy and showed no signs of slowing down as she hit the ground running on the first day of the trip. Climbing into a helicopter to fly deep into Morocco's Atlas Mountains for a charity that provided educational opportunities to girls from rural parts of Morocco, Education for All, Meghan put on her noise-isolating headphones, held Harry's hand, and took a deep breath as the chopper took off. "Her energy is boundless," British Ambassador to Morocco Thomas Reilly, who escorted the duke and duchess on their three-day visit to the country, said. "Here's a woman jumping into a helicopter to fly 1,400 meters [almost 4,600 feet] high, still smiling and ready to do it all, ready to push the issues that matter."

While at one of the charity's boardinghouses in the small town of Asni, Meghan impressed the accompanying press with her ability to put some of the nervous students at ease, even asking a few questions in French. "No girl in this country should get left behind," Meghan said of the visit. "It's important that every girl has access to further and higher education."

From gender equality and universal education opportunities to social entrepreneurship and female empowerment, the visit's three-day itinerary shone a spotlight on the issues most important to Meghan. Prince Harry, already established as a humanitarian force of his own, often let Meghan take the lead during their nine Moroccan engagements, leaning into her ear periodically to see if his wife was feeling "okay" along the way.

There was even an appearance for *Together: Our Community Cookbook* with a Moroccan chef. The collection of fifty recipes from women impacted by the 2017 Grenfell Tower fire included a foreword written by Meghan and had hit the top of Amazon's list within hours of its publication five months earlier. It was one of Meghan's biggest royal achievements to date, but it had all started with a private visit to a small West London community kitchen that helped families affected by the tragic fire that left seventy-two dead and hundreds homeless.

Meghan threw on an apron to help a group of women at the Al Manaar Muslim Cultural Heritage Centre, though the plan was never to do anything more than volunteer at the space where women cooked food for families and the local community. "She just wanted to help," Zahira Ghaswala, the kitchen's coordinator, said. "Within moments of arriving the first time, she was helping wash the rice, make chapatis, serve food."

By her second visit, Meghan came up with an idea to raise money for the kitchen, which at the time was only able to run two days a week. "We should do a cookbook," she told the women. Inspired by her ambition, the women worked closely with the duchess. "We didn't think it would move so quickly!" Zahira said. With Meghan on first-name terms with all the women at the kitchen, it wasn't uncommon for her to pop by unannounced, always greeted with kisses and hugs. "She is like family," the kitchen's project manager Intlak Al Saiegh said. "The children love her, too. She would always sit them on her lap and talk to them."

The feeling was mutual. "I immediately felt connected to this community kitchen; it is a place for women to laugh, grieve, cry, and cook together," Meghan wrote in the cookbook's foreword. "Melding cultural identities under a shared roof, it creates a space to feel a sense of normalcy—in its simplest form, the universal need to connect, nurture, and commune through food, through crisis or joy—something we can all relate to."

At a book party held at Kensington Palace, Doria made a surprise appearance, flying in from LA to stay with her daughter and son-in-law for a few days. "Hi, I'm Meg's mom," Doria said to the women from the kitchen gathered at the event. "I've heard a lot about everyone here . . . It's great to be able to see you all."

After showing her mother around, Meghan gave an off-the-cuff speech. "I had just recently moved to London, and I felt so immediately embraced by the women in the kitchen," she said. "Their warmth, their kindness, and also the ability to be in this city and to see in this one small room how multicultural it was . . . I feel so proud to live in a city that can have so much diversity. [There are] twelve countries represented in this one group of women! It's pretty outstanding." Doria was suitably impressed. "The power of women," she said. "We make things happen. We're curious. We say yes, we show up. I'm inspired."

By the time Harry and Meghan were on their tour of Morocco, *Together: Our Community Cookbook* had become a *New York Times* bestseller, with 71,000 copies sold in its first seven weeks. In an afternoon cooking with the Moroccan chef Moha Fedal, the couple made a Moroccan pancake recipe from the cookbook with disabled staff who work at a specially designed restaurant in the capital of Rabat. "They'll be so proud to see this," Meghan said of the book making its Moroccan debut. "The message has traveled far."

After the overseas trip, Meghan began to slow down ahead of her maternity leave. Air travel was now off-limits. Given the continued negative commentary in sections of the British press, being back in England wasn't necessarily much more restful. While Meghan had never gotten accustomed to all the reporting on her, by the end of her pregnancy, she couldn't bear the unnecessary criticism. The maternity clothes she chose or how she held her bump were all fodder for the tabloids. It was as if she couldn't even be pregnant in a way that was acceptable to the media. She likened the attacks to a friend as "death by a thousand cuts."

Meghan was suffering terribly. As she anxiously expected the arrival of her first child, she felt fragile and very emotional. Harry tried his best to be everything his wife needed, but he felt this was the moment for his family to step in. But no one in the royal family made that move.

There were plans for Meghan to attend a couple of engagements in the final weeks of her pregnancy, including Harry's tree planting in support of the Queen's Commonwealth Canopy forest conservation initiative on March 20. But in the end, Meghan didn't feel up to it—she was more comfortable doing other work from home.

There was never any pressure on Meghan to work, but as a friend, who jokingly called her "Super Meg," said, "It takes a lot to put [her] out of action." Communications secretary Sara Latham often dropped by for meetings at Frogmore Cottage, which she and Harry moved into the first week of April. Despite reports of over a monthlong delay to the renovation works, the couple moved into the house only nine days later than expected—quite a feat considering the gut renovation started in early October 2018.

Meghan's spirits were buoyed by the visits of close friends, including Daniel, who arrived at the cottage on April 6 to find Meghan "incredibly calm and just enjoying the last days with the bump." Harry and Meghan cooked for the makeup artist—with Harry doing most of the work in the kitchen. "There was no nervousness, and she and Harry seemed so happy at the new house," he said.

Doria arrived at Frogmore on April 16 to help out as her daughter's due date of April 28 neared. On her commercial flight from LA, a passenger approached her to ask if she was Meghan's mother. "I'm the proud mom!" replied Doria, who as soon as she landed at Heathrow was driven straight to the cottage.

While it was a comfort to have her mom with her, Harry was constantly looking after his wife as well, making sure she was physically comfortable and getting her snacks. Guacamole and crudités was as close as she got to junk food. Not because she doesn't like it; she just didn't crave it.

While she didn't worry about her weight, Meghan jokingly called herself "a balloon" to a friend as her due date came and went. Her engagement ring no longer fit. As her pregnancy went on into the first week of May, she stuck with the modified yoga routine she had done every morning throughout. She also made long walks with their two dogs part of her daily ritual upon moving to Frogmore.

Despite being overdue, the couple still had people stop by at the house to visit. Sara kept up her visits, including one on Friday, May 3, where she described Meghan as "calm and content." The next day, Gayle King, in Windsor to film a CBS documentary for Harry and Meghan's one-year anniversary, popped by for an hour. Gayle left impressed at how much energy the duchess still had.

By May 6, Meghan was several days past her due date. "The longest eight days of her life!" a friend said. "But her patience and calm were amazing during that time—she just said, 'The baby will come when it comes.' And that was that."

20

Welcoming Archie

Harry jumped behind the wheel of the navy blue Range Rover where Meghan and Doria were waiting in the back seat on the night of Sunday, May 5. With a protection officer also in the car and a team of them in an accompanying Range Rover, the prince started off on the twenty-eight-mile route from Frogmore Cottage to the Portland Hospital in central London.

While Meghan was originally interested in a home birth, as she entered her final trimester she chose to deliver in a hospital. Although there were reports that Meghan was "devastated" to have her dream home birth plans dashed at the last minute, a source said that by the time Meghan went into labor, those plans had long been put to rest. "I know there were stories about a home birth, and it was certainly something that was discussed early on," the source said, "but Meg knew it would be a hospital birth for a few months.

"All she cared about was having the baby in the safest way possible," the source added. "She was more and more nervous as she approached the due date, so I would say in some ways it was a relief for her to be doing it in a traditional hospital."

Also contradictory to reports, Meghan never considered giving birth at the Lindo Wing, where Kate delivered all three of her children, Diana had William and Harry, and Princess Anne had Peter and Zara. Meghan wanted somewhere more discreet than St. Mary's Hospital.

The Portland Hospital—a US-owned hospital popular with celebrities and the expat American community in London—was where Beatrice and Eugenie were born. It offered not only state-of-the-art care but also an underground entrance, where blacked-out SUVs driving in and out were the norm. Harry and Meghan, who were never spotted entering or leaving Portland, didn't tell anyone about their hospital choice, not even their closest aides or friends.

The only people who did know were Doria and Meghan's medical team, which included her ob-gyn, Penelope Law, who was one of Portland's top obstetricians—as well as a countess (she was the wife of the seventh Earl of Bradford). Still, she told her patients to call her "Dr. Penny." Despite her reputation at the hospital of being "too posh to pull," referring to the high rate of C-sections she performs, she is pro–natural delivery. Meghan did not deliver by C-section, although the couple refused to comment on the details of the birth. A source said that Meghan "took the advice" of doctors, who attended Frogmore Cottage every day in the days leading up to her hospital admission—and at 5:26 a.m. on Monday, May 6, Archie Harrison Mountbatten-Windsor, seventh in line to the throne and weighing seven pounds, three ounces, was born in an uncomplicated birth. Meghan was simply relieved it had gone well—and to have her "beautiful, sweet little boy" in her arms for the first time.

"Archie was alert as soon as he arrived—eyes wide-open," a friend said. "Meghan described the moment she first held Archie as 'ecstasy . . . total bliss and contentment.'" A trusted confidant added, "Like any new mother, you can't fully know what to expect until you have been through it."

Harry and Meghan already had a name ready to go when Archie was born, because the couple had known all along that they were having a boy. According to a source, they settled on their son's name some time during the final week of her pregnancy. The couple wanted something traditional, a name that was powerful even without a title in front of it. Archie, meaning strength and bravery, fit the bill. "They thought about Archibald for all of one second," a friend of the couple said with a laugh. "He was always going to be little Archie." (Mountbatten-Windsor is the surname used by all male descendants of the Queen and Prince Philip. Royals with titles don't typically use surnames.)

Harry and Meghan—who were going to register Archie for dual citizenship—decided to forgo a title for their son, because they wanted him to be a private citizen until he was at an age where he could decide which path he would like to take. A source said the pair both worried about the day Prince Charles becomes king and Harry's children could inherit the titles of prince or princess. They shared their concerns with Charles, who said he would consider when he became king issuing a new letters patent, a legal instrument in the form of a written order issued by a reigning monarch, that would change this style. "To not have a senior role in the royal family but have a title," a senior aide close to the couple said at the time, "is just a burden."

Harry took to texting and calling friends (including Skippy, who he was speaking with more regularly at this point) and family with the happy news of Archie's arrival. He started with the Queen and Prince Philip, who were the first to hear the news about the arrival of their eighth great-grandchild. He then sent his father and brother texts alongside a photo of his new son, before notifying other family members—including Princess Anne's daughter,

Zara, and her husband, the rugby legend Mike Tindall—through the special cousins-only WhatsApp group that all royals were a part of. Harry also made sure he was the one to tell all of Diana's family—his two aunts Lady Sarah McCorquodale and Lady Jane Fellowes and his uncle Earl Charles Spencer. He also couldn't forget Tiggy, who he had wanted to pick as a godmother to his son or daughter long before he became a father.

Doria messaged Thomas with the news, which Meghan had asked her to do. The new mother did not want him to find out after the rest of the world. But she didn't want to know whether her father replied to her mother's text.

Lastly, Harry had Palace aides to inform, including Sara, which he did at 9:30 a.m., just as they were leaving to return to Frogmore Cottage. It was soon after Archie was born, but Dr. Penny had given the all-clear, and Meghan felt up to getting back home, where she would continue to be monitored.

Although Meghan spent just a short time in the hospital after Archie's birth, when she texted her friends with the news back home while the baby slept, she described being elated, if tired and a little overwhelmed. "A pinch me moment," she told one pal.

The new mom marveled at how calm her baby was. "He's barely cried," she said to a friend. "He's an angel."

In a text to another dear pal, Meghan wrote, "If my son is half of what your children are, I will be so happy."

When it came to letting the public know about Archie's birth, Harry wanted to do so himself. "Harry didn't want his office to give the info to the papers to put out, and he didn't want to lose control of this precious moment," a source close to the prince said. "He wanted people to hear it in his own words, no statement, no formal announcement . . . just him, off the cuff and candid." Sara made the necessary arrangements.

Standing in front of Windsor Castle's Mews with two horses

sticking their black heads out of the stable doors, Harry said, grinning, "I'm very excited to announce that Meghan and myself had a baby boy early this morning, a very healthy boy. Mother and baby are doing incredibly well. It's been the most amazing experience I could ever have possibly imagined. How any woman does what they do is beyond comprehension, but we're both absolutely thrilled and so grateful to all the love and support from everybody out there. It's been amazing."

As he talked about the "first birth" he attended, Harry gushed about his wife and baby. "This little thing is absolutely to die for. So, I'm just over the moon," he said.

Two days later, Archie made his global debut at Windsor Castle during an intimate media call—just two photographers, one agency reporter, and three video cameras pooled together to feed to every news outlet under the sun.

As Harry and Meghan walked into St. George's Hall, where they had celebrated their wedding reception nearly one year earlier, the cameras clicked away to capture the newborn royal, wrapped in the G. H. Hurt & Son shawl traditionally worn by royal babies. (Prince George, Princess Charlotte, and Prince Louis all wore the same brand for their debuts).

Unlike their engagement photo, this time it was Harry giving Meghan the quick pep talk before stepping out. "You look beautiful," he told her. Meghan selected a Wales Bonner trench dress, Manolo Blahnik pumps, and one of her favorite gold-and-turquoise Jennifer Meyer necklaces for the occasion. She also sported her engagement ring, which she hadn't been able to wear in the final seven weeks of her pregnancy. Prior to arriving, she admitted she was exhausted but excited to share such a happy moment.

The family had originally planned to pose on the steps behind Windsor Castle to echo their wedding photo taken before their reception, but light rain at Windsor meant that the Palace put their "wet weather scenario" into place, with Harry, Meghan, and the baby posing inside St. George's Hall instead.

Sara and assistant communications secretary, Julie Burley, who rushed to pick a few lint pieces off the bright red hall carpet just before the couple arrived, instructed the small camera pool that they had just ten seconds for photos before three vetted questions were asked. Yet the duke and duchess seemed happy to stay and chat for longer about their new son.

"I have the two best guys in the world," Meghan said. "I'm really happy."

When asked about what kind of baby Archie is, Meghan answered, "He has the sweetest temperament. He's really calm."

"Don't know where he gets that from," Harry quipped.

The couple were candid about their feelings for their son but not his name. They had yet to reveal the name they'd chosen for Archie publicly, because they wanted the Queen to hear it first and give her approval. This wasn't out of ceremonial necessity but simply because Harry was respectful of his grandmother.

After finishing with the press, Harry, Meghan, and Archie went straight to Windsor Castle to meet his great-grandmother, the Queen. They had already bumped into a cheerful Prince Philip on the grounds before entering the media call, but this was to be his first proper moment to meet his great-grandson.

Also on hand for the meeting with Queen Elizabeth II was Archie's proud grandmother, Doria. The moment was later shared in a photo on social media. All five adults around Archie, the first biracial grandchild of the Queen. The picture, taken by the couple's personal photographer Chris Allerton, was a hugely significant moment for the royal family. There, for the first time, was much-needed visibility around race and inclusion at the heart of the monarchy. "That made me proud," Meghan told a friend.

Doria remained close at hand to support her daughter. "Doria was looking after Meghan while Meghan looked after Archie," said a friend, who added that Doria helped prepare meals and do other things around the house so Meghan could devote all her energy toward caring for her son, including nursing him.

Harry was also "super eager to do as much as he can," a friend of the couple said. "Meghan loves that he wants to do so much. He's been changing most of Archie's diapers—he likes having it as his 'job,' especially as Meghan has so much more to do."

In being a hands-on dad, Harry was very much like his brother, William, who was involved in every aspect of raising his three children—including school drop-off and pickup, as well as homework. He and Kate, who had an equal partnership when it came to the house, were modern parents. William prepared meals just as much as Kate did.

In this way, William was continuing his mother's legacy. Princess Diana was one of the first royals to make the kitchen in their apartment a place where the family convened. This was during a time when most other members of the royal family had barely stepped foot in the kitchen. When William and Kate took over the apartment at 1A, they wanted the kitchen to be at the heart of the home. It wasn't just practical; it was also symbolic. Like his mother had wanted for him, William desired relatively normal childhoods for his kids, even if his eldest son was destined to be king.

Harry was just getting to know his own son. The couple couldn't quite get over how silent their new baby was. Meghan told a friend that Archie slept so quietly she sometimes wanted him to make noise so she knew he was okay. Archie had a nursery, of course, but also slept in a bassinet in Harry and Meghan's bedroom.

Meanwhile, gifts poured into Frogmore. Their home, particularly their kitchen, was filled with flowers from around the world: the Clooneys, the Cordens, and New Zealand prime minister Jacinda Ardern all sent arrangements. Oprah sent the couple a very special gift—a huge library of children's books, all labeled with customized "Archie's Book Club" stickers.

One of Archie's first storybooks for his nursery bookshelf was *The Giving Tree*, by Shel Silverstein, one of Meghan's favorites read to her by Doria as a child. The Mulroneys sent a top-of-the-line bassinet stroller as a gift, which Meghan used to take Archie on walks around the grounds of Frogmore every day, dogs Guy and Pula often in tow.

The extra precautions the new parents took with their cyber security didn't stop Harry and Meghan from showing off pictures of their baby as any new parent would. On British Mother's Day— which Meghan started with breakfast in her bedroom with her mother and Archie—Harry shared another photo of Archie with the world via Instagram. This one was the baby's little feet in his mother's hand.

The forget-me-nots, Princess Diana's favorite flower, in the background of the photo were an intentional nod to his late mother. Understandably, she had been "very much on Harry's mind" since he became a father.

21

@SussexRoyal

On the anniversary of their first year of marriage, Harry and Meghan enjoyed a traditional Sunday lunch with Doria, her last meal before traveling back to LA. Her five weeks at Frogmore had flown by, but she had to get back to work.

Meghan was grateful for all the love and support her mother provided during the last weeks of her pregnancy and the first weeks of Archie's life. As a friend said, "Meg has taken to motherhood like a duck to water, but it definitely helped having Doria with her to double-check things with. It's all so new to her." Plus, having her own family in those first weeks was important to share the earliest baby memories.

On May 19, 2019, Harry also surprised his wife of one year with the gift of a ring that he had created with jeweler-to-the-stars Lorraine Schwartz, a favorite of Meghan's. The conflict-free diamond eternity band paid homage to the family of three with Meghan's, Archie's, and Harry's birthstones (peridot, emerald, and sapphire, respectively) on the underside of the ring. "Harry wanted to make it special," the jeweler shared. "He's the loveliest person ever. So romantic, so thoughtful." (So much so that Harry also thought to have Lorraine resize and reset Meghan's engagement ring with a new diamond band.)

The couple never imagined their first year would go so quickly and that they would achieve so much in such a short period. "It was their dream to be having their one-year anniversary as parents, but they knew that things don't always happen the way you plan," a source close to the couple said. "Both of them feel incredibly blessed. Meghan has thanked God every day for blessing them with Archie.

"They couldn't believe they had this beautiful son with them all of a sudden. They had this moment where they looked at each other like, 'We did this.' Suddenly they were a family of three."

In their first weeks home as a new family, Harry and Meghan welcomed friends from far and wide. Jessica and her daughter, Ivy, took a mother-daughter trip to London and made time to meet Archie for the first time. Serena and Alexis, with their daughter, Alexis Olympia, were also guests for an afternoon. And Charlie van Straubenzee and wife Daisy Jenks, paid them a visit. Also spending time with the couple were Ellen DeGeneres and wife Portia de Rossi, who stopped by for an afternoon in August. "Cutest couple and so down to earth," Ellen later revealed.

And there were many visits by family members, close and extended. William and Kate stopped by eight days after Archie's birth, without their children, to meet the new arrival. Both of Diana's sisters, Lady Sarah and Lady Jane, also stopped by with gifts, as did Harry's younger cousin Celia McCorquodale and her husband, George Woodhouse. And a "thrilled" Prince Charles paid two visits, one by himself and one with Camilla.

Charles made the effort to see Archie as much as his schedule permitted, dropping by three times in the first four months of his grandson's birth. While Harry and his father were now closer than ever, busy schedules made it difficult for them to spend regular time together. Charles tended to be more of a presence at big family events. "This isn't a family that pops by to say hi or text each other to see how they're doing," a source said. "There's a formalness there."

Great-grandmother "Gan-Gan" (as the Queen is known by the Sussex and Cambridge children) saw much more of Archie. Spending a lot of time on the Windsor estate (her castle apartments are about a one-mile walk from Frogmore Cottage) made doing so a lot easier. Archie also had several visits from Eugenie and Jack.

Although Harry and Meghan had initially chosen to forgo a full-time nanny, Doria had just flown back to LA, and so they decided to hire a night nurse to establish a sleep schedule and be an extra pair of helping hands. But their time with the couple was brief. Meghan and Harry were forced to let the nurse go in the middle of her second night of work for being unprofessional and irresponsible.

The new parents went on to hire a second night nurse, who did a fine job, but because of the incident with the first nurse, neither found themselves comfortable sleeping through the night without going to check on Archie regularly. After a few weeks, they decided to take on the nights themselves and went without a night nurse entirely. Instead, they hired a nanny to work weekdays. The nanny joined Harry and Meghan's Frogmore staff, which consisted of an assistant and a housekeeper, neither of whom were live-in.

Harry and Meghan had agreed they didn't want their home filled with staff. Harry had seen that situation at William's home (the Cambridges had a live-in housekeeper and a full-time, live-in nanny), and didn't want the same for his own family. He and Meghan liked the idea that when they went to bed at night, it was just the three of them in the house. Cozy and private.

In the mornings, Harry usually made his own coffee. When they had meetings at the large kitchen table with staff members, it was often Meghan who made a pot of tea and put chocolates or energy balls on a plate for nibbling.

Meghan remained on maternity leave for the summer, making only intermittent appearances at a select few important engagements and stepping out for family events. Trooping the Colour, the Queen's official birthday parade, was Meghan's first post-birth engagement, on June 8. Harry forwent the two-week paternity leave that was typical in the UK. Instead, he worked a greatly reduced schedule of just one or two engagements a week to fulfill preexisting commitments and keep the public eye focused on the causes important to him and Meghan. There wasn't much that could drag the new parents away from their son. Harry almost immediately realized how quickly children grow when he said to friends about Archie, "He was so tiny when we brought him home, but he's already gotten big!"

However, helping other less fortunate kids became an even more important part of the couple's calling. Harry flew to the Netherlands on May 9 to launch the official one-year countdown to the Invictus Games taking place in The Hague. Five days later, he was in Oxford to highlight work at a children's hospital and visit the OXSRAD disability center his mother opened in 1989.

On May 24, Harry headed to Rome, Italy, for two nights to play in the Sentebale ISPS Handa Polo Cup. The charity provided education, health, and psychosocial programs to help children struggling with the misperceptions about AIDS and HIV in southern Africa since its founding in 2006. It also hosted clubs, camps, and programs to over 4,600 adolescents coming to terms with living with the virus, and more than two thousand children were accommodated at their Mamohato Children's Centre in Lesotho.

Polo matches were an essential way for William and Harry to raise money for many of their philanthropic endeavors. Harry, a keen polo player, had spent two weeks preparing for the event by regularly riding his horse in Windsor Great Park. And the training paid off. His team won, 9–6. The match and evening reception at the St. Regis Hotel, where Harry stayed for two nights, raised over a million dollars.

At a private dinner that evening, Harry explained what he hoped to achieve with Sentebale. "These children receive help and support to understand that HIV is no longer a death sentence, that they are not alone in this fight, and that they truly can thrive rather than just survive," he said. "Our camp not only gives these young people the confidence and reassurance they need to live life with HIV, but also empowers them to speak out about the virus and encourage their peers to learn about it and prevent it from spreading."

Before the match, Harry's close friend, Sentebale ambassador, and polo teammate Nacho Figueras shared how Harry had already been moved by fatherhood. "He seems to be very, very happy," Nacho said. "He was ready for it, and I think he's loving it. I always thought that he would be an amazing father because he has a great affinity for children."

Harry, who shared in the responsibilities of Archie's night feedings, got his first full night of sleep since his son's arrival during that event, which Nacho also remarked on in the interview. However, the conversation turned quickly when a reporter at the event asked, "Not many fathers go abroad within two weeks of a birth. Any word on that from the mother?"

"How dare that guy tell a father who loves his child and is leaving the house for just twenty-four hours to go raise money for thousands of vulnerable children in Africa, how dare he say something like that," Nacho fumed on CBS a few days later. The polo player wasn't the only one angry at the insinuation. Harry's team at the Palace was furious, as Harry's efforts in the area of the AIDS crisis were not about only working for the greater good but also carrying on his mother's memory.

"After my mother and many others campaigned for years highlighting this epidemic, we are finally at a tipping point," Harry said. "We either finish what they started and solve this problem once and for all, or we face the humiliation at being complacent and allowing this virus to strike back just when we were starting to get on top of it."

For Harry, the mission was intensely personal—carrying on the work his mother, Princess Diana, never got a chance to finish herself. "Our hope is that this generation will be the generation that turns the tide on the stigma," he continued. "This will be the generation who will talk about safe sex. The generation who will support those who are living with HIV. And the generation that stops HIV from spreading once and for all."

Whatever grief Harry received for going to Rome to play polo after his son's birth was nothing compared to the backlash the Sussexes received after their family's summer travels. The trouble began when the famously eco-conscious prince used a private jet to visit three different destinations within a month.

His first stop was Google Camp—a three-day event, held in the last week of July at an exclusive Sicilian seaside resort, where high profile entrepreneurs, philanthropists, and movie stars such as Barack Obama and Leonardo DiCaprio focused on fighting climate change. The tech giant footed the bill for everything, including travel to the resort and back. Harry's original plans were to fly commercial, there and back on the same day, but while at the event he accepted a lift back to London on an attendee's private jet so he could stay a day longer and discuss his work on an unannounced sustainble tourism initiative.

Following Meghan's thirty-eighth birthday on August 4, the family of three set out from London to the Spanish island of Ibiza, where they stayed at an upscale gated complex. From Ibiza they flew in Elton John's private jet to the singer's house in Nice. The singer had invited them to stay for a while.

A firestorm erupted over the so-called hypocrisy of the prince, seemingly touting the virtues of conservation while flying on gas-guzzling private jets. Not to mention the fact that the Sussexes had decided against a trip to visit the Queen at Balmoral with Archie earlier in the summer, reportedly saying the infant was too young for the travel. Some of the press latched on to this, calling it a snub instead.

Elton John immediately came to the couple's defense, stating that he had paid for the jet trip and its carbon offsetting (a practice that allows passengers to invest in projects like solar panels and sustainable forests, which would reduce the same amount of carbon dioxide as was released into the air by their private flight).

"I'm calling on the press to cease these relentless and untrue assassinations on their character that are spuriously crafted on an almost daily basis," the singer tweeted.

With the controversy reaching its apex just days before the launch of Travalyst, the sustainable-tourism initiative he had been working on for most of the year, Harry regretted not heeding the advice of Sara. She had warned him about a potential media storm if he flew back on a private jet from Google Camp, which he attended to preview Travalyst. The earnest prince was the first one to admit when he made a mistake.

Meanwhile, Buckingham Palace had no comment, which only sought to reinforce Harry and Meghan's desire to change their working model. At the core of their issues was their inability to speak for themselves. Instead, they had to rely on a large, slow-moving machine that was the institution of the monarchy. For an independent American woman like Meghan, this was especially frustrating, which was why she was so excited about the Instagram account @SussexRoyal that she and Harry had made public earlier that spring.

"Launching the account was a somewhat liberating experience for Meghan," an aide shared. "Not having a platform of her own to talk directly to the public was one of the toughest changes for her, especially after building so much of her own brand on Instagram and her blog. @SussexRoyal meant that she finally had a place to curate."

The couple began planning the account around the time they announced they were getting their own office under the auspices of Buckingham Palace. Instagram was nothing new to the Palace. William, Kate, and Harry had established @KensingtonRoyal in 2015. When Meghan married Harry, she began posting to the shared account as well. Even the Queen had shared on the platform, hitting send on her first post (a photo from the British Science Museum's Royal Archives) in March that year.

For the Duke and Duchess of Sussex, the social media platform was more than a way to reach a new generation of royal watchers.

"People can get the news directly from us," Meghan said at an early planning meeting with staff, during which several hues were considered before she and Harry picked the perfect shade of blue for their social media branding. In addition to deciding on the photos that *always* had to have a white border, Meghan drafted a lot of the posts herself in the early days. It was one of the things that kept her occupied during her final days of pregnancy.

The couple's savvy social media manager, David Watkins, who had moved to the royal household from Burberry, was often spotted at engagements, shooting exclusive content for the couple, who wanted their account to feel informal and approachable. David was recommended by Isabel May, the former director of communications at Burberry and one of Meghan's close friends in the UK since the two women were introduced by Markus in 2017. Isabel (or just Izzy to friends) was Meghan's close confidant and also reportedly one of Archie's godmothers, and she made regular visits to Frogmore Cottage. She became one of the few people in the UK who Meghan felt she could trust with "anything."

As part of the new social media account, Harry and Meghan

worked with a Palace aide to put together a slide show of unseen behind-the-scenes photos from their wedding the week before their first anniversary. The couple loved the process of looking back on moments captured on film from a year earlier and even watching video clips of their special day for the first time since it happened.

Instagram quickly become a vital part of the Sussexes' new media strategy. They beat out the pope to break the Guinness world record for the fastest accumulation of one million followers in twenty-four hours. In fact, within a day, they had 2.1 million. And they kept pace with William and Kate's account, which remained @KensingtonRoyal.

"It took a little time, but I'm starting to see Meg's mark on so many things," a friend said. "Sometimes those posts on the account remind me of her *Tig* days, and I love that. Her voice is getting louder every day."

While Harry and Meghan's Instagram account might have proved a powerful tool for gaining control over the narrative, it was also a place to share some of their favorite moments, like when they met Jay-Z and Beyoncé at the European premiere of *The Lion King* in London's Leicester Square on July 14. Having Beyoncé hold Meghan's hand while saying, "We love you guys," made the fact that she had to carefully plan their three-hour outing around feeding times totally worth it.

The premiere provided yet another example of information about Harry and Meghan being skewed after the prince was videoed talking to Bob Iger on the red carpet.

He was overheard joking to the then-Disney CEO, "You know she does voiceovers . . ." in reference to Meghan, who had agreed to narrate a Disneynature documentary, *Elephant*. When the clip surfaced in January 2020, tabloids spun it into an example of the couple "shilling themselves" to a Hollywood executive. In reality, however, Meghan had already signed on to the project that she recorded in the fall of 2019 in return for a donation by Disney to the conservation charity Elephants Without Borders.

Instagram was another way for the couple to highlight their charities and patronages, such as the Diana Awards' National Youth Mentoring Summit, which Harry addressed on July 2. "Being a role model and mentor can help heal the wounds of your own past and create a better future for someone else," he said. "On a more personal level, it's the power to change the course of a life, to be the North Star for a young person having trouble navigating their own path."

Harry and Meghan enjoyed calling their own shots, which they were now getting the chance to do, to some degree. "Harry and Meghan liked being in control of their narrative," a source said, which is why agreeing to fold their household into Buckingham Palace, instead of creating their own independent court at Windsor as they wanted, proved a big disappointment to them.

Harry, who wanted to do so much in the world, was growing frustrated that he and Meghan often took a backseat to other family members' initiatives and priorities. While they both respected the hierarchy of the institution, it was difficult when they wanted to focus on a particular project and were told that a more senior ranking family member, be it Prince William or Prince Charles, had an initiative or tour being announced at the same time—so they would just have to wait.

As their popularity continued to grow, so did Harry and Meghan's difficulty in understanding why so few were looking out for their interests inside the Palace. They were a major draw for the royal family. According to a *New York Times* article that compared the online popularity of the Sussexes to the Cambridges from November 2017 to January 2020, "Harry-and-Meghan-related searches accounted for 83 percent of the world's curiosity in the two couples."

The couple tried to air these frustrations internally, but the conversations not only didn't lead anywhere, the details of them would usually leak to one of the British newspapers. At this point there were just a handful of people working at the Palace they could trust, including Sara, communications aide James Holt, communications secretary Marnie Gaffney (who was made a member of the Royal Victorian Order by the Queen, an honor recognizing personal service to the monarch or members of the royal family, during a June 2019 investiture), and their top aide, private secretary Samantha Cohen. Outside this core team, no information was safe. A friend of the couple's referred to the old guard as "the vipers." Meanwhile, an equally frustrated Palace staffer described the Sussexes' team as "the squeaky third wheel" of the palace.

That was their dysfunctional backdrop when in late September Harry, Meghan, and twenty-week-old Archie flew to Cape Town, South Africa, to begin a four-country royal tour of southern Africa.

Arriving at the start of their tour in Cape Town's Nyanga township, Harry and Meghan received a lively welcome from local performers and youth who had gathered to chat, dance, and exchange hugs. The atmosphere was a far cry from the negative stories that dogged the couple on a near-daily basis during the summer.

There was no airport arrival complete with red carpet as is usually seen on official royal visits. The ten-day tour was more familiar and casual. In a decision the Sussexes made together, Meghan—who brought a wardrobe of simple pieces she picked for comfort or had worn at previous royal engagements—left her engagement ring back in the UK. Their goal was not to impress people with their royal lifestyle but to connect to locals on a real level.

"May I just say that while I am here with my husband as a member of the royal family," Meghan said in her address to the Nyanga township, "I want you to know that for me, I am here with you as a mother, as a wife, as a woman, as a woman of color, and as your sister."

The tour was also an opportunity for the world to see Archie for the first time since his christening on July 6 in the Queen's private chapel in Windsor Castle. At the ceremony—attended by 22 guests, including the Cambridges, Charles and Camilla, Doria, Princess Diana's sisters, Archie's godparents, and a few friends like Genevieve and Lindsay—Archie wore the same christening gown donned by George, Charlotte, and Louis at their baptisms. The Honiton lace gown is a replica of a dress that Queen Victoria commissioned for her firstborn child, which was worn by 62 royal babies—including five monarchs—over 163 years. Archie's christening had been kept a completely private affair, which angered some of the media who were used to receiving access to the guest arrivals. Days of commentary were dedicated to fact that Archie's baptism "broke tradition" and went against an unspoken deal that the royal family have with the tax-paying public who part-fund the Monarchy. "We have a public right to see Archie," a morning television pundit argued. Not that Meghan cared. "The same people who have been abusing me want me to serve my child on a silver platter," she told a friend. "A child who is not going to be protected and doesn't have a title. How does that make sense? Tell that to any mother in the world."

Similarly, the couple kept the 380 members of the press covering the tour in Africa away from their intimate meeting with Archbishop Desmond Tutu, instead opting to take their own picture that they released. At almost five months old, Archie (or "Bubba" and "Arch," as his parents like to call him) gurgled and giggled to the delight of the Anglican cleric.

For Archie's sake, Meghan based herself in South Africa with two aides for the duration of the tour, leaving Harry to travel to Malawi, Angola, and Botswana solo. In Angola, Harry shone a spotlight on landmine clearance, continuing the work his mother began in 1997 (when she famously walked through an Angolan minefield cleared by the Halo Trust to highlight the plight of local people seriously injured by military IEDs). Diana's work had impact—a year after her death, an international treaty was signed to ban all IEDs, and in 2013, Harry vowed that he would continue her life-long mission.

Meghan's work schedule revolved around feeding and nap times. "It's a handful, but every moment is so precious," Meghan told a friend. Earlier in the summer, Archie started take baby swimming classes (after his parents anxiously looked up videos on YouTube about how babies hold their breath under water). During the trip, he continued to achieve new milestones, including mimicking the sound of a animals during their stay at the high commissioner's residence in Cape Town.

After traveling over five thousand miles in five days (the longest he had ever been apart from Archie), Harry rejoined his wife and son. While he shared a few remarks to cameras throughout the trip, the prince kept most of the traveling press pack at arm's length. Though he was pleased that the coverage of the tour had been posi-tive, he also struggled to stay upbeat around representitives of pub-lications he felt had spent much of the past two-and-a-half years writing negative, and sometimes false, stories about his wife and family. For nine out the ten days of the tour, Harry kept his feelings to himself. But the truth came out on October 2, when he dropped a bombshell statement that few had known was coming.

22

Half In, Half Out

At 7:13 p.m. on October 2, with just two days left of what was unanimously considered a highly successful tour of southern Africa by the Duke and Duchess of Sussex, a message from their communications team dropped on the #SussexRoyalAfrica WhatsApp chat group. The text chain had been created for aides to update around twenty-five accredited reporters on the trip with logistical information such as bus times and flight itineraries.

"Evening all, for your information," read the vague message that contained a link to a website, sussexofficial.uk, which no members of the media, whose job it was to follow the royals, had ever seen—because it was created for that very moment: an open letter from Harry accompanied by a legal case filed against the *Mail on Sunday*.

"Unfortunately, my wife has become one of the latest victims of a British tabloid press that wages campaigns against individuals with no thought to the consequences—a ruthless campaign that has escalated over the past year, throughout her pregnancy and while raising our newborn son," the letter read.

"There is a human cost to this relentless propaganda, specifically when it is knowingly false and malicious, and though we have continued to put on a brave face—as so many of you can relate to—I cannot begin to describe how painful it has been. Because in today's digital age, press fabrications are repurposed as truth across the globe. One day's coverage is no longer tomorrow's chippaper" (a reference to the fact that in the UK, fish and chips used to be served in newspaper).

"Up to now, we have been unable to correct the continual misrepresentations—something that these select media outlets have been aware of and have therefore exploited on a daily and sometimes hourly basis.

"It is for this reason we are taking legal action, a process that has been many months in the making."

The battle was on.

The attached lawsuit brought by Meghan was for invasion of privacy, breach of data protection, and copyright infringement claims against the *Mail on Sunday* for printing extracts from the private letter she wrote to her father in August 2018.

Although Harry didn't announce them with the news of Meghan's lawsuit, he had also filed lawsuits at the same time against *The Sun* and *The Mirror* regarding their alleged illegal interception of his voicemail messages between 2001 and 2005. Though the royals traditionally used lawyers at Harbottle & Lewis, Harry and Meghan wanted to keep their legal proceedings separate—and away from prying eyes within Buckingham Palace, where they had been advised not to take legal action—so they enlisted Clintons for him and Schillings, the UK's leading law firm in defamation and media-related cases, for her.

The duchess's lawyers (who included barrister David Sher-

borne, who once represented Princess Diana) were prepared, setting out an extensive list of "false" and "absurd" stories to highlight
a pattern of mistruths. There were plenty of articles that offered
inaccurate details about their Frogmore renovations, including
the addition of a tennis court and yoga studio, £500,000 spent on
soundproofing their home, and another £5,000 for a copper bath. In
the court papers, her lawyers also addressed a feature that attacked
Meghan for enjoying avocados: "The connection made between the
fact that the Claimant likes eating avocado and made avocado on
toast for a friend who visited her with human rights abuses, murder,
and environmental devastation is another highly tenuous and delib-
erately inflammatory one."

Royals filing lawsuits against publishers was nothing new. In
1849, Prince Albert established the "law of confidence" with a
lawsuit against a British printer who had made bootleg copies of
etchings he created with Queen Victoria. Princess Diana used that
precedent against the *Sunday Mirror* in 1993 for publishing photographs of her working out in a gym in leotard and leggings, winning
approximately £1.5 million. Even the Queen has sued. She went
after *The Sun* for publishing a leaked copy of her 1992 Christmas
broadcast speech.

Harry and Meghan's lawsuits were different from anything in
Palace history. Or at least how they went about the process. An
announcement of this sort was usually issued in formal correspondence on Palace email and then hosted on royal.uk, the official
royal family website—such as when William sued a French tabloid magazine *Closer* for publishing topless photos of Kate in 2012.
But this new move wasn't supported by many at the Firm, and the
couple was left to take matters into the their own hands. None of
the press in Africa were expecting to receive major breaking news
in a WhatsApp message.

The media was also perplexed about the timing of the state-

ment considering how well the tour had gone. But there was a reason for the awkwardly timed announcement.

Changes to procedures at London's High Court starting on October 1 would have meant their cases would have been heard in a
division with judges who tended to side with publishers. Sources
confirmed that Harry and Meghan's lawyers rushed the lawsuits
out at the end of September in an effort to keep the case before a
more privacy-friendly Division. "Both were incredibly nervous," a
source said. "They needed to go in strong."

Whatever the reason for its timing, Harry was determined for the
statement to make uncomfortable reading for many members of the
press, including those in Africa with him. The prince said he was
tired of playing the "game," in which royals trade exclusives with
the tabloids in exchange for some peace and privacy. He was also
sick of the hypocrisy of the media outlets that glorified Meghan one
day and tore her down the next.

"The positive coverage of the past week from these same publications exposes the double standards of this specific press pack
that has vilified her almost daily for the past nine months," Harry
wrote. "For these select media this is a game, and one that we have
been unwilling to play from the start. I have been a silent witness
to her private suffering for too long. To stand back and do nothing
would be contrary to everything we believe in."

According to a friend, Harry wanted to protect his wife and
family, but he also had ambitions to ring in a more honest and fair
media. Princes and princesses weren't the only ones who had been
at the mercy of dishonest press practices. A phone-hacking scandal
had rocked England in 2011, when it was revealed that employees of
the *News of the World* tabloid and other British newspapers owned
by media titan Rupert Murdoch listened to the private voicemails
of celebrities, crime victims, and politicians. The illegal method of
getting stories resulted in the shuttering of the 168-year-old *News*

of the World and one of the most expensive investigations and trials in British legal history.

"Harry feels that the mass-market tabloid press in the UK is a toxic part of British society that needs to be addressed," the prince's friend said.

Despite the risk that she would be called to the stand, Meghan was determined to see the *Mail on Sunday* lawsuit filed. It came as little surprise that Thomas Markle later announced in the *Mail on Sunday* that he would be willing to testify against his own daughter. Legal documents later revealed that the newspaper planned to rely on evidence from Thomas, who felt he "had a weighty right to tell his version of what happened between himself and his daughter including the contents of the letter."

Meghan no longer recognized Thomas as the man who raised her. He went on to spend six days with filmmakers for a 90-minute documentary, *Thomas Markle: My Story.* "For what I've been through," the 75-year-old said, "I should be rewarded." Neither Harry nor Meghan watched the show, which attempted to paint a portrait of a man wronged by the Sussexes. "It is his own behavior that he is truly the victim of," said a friend of the couple.

Even before they announced their lawsuits, Harry and Meghan attempted to change the way they worked with the press. They questioned the firm hold the royal rota (the group of British newspaper journalists who decide which UK representative attends royal engagements on the understanding that they will share all material obtained) had on their coverage. "It makes no sense to me," Meghan remarked when told by senior aides that letting US press receive the same access as the British-only newspaper rota was not an option despite her nationality. The same rule also froze out grassroots and international media interested in their charitable endeavors. The rule of giving exclusive access to the rota also meant that the couple was expected to share personal photos with

British newspapers, four of which were tabloids, that they would have rather put on their own social media exclusively. They didn't like having such little control over their personal content.

"I'm tired of people covering engagements and then going off to write some rubbish about what someone is wearing," Harry said to a friend.

The only way they could truly change things was if the couple started to pay for their events themselves, rather than taking from the Sovereign Grant, the government- and taxpayer-provided purse that funded the royal family. "Sure, if money was no object," Harry remarked. It was a catch-22. He and Meghan didn't receive salaries, but as full-time working royals, they were unable to earn money.

The couple wasn't ready for such a drastic step as leaving the monarchy. Instead, they quietly decided to take whatever control was within their power, including using their new Instagram account to tighten up access to staple media fodder like pictures of their baby. They figured out a way to occasionally work around the royal rota by holding "private engagements" that differed from public ones. When Meghan only shared on Instagram and with one other outlet photos of her visit to London's Luminary Bakery, a bakery that provides underserved women with jobs and training on social media, the other newspapers were furious. It was a small victory for the couple over "The Cartel," as they had come to jokingly call them.

Taking on the most powerful media organizations in the world was not without serious peril. "It's a death wish," a senior aide at Buckingham Palace said about Harry and Meghan's war on the tabloids. "You just don't take on the British press." Harry had hoped his family would be willing to show support for their decision, but the silence was deafening. Though Charles privately respected his son's decision, the Prince of Wales also depended on the press to back him when he one day became king.

"Though this action may not be the safe one, it is the right one," Harry said in his original statement announcing Meghan's lawsuit. "Because my deepest fear is history repeating itself. I've seen what happens when someone I love is commoditized to the point that they are no longer treated or seen as a real person. I lost my mother and now I watch my wife falling victim to the same powerful forces."

His emotions were on full display on October 15 when Harry choked up while addressing the audience of the WellChild Awards. "Last year when my wife and I attended we knew we were expecting our first child—no one else did at the time, but we did," he said at the awards ceremony hosted by the UK charity supporting children and young people with exceptional health needs. "I remember squeezing Meghan's hand so tight during the awards, both of us thinking what it would be like to be parents one day, and more so, what it would be like to do everything we could to protect and help our child should they be born with immediate challenges or become unwell over time."

Bowing his head, Harry had to stop speaking for a few seconds to regain his composure. Amid applause from the crowd, he continued. "And now, as parents, being here and speaking to all of you pulls at my heart strings in a way I could have never understood until I had a child of my own."

Harry wanted to create a safer world for all children, including his own. For his son, that meant Archie growing up away from the particular kind of struggles the prince has had to face.

The statement and lawsuits were just the beginning of the couple's campaign. Jaws dropped around the world on October 20, when British network ITV aired a documentary of the Sussexes' southern Africa travels where Harry and Meghan dropped a number of bombshells.

"It's not enough to just survive something, right? That's not the point of life. You've got to thrive, you've got to feel happy. I really tried to adopt this sensibility of the British stiff upper lip, but I think that what that does internally is probably really damaging," Meghan admitted on *An African Journey*. "I never thought this would be easy, but I thought it would be fair."

When the documentary host, ITV news anchor and friend of the couple Tom Bradby, asked Meghan how she was coping, she replied, "Thank you for asking because not many people have asked if I'm okay."

Palace aides took this comment as a dig at the family for not providing her enough support as a new member of the Firm.

"And the answer is, would it be fair to say, not really okay?" Tom said. "That it's really been a struggle?"

"Yes," Meghan replied.

Harry also admitted during the special for the first time publicly that there *was* tension between him and his brother, William. "Part of this role, part of this job and this family being under the pressure it is under, inevitably stuff happens," he said. "But look, we are brothers, we will always be brothers. We are certainly on different paths at the moment, but I will always be there for him, and, as I know, he will always be there for me. We don't see [each other] as much as we used to because we are so busy, but I love him dearly, and the majority of stuff is created out of nothing. As brothers, you have good days, you have bad days."

The day after the documentary aired, William's thoughts were revealed by a palace courtier. Several outlets, including the BBC and *The Sun*, quoted a Kensington Palace aide stating that Prince William was "worried" about his brother. He felt the couple was "in a fragile place."

A source close to Harry later said, "It's these games the couple were eager to get away from. Rather than reaching out to them, someone close to William briefed the press on his views about Harry's mental health. He thought it was low to be sharing opinion like that so publicly." A friend of the prince added, "Harry felt that

William and the people around him were too concerned with press coverage."

Highly emotional and fiercely protective of his wife and son, Harry was drained by the unique circumstances of his family, which, as a source described, "doesn't have the opportunity to operate as an actual family." While politics are part of every family dynamic, they are at a whole other level for William, Harry, and the rest of the royals.

"Every conversation, every issue, every personal disagreement, whatever it may be, involves staff," the source said of the aides who invariably send and receive messages between the royal households. "It creates a really weird environment that actually doesn't allow people to sort things out themselves."

No one could deny the fact that the couple was emotionally exhausted, whether they had brought it on themselves or were victims of a merciless machine. "They felt under pressure," a source said. "They felt that they were alone."

With so much stress in their life, their sole source of joy was Archie. Growing "at the speed of light," by the southern Africa tour, he had two teeth and was crawling. He loved being read to by his parents and particularly enjoyed the riddle-and-rhyme book *Is Your Mama a Llama?* by Deborah Guarino. Like many new parents, Meghan enjoyed taking him to classes, like the Happy Clappy music class in Windsor she brought Archie to by herself in October (her protection officers stood outside). All the moms, and two dads, in the room were wide-eyed as the Duchess of Sussex joined their circle with Archie, who went straight for a tambourine and, according to his mom, "loved it."

Archie was also their reason for wanting to start working on changing some of what they called "negative forces" in their lives. As the fall wore on and tensions with certain sections of the Palace grew, Harry and Meghan decided they needed to get out of the country for a while. Christmas was right around the corner, and spending it at Sandringham surrounded by members of the royal family did not sound like a holiday.

The couple decided that for the second half of November and all of December they would base themselves in Canada. They considered going to the United States but felt a Commonwealth location was more appropriate at the time. There was ample precedent for royal family members skipping out on the traditional Sandringham festivities. In 2012 and 2016, the Cambridges celebrated with the Middletons at their home in Berkshire instead. In 2017, Zara and Mike Tindall passed the holidays with his side of the family in Australia. Still, the press eviscerated the Sussexes when they made the same choice.

Battered and bruised from the tabloid attacks and lack of support from members of the royal family, Harry and Meghan headed for the $18 million Vancouver Island estate that pal Ben Mulroney helped secure for them through the music producer David Foster. Foster was close friends with the wealthy investor who had put the property up for sale and was willing to rent it to the royal couple for far below market value.

Mille Fleurs—the Vancouver property in North Saanich, close to Victoria, British Columbia—with two private beaches on four acres of land, provided a tranquil landing for the shell-shocked couple. Doria's visit for the Thanksgiving holiday was much welcomed. (Despite reports in the press that she had quit her job, she took only a brief vacation to spend with them.)

Through December, their days were spent mostly enjoying quiet family time with just the three of them. They took long walks outside with both of their dogs (which traveled over with the couple). Though they had a housekeeper and a nanny, the couple did most of the cooking, making great use of the pizza oven in the mansion's kitchen. On a couple of occasions, Harry and Meghan had a date night at the Deep Cove Chalet restaurant. While many of the area's wealthiest residents are known to fly in by helicopter, Harry and

Meghan turned up at the five-star restaurant on foot. Otherwise, they barely left the compound.

Away from the courtiers and all things royal, they could think for themselves. They went over the events that had unfolded since the wedding and talked about how and if they could possibly create a situation that would make for a better future. That future also included an even greater focus on their humanitarian work.

"I don't need to have that movie moment where we get out of a car and wave to a hundred photographers before going into a building," Harry told a friend about some of the frustrations of his current role. "It should just be about the work happening inside. Let's focus on what really matters."

Before leaving the UK, Harry had spoken a handful of times with his grandmother and father and a number of key aides about the urgent need to change things for him and his wife within the Palace structure. He felt at once used for their popularity, hounded by the press because of the public's fascination with this new breed of royal couple, and disparaged back within the institution's walls for being too sensitive and outspoken. He and Meghan didn't want to completely walk away from the monarchy; rather, they wanted to find a happy place within it.

In fact, they hoped to use part of their time away to put the finishing touches on the Sussex Royal Foundation to launch in 2020, which, like the Royal Foundation, would serve as an umbrella organization for all their charitable interests. That included setting up a website, SussexRoyal.com, to launch the foundation. They had hired a team outside the Palace to keep their plans confidential. Meghan worked with Made by Article, the same Toronto-based design company that successfully produced her shuttered lifestyle blog *The Tig*, as well as a small group at Sunshine Sachs, her original PR team before becoming a royal.

They took some time out for visits by friends like actress Janina Gavankar, a longtime friend of Meghan's who, meeting Archie for the first time, took a picture of him and his parents that wound up becoming the Sussex Christmas card photo.

As the weeks went by, the couple realized they couldn't go back to the way things had been at home before they left. As hard as the decision was to make, they had come to a conclusion: Harry and Meghan were going to step back from their roles as senior royals—and cut themselves off from access to the Sovereign Grant. Making a living on their own to support their philanthropic endeavours was a daunting but exciting prospect. Harry and Meghan were used to big projects and big impact; Harry turned the first Invictus Games around in less than a year, and Meghan's projects had all broken records. Now, they were ready to do even more of that, at their own pace. By essentially moving away from their current working model, it would also allow them to live part-time in North America, far away from the British tabloids and the negativity within the institution. That made the challenge worthwhile.

Despite the change, they still wanted to carry out their duties for the Queen. That was the one thing that they did not want to end—not just because of Harry's love and respect for his grandmother, but also because Meghan felt she had given up so much to take her life down a path of service to the monarchy. She didn't quit when she signed up for a task. Then at ninety-three years old, the Queen needed the support of younger family members to maximize her legacy, and the couple wanted to proudly represent that by carrying out works for the monarchy in the UK and across the Commonwealth. They hoped that family members such as Prince Michael of Kent—who had formally represented the Queen on occasions abroad and carried out thousands of royal engagements in the past decade, but didn't receive any parliamentary allowances in return for being able to earn his own living as chairman of his own consultancy company—provided a precedent for combining private work with duty.

They knew there would be hurdles, such as discussions over the security that was currently provided by the Metropolitan Police for "internationally protected people." But they were confident enough that before Christmas, Harry emailed his grandmother and father to say that he and Meghan had come to the decision to change the way they worked—to step back and spend more time abroad. He didn't get into much more detail than that, worried that the news might leak via a member of staff. The rest, he said, they would discuss in person.

With both family members informed, Charles's private office was requested to schedule a time for the two to meet the Queen, who was based at Sandringham for the holiday season, as soon as the Sussexes returned to the UK on January 6. Their trip to London was going to be short, but Harry was keen to ensure that by the time they returned to Canada at the end of the week, their new chapter had been secured.

Harry was right to be worried about leaks. Certain details from the email soon ended up in the hands of a tabloid reporter who began inquiring at the end of the year about the couple's plans to spend more time in Canada. But that was the least of his worries. Despite repeated follow-ups with his father's office, he was unable to secure time with the Queen. The monarch, he was told, would not be available until January 29. "He felt like he was being blocked," a source close to the prince said.

As their Air Canada flight made its early morning touchdown at Heathrow Airport, and still with no appointment to see Her Majesty, Harry and Meghan toyed with the idea of driving straight from the terminal to see the Queen. Not wanting to cause problems for themselves (arriving unannounced would have ruffled feathers), the couple instead called for a team meeting at Frogmore Cottage. With senior aides Sara and private secretary Fiona Mcilwham in front of them, Harry and Meghan revealed for the first time details of their plans to the team. Whether their speedy approach was right or not, Harry and Meghan were more determined than ever. "At this point they felt like they had brought up the subject enough times with family members over the past year and they were fed up of not being taken seriously," a source close to the couple said. "Everyone had their chance to help but no one did."

Few things remain secret between Royal Households and it didn't take long after Harry's initial email for the Sussexes' grand plans to be the topic of conversation among most of the aides and family members. Worried about losing control of the situation, Harry contacted his grandmother to explain his concerns, and she signed off on putting together a jointly agreed statement. The couple hesitated about involving the other Households, not knowing if everyone involved would have their best intentions, but agreed for aides to meet up the next day and get on the same page.

With a plan in place, Harry and Meghan put on big smiles the following day as they chatted to dignitaries and tasted Nanaimo bars at an engagement with Janice Charette, high commissioner in Canada to the UK. But as they thanked her and her staff for the warm reception they received during their stay in Canada, privately they were both nervous about what was about to happen. They had already seen a draft of what Buckingham Palace planned to put out in a statement that would follow theirs and the "lack of warmth" in the response that was being prepared was a clear sign that not everyone supported their decision.

But there was little time to dwell, just a few hours after leaving Canada House, a story about their plans to stay in Canada broke on *The Sun*'s website. Details were missing, but it was clear that someone within the Palace had briefed the tabloid. A royal source absolutely denied the charge, blaming the couple themselves for the leak, "because they were frustrated at the Palace in the talks that were going on . . . They wanted to force the decision, to break it open." The couple deny this claim.

With the news out there and almost every major media organization in the world now contacting the Palace for comment, a statement needed to be issued fast. On January 8, the couple took to Instagram to share their news with the world.

"After many months of reflection and internal discussions, we have chosen to make a transition this year in starting to carve out a progressive new role within this institution. We intend to step back as 'senior' members of the Royal Family and work to become financially independent, while continuing to fully support Her Majesty The Queen," the statement read. "It is with your encouragement, particularly over the last few years, that we feel prepared to make this adjustment. We now plan to balance our time between the United Kingdom and North America, continuing to honour our duty to The Queen, the Commonwealth, and our patronages."

Alongside their announcement, they launched their website, SussexRoyal.com, which was now no longer a landing page for their new foundation but a detailed roadmap of the "new working model" they hoped to espouse. The website offered clarity on their decision to be financially independent, which was not only to have more freedom in their work but also to remove the tabloids' justification in having access to their lives. Public money means you are public property.

The website took everyone, even their communications team, by surprise. Aides and family members knew the couple wanted to step back, but the public website, which laid out the details of their new half-in-half-out model as if it were a done deal, put the Queen in a difficult position.

Flustered Buckingham Palace aides ditched their original statement and put out a short media release fifteen minutes after the Sussexes released theirs: "Discussions with The Duke and Duchess of Sussex are at an early stage. We understand their desire to take a different approach, but these are complicated issues that will take time to work through."

The aides, including the Queen's private secretary, Edward Young, were furious. "The private offices don't like that type of behavior," a source familiar with the negotiations said. "It is deeply unhealthy and unwelcome."

More unsettling however, was the reaction from the family to the website they had launched. "The element of surprise, the blindsiding of the Queen, for the other principals who are all very mindful of this rightfully, it was deeply upsetting" according to a senior member of the Household. Several in the family shared that both the Queen and Prince Philip were "devastated."

"The family is very private and bringing it into the public domain, when they were told not to, hurt the Queen," the source continued. "It was laying out what the Sussexes wanted in a statement without consulting with Her Majesty first—and she's the head of the institution."

The Palace scrambled to figure out if all of the requirements in the couple's roadmap could even work logistically, including having the "future financial autonomy to work externally." This was very different from the simple idea of spending more time abroad that had originally been presented. There were security and funding issues, tax implications, and visas. How could they legally take on commercial endeavors and still represent the Queen? "It was a huge headache," said an exasperated aide.

Even a source close to the couple admitted that while Harry and Meghan had put a lot of thought into this immense transition, they could also be "impatient and impulsive."

"They run hot in a way," the source said. "The reactions in individual moments are definitely not the same, a month, a few weeks, down the line."

The Queen was anything but fevered. Despite her sadness at the thought of losing the Sussexes as working royals, she could see it was necessary for the couple to completely separate from the institution. No one should be forced into something they don't want to do. But if Harry thought that their public proposal would result in their getting exactly what they wanted, "he was sorely |mistaken," said a senior courtier. "The Queen understood the difficulties they faced, but the rules don't bend for *anyone*." Buckingham Palace issued a further statement stating that a solution to Harry and Meghan's requests would be reached "within days, not weeks."

After three days of discussions between the royal households and government officials, including the Canadian government, the Queen requested that Harry travel up to Sandringham to meet with herself, Charles, and William.

At the "Sandringham Summit," as the press dubbed it, the four of them would sort out the future once and for all.

23

The Family Meeting

As the Range Rover pulled up the driveway to Sandringham House, Harry felt himself getting nervous. The estate, where the Queen was currently in residence and so many Christmas memories had been made, was now the setting for the most important meeting of Harry's royal life.

It was also the hardest. In trying to find a sustainable way of life for him and Meghan, he found himself more at odds with his family than ever. It wasn't an easy decision to stand up to the age-old rules of the monarchy, but for Harry, this was his only option in "making things right for his own little family," a source close to the couple said. "This is tearing him apart. He loves the Queen, but his wife feels aggrieved, and he adores his son. Harry's whole world is Archie. He's the most amazing father."

Meghan wasn't there for the January 13 meeting, having returned to Canada, where Archie had remained with Jessica and his nanny. He did have by his side his private secretary, Fiona, and Samantha Cohen, or "Sam" as Harry called her. Although Samantha

had left the Palace in October after two decades of service to become Chief Executive of the Commonwealth Enterprise & Investment Council and co-chair of the board of trustees at Cool Earth,
she remained a trusted voice inside the institution after her service
as one of the Queens closest aides and running the Sussexes' office.
Harry needed her support for this. She was one of the few people
who knew all parties, and he had always been able to trust her for
sound advice.

The three had spent the morning going over all the points
Harry wanted to bring up in the meeting. He hoped that allowing
only private secretaries (chiefs of staff) from the Queen, Prince
Charles, and Prince William's offices, would prevent information
being leaked. Although it was a business matter for the Firm, it was
also a private one Harry wanted to keep in the family.

Harry was still facing the Queen, Charles, and William for the
first time since he and Meghan had released their full plans to
the world. (Although Prince Philip had been widely expected to
participate in the meeting, he left for his farmhouse located on the
estate shortly before discussions got underway.)

In the days since launching SussexRoyal.com, Buckingham
Palace's dismay had turned to resolve in repairing the situation by
finding an appropriate structure and moving on as quickly as possible. While the hybrid model of royalty that Harry and Meghan
suggested posed a huge challenge that few thought could be overcome, one source said, "The drama and division is doing the most
damage."

Prior to the meeting, aides had assured Harry that the Queen
wanted to help the Sussexes find a resolution, even if they might not
get *everything* they wanted. Despite the reassurances, Harry wasn't
sure who to believe anymore. But he took some comfort in the fact
that his grandmother would be sensitive to his concerns.

Charles, William, and Harry joined the Queen in the library, one of the more relaxed spaces at the property. The cozy room had been converted from a bowling alley in 1901, a change which Queen Alexandra (who called Sandringham home until her death in 1925) had always regretted. Meghan was on standby in Vancouver, ready to join the meeting via conference call. But when Harry offered to call her, it was deemed unnecessary.

What a source described as a "practical workmanlike approach" permeated the room as the royals set out to form a deal. Harry felt as though he and Meghan had long been sidelined by the institution and were not a fundamental part of its future. One didn't have to look further than the family photos displayed during the Queen's Speech on Christmas Day. In the Green Drawing Room at Buckingham Palace, where the Queen delivered her address, viewers glimpsed photos of the Cambridges and their children, Charles and Camilla, Prince Philip, and a black-and-white image of the sovereign's father, King George VI. Noticeably absent was a photo of Harry, Meghan, and their new baby, Archie. Palace sources insisted that the photos were chosen to represent the direct line of succession, but for Harry and Meghan, it was yet another sign that they needed consider their own path.

Charles made it clear to Harry that he and Meghan were very much part of the future for the royal family despite calls for a "slimmed down monarchy" with fewer senior working royals. "The Prince of Wales' vision always included Harry as part of slimmed down monarchy," a source close to the family shared. "His vision included both his sons. William will always be more important than Harry but that's a fact only because of birthright."

Though William had not taken the original news of his brother's plan well, his fate was up to the Queen, and she was very aware that the outcome of the meeting would set the standard for generations to come.

Finally, she made it clear that their quasi-royal vision would not work. "It was untenable," a Palace source said. "If Harry and Meghan had been semi-working royals, there would have had to have been oversight in everything they did in their independent sphere, a committee to approve events and deals."

When the meeting was over, Harry immediately debriefed Sussex aides before sending a text message to Meghan. Later that evening, the Queen put out an exceptionally candid and personal statement. "My family and I are entirely supportive of Harry and Meghan's desire to create a new life as a young family," the statement read. "Although we would have preferred them to remain full-time working Members of the Royal Family, we respect and understand their wish to live a more independent life as a family while remaining a valued part of my family."

The official communication also announced that Harry and Meghan no longer wanted to rely on public money during the coming period of transition, during which time the couple would live in both Canada and the UK.

"These are complex matters for my family to resolve, and there is some more work to be done," the Queen stated, "but I have asked for final decisions to be reached in the coming days."

"More work" was an understatement. Harry spent the next several days holed up in intense meetings and conference calls with top aides from all three Royal Households, Buckingham Palace, Clarence House, and Kensington Palace, which were led by Charles's private secretary Clive Alderton. William was more than happy to leave the matter up to staffers." The *Sunday Times* quoted the Duke of Cambridge telling a friend, "I've put my arm around my brother all our lives and I can't do that anymore; we're separate entities."

That held true for Meghan and Kate as well. The two duchesses' relationship had struggled to move past the distant politeness of when they first met. Their cordial but distant rapport was apparent when the pair appeared alongside each other at the King Power

Royal Charity Polo Day the previous summer. While the doting mothers were photographed next to each other with their children, the two appeared to barely exchange a word. However, a few final memories were made after it was suggested by aides that the two women attend Wimbledon together three days later. Both had plans to go to the tennis tournament. Meghan was going to support her friend Serena Williams in the Ladies' Final, while Kate is patron of the All England Lawn Tennis Club. At the match, which Kate's sister Pippa also joined, the women laughed and chatted in the Royal Box on the Centre Court together. Kate even rubbed Meghan's back in consolation when Serena lost. "They had a wonderful time," a source close to the Duchess of Cambridge said. "The whole day was lovely."

The state of affairs between the two women was just an offshoot of the real issue at hand: the conflict between Harry and the institution. Harry likened his meetings throughout the week to standing in front of a firing squad. "There was a lot of finger pointing in both directions with things leaking," an aide said. "It was all very unhealthy."

When Harry described how he didn't feel supported by his family, this was what he was referring to. They did their bit in the family meeting at Sandringham, and then they left him to defend himself against and negotiate with their aides, which is exactly what he didn't want to happen. "He feels that there were so many occasions when the institution and his family could have helped them, stood up for them, backed them up, and never did," a source said.

Courtiers viewed Harry's position as completely unrealistic. While it was easy to say they wouldn't take money from the Sovereign Grant, it was quite another thing to follow through. "The biggest row was over money, because it always is," a source familiar with the negotiations said. One aide made a catty joke about Meghan launching a line of beauty products.

More accurately, the couple hoped to earn a living through

smart speaking engagements, production deals, and other commercial endeavors that had social impact. Still, there were some difficult calculations to be made. If Harry and Meghan did some official work, they would have to figure out how much of their expenses—such as office-related costs and money for security or clothes—were private rather than subject to tax relief. "They've created a complete headache for everyone," an exhausted aide complained on the fifth day of meetings.

More difficult than challenging tax formulas were the hurt feelings on both sides. Even sources close to Harry and Meghan had to admit that the way the couple were forced to approach the situation (mainly in the act of keeping the family and their team in the dark about their website) "created a lot of ill will in the household and especially in the family."

"Harry and Meghan would have reached a more beneficial agreement to allow them to live the life they wanted if they had handled things in a private, dignified way," explained a senior Buckingham Palace aide. Added another courtier, "They oversimplified what they were asking for. They thought they'd give Charles their rider, negotiate over email, rock up to London, give three months notice and fly back to Canada."

Harry and Meghan, however, felt that they had been patronized by other family and staff members for too long. People had humored them when they brought up their grievances, never thinking the couple would actually do anything drastic. The explosive reaction was a direct result of their growing impatience. If other members of the family and those working with the Households had taken their requests more seriously, it wouldn't have reached that point.

Either way, the source said, "The courtiers blame Meghan, and some family do."

The media speculated that Meghan was behind the decision for the couple to step back, but few knew how much she sacrificed to try and make it work. As Meghan tearfully told a friend in March,

"I gave up my entire life for this family. I was willing to do whatever it takes. But here we are. It's very sad."

While the British media often blamed royal wives, in Harry's case, he was very much on board with distancing himself from the public eye. It's why he gravitated toward the military, avoided the pomp as much as he could, and didn't give his child a title. He long craved a life away from the prying eyes of the media. Meghan simply emboldened him to make the change. She supported him no matter what. "Fundamentally, Harry wanted out," a source close to the couple said. "Deep down, he was always struggling within that world. She's opened the door for him on that."

In the evenings, after hours of meetings, Harry was drained. Back in Canada, Meghan did her best to stay busy, even boarding a seaplane on January 14 to visit the Downtown Eastside Women's Center in Vancouver, a shelter for women and children in one of Canada's poorest areas. Work kept her preoccupied, and she was eager to get to know some of the women's charities close to their new home. Deep down she felt helpless as she received occasional updates from an exhausted Harry back in England. She regularly tried to lift his spirits with photos of Archie, including a video of the first time he saw snow.

Five long days after the original meeting, the Queen issued a statement that a plan had emerged for "a constructive and support-ive way forward for my grandson and his family" to take effect in the spring of 2020. This was followed by a statement from Harry and Meghan. Both outlined the terms of the deal, which stipulated that the couple would completely step back from royal duties. No longer working members of the royal family, they would no longer be able to use their HRH titles or the word "royal" in any of their future endeavors. Harry would lose his military honors, and his role as Commonwealth Youth Ambassador was also pulled.

Harry and Meghan were allowed to maintain their private pa-tronages. Although they could no longer formally represent the

Queen, they "made clear that everything they do will continue to uphold the values of Her Majesty."

As to the issue of money, Harry and Meghan would no longer receive public funds for royal duties. The couple took it even further, stating, "The Duke and Duchess of Sussex have shared their wish to repay Sovereign Grant expenditure for the refurbishment of Frogmore Cottage, which will remain their UK family home."

That was £2.4 million of taxpayer money that sections of the British public were furious about when the number was confirmed in the 2018–2019 Sovereign Grant Report, released the previous July. Constant negative press coverage surrounding their renovations did little to help. It felt good to put that behind them. Offering to repay the money was a symbol of how much Harry and Meghan wanted to cut any ties. Privately, Prince Charles said he would help them financially, out of his own personal money, if they needed it. That was him being a caring father, not the Prince of Wales.

Perhaps the most meaningful show of support, however, came from the Queen in her statement. "I recognize the challenges they have experienced as a result of intense scrutiny over the last two years and support their wish for a more independent life," she said.

Throughout all the drama and the couple's unhappiness, the Queen had always tried to be sensitive to her grandson's needs. That one sentiment meant a lot to Harry, because it proved she had heard him during the summit when he, once again, expressed his frustration and anger that no one in the Palace had ever truly acknowledged what he and Meghan had experienced ever since their relationship was revealed.

If his grandmother's validation of his experiences served as encouragement, the most demoralizing aspect of the new deal was his being stripped of the honorary military appointments that had been awarded to him as a senior royal. As a retired serviceman, Harry would always be able to wear his medals, but no longer could he wear uniform as Captain General of the Royal Marines, Honorary

Air Force Commandant of the Royal Air Force Base Honington, and honorary Commodore-in-Chief of the Royal Navy's Small Ships and Diving Operations. Those roles had come to an end. "That's been a tough pill to swallow, and one that has been most painful to Meghan witness him go through," a source close to the couple said. "It's the one that made Harry emotional."

Harry put that emotion on display on January 19, a day after the statements came out, when he addressed those attending a dinner in central London to benefit Sentebale. He was forthright about his "sadness" at stepping down as a working member of the royal family, a decision he and Meghan did not take "lightly." He was also clear to explain that he wasn't "walking away" from his commitments, including to Sentebale, but would "continue the work to make real long-lasting impact for all those that have been left vulnerable."

"It has been our privilege to serve you, and we will continue to lead a life of service. I will always have the utmost respect for my grandmother, my commander in chief, and I am incredibly grateful to her and the rest of my family, for the support they have shown Meghan and I over the last few months," Harry said in his speech, which was also shared to the Sussexes' Instagram account. "I will continue to be the same man who holds his country dear and dedicates his life to supporting the causes, charities, and military communities that are so important to me. Together, you have given me an education about living."

The last line was similar to one his mother said in December 1993, a year after it was announced in Parliament that Diana and Charles were separating. Princess Diana, too, announced her withdrawal from public life in a speech at a charity benefit (for Headway, the National Head Injuries Association for which she was a patron).

"In the past twelve years, I can honestly say, that one of my greatest pleasures has been my association with people like yourselves," Diana said. "During those years I have met many thousands of wonderful and extraordinary people, both here and around the world. The cared for and the carers. To the wider public, may I say that I've made many friends. I've been allowed to share your thoughts and dreams, your disappointments and your happiness. You have also given me an education. By teaching me more about life and living than any books or teachers could have done."

The similarities between mother's and son's speeches weren't a coincidence. Before writing his remarks, Harry refreshed his memory on what his mother had to say on the occasion of her making the decision to leave a life he now knew she felt privileged to be a part of but also trapped by its circumstances.

At thirty-six, almost the same age his mother was when she died, Harry had received the same "education."

24

Finding Freedom

While the hours crept closer to the couple's final day as working royals on March 31, it was as important as ever to Harry and Meghan to continue working. Commitments that had been made long before their January announcement still needed to be carried out, and for both of them, it was important not to let anyone down. Plus, they were at their best when they were busy.

While they had spent most of their time since the announcement in Canada, a final slew of engagements was in the diary for the Sussexes back in the UK. Because the coronavirus outbreak in China was threatening Europe by then, neither felt it would be safe to bring Archie. They also weren't fans of taking their baby on long-haul flights if it wasn't necessary. So they agreed that Meghan would stay back until she needed to join Harry in a week's time.

Harry's return to the UK on February 25 was an immediate reality check. Having flown into Heathrow, Harry continued his journey up to Scotland via train with a couple of protection officers who had flown over with him from Canada. Arriving at Waverley Station in Edinburgh, the prince was immediately confronted by three photographers, who had received a tip to his whereabouts. Harry grimaced at the sound of the camera shutters. "Come on, guys, what's the point?" he said, as one of the paparazzi told him to smile. The prince gritted his teeth and picked up the pace until he reached the awaiting Range Rover. It was exactly the kind of homecoming he expected.

Harry was in Edinburgh for his sustainable-travel initiative, Travalyst, which he had launched the previous summer with heavy-weight industry partners Tripadvisor, Visa, Booking.com, and Skyscanner. He was now bringing the ambitious project into its next phase at a working summit, where he planned to unveil a new online scoring system to not only show travelers how eco-friendly their trips were but also guide them into how to make a positive impact on the destinations they visited. Harry had been inspired by his many trips to Botswana. Specifically, he told the authors of this book, that every time he returned to the African country his experience as a tourist improved, but the community creating that experience remained the same. "Seeing how little money was going back into communities was really surprising," he said. "You have these big companies benefiting from tourism, but for the people living in these areas, that's not often the case. The money from tourism needs to feed back appropriately into the communities people are visiting."

The following day, Harry was confident as he took to the stage to speak in front of a hundred representatives from the tourist and travel industry in Scotland. Gone were the Palace aides and the usual throng of accredited photographers outside waiting to take photos of him upon entering. By his side were just two aides—former Royal Foundation communications officer James Holt, who continued to work with Harry in a private capacity, and Heather Wong, his former deputy private secretary, who now worked on his

Travalyst initiative. "It's good to be back focused on the work," he said. "That's what matters."

(Later in March, Harry chose to add another area of focus to Travalyst in response to the coronavirus pandemic. With the whole world *not* traveling, he explained in a meeting, there would now be a "fundamental shift" in the way people travel in the future. He wanted the initiative—now a nonprofit independent from the monarchy—to aid in global recovery and help guide consumers in supporting communities most in need when they start traveling to destinations around the world again. "There's an opportunity to change the game for the better," he said.)

Scotland was a success, as well as a reminder that, despite losing so much, Harry still had much to offer. His own legacy was taking shape, away from the royal family. Arriving back at Frogmore Cottage in Windsor, though, Harry didn't feel the same warmth in the house that he had during his first months there with Meghan and Archie. The home, although still full of their belongings, was empty and cold. The lush grounds surrounding the property were still in the final days of winter, with little sign of spring around the corner. As he told a friend, "So much has changed since we were last here."

While Harry spent much of his time in the UK in meetings with Palace staff to tie up final details, he did make time for family. He had barely exchanged words with his brother since they had last seen each other at Sandringham, but Harry did enjoy chats on the phone with his father, whose private secretary Clive Alderton continued to oversee the final elements of Harry and Meghan's transition. The line between family and institution was more blurred than ever, but it was perfectly clear who was playing what role when the Queen invited Harry over to lunch on March 1. Though his last time with Her Majesty had been in a more formal capacity, this time it would just be the two of them for Sunday lunch. "No titles," an aide said. "Just granny and grandson."

Sitting at the Queen's dining room in her Windsor Castle apartment, it was just like the old days. During Harry's lonelier years, he would often look forward to spending time with his grandmother, be it for tea or a meal. Despite the strange dynamics of his family, which many outside the royal bubble struggle to understand, he would always love his grandmother. While he had lost respect for parts of the institution, and even certain family members at points, the Queen was still one of the most important women in his life. As they tucked into a roast lunch, the Queen made it clear to Harry that she would always support him in whatever he decided to do. Though a twelve-month trial period had already been promised to Harry earlier in the year, their conversation was also a reminder that should he and Meghan ever want to return to their roles, they were always welcome.

"It's been made very clear they can come back whenever they want, when they're ready," a source who had been involved with the negotiations said.

Two days later, Harry was reunited with Meghan. (Archie was back at Vancouver Island, with the nanny and Jessica, who had flown again from Toronto to help out.) That afternoon the couple took their fifteen-person Buckingham Palace team out for lunch in London at the Goring Hotel, a favorite of the Queen's and home to arguably the best beef Wellington in the city. It was one of the final times they would be with all the private aides and communications staff in one room. While the couple were appreciative for all the support they had received from the dedicated group, moving abroad and cutting themselves off from the Sovereign Grant meant they were unable to move forward with the same team. Both Harry and Meghan took turns to express their thanks and gratitude for everyone's service, especially through what Meghan had called a "difficult and testing time."

The following evening marked their arrival at the Endeavour Fund Awards, which served as a showstopping reminder of their ability to command the world's attention. Earlier in the day Daniel Martin (who, when planning all her looks for the week, had joked, "Go out with a bang!") had done her makeup and George Northwood her hair.

The event was in honor of wounded, injured, or sick service personnel and veterans who have gone on to use sports and adventurous challenge as part of their recovery and rehabilitation. The pictures of the couple beaming under their umbrella as they arrived at the event went viral around the world. The sparkling rain in the frame was pure coincidence, but the confident walk into the Mansion House venue, and Meghan's blue midi dress by Victoria Beckham, were carefully planned. Despite all eyes being on them outside, the focus of the ceremony inside was firmly on the veterans, all of whom in turn spoke highly of the duke—or Captain Wales, as he's known in the veteran community. His mission to support servicemen and servicewomen had seen Harry pledge to continue to support the community in his new non-working royal life in the UK and North America as well. The first task? Bringing together the work of the Endeavour Fund and Invictus Games, both of which he helped establish. "He's deeply committed to these causes," a friend said. "Though he lost his honors in this move, that doesn't change his unwavering advocation."

Harry's lifelong commitment to the military was why the Mountbatten Festival of Music three days later was a particularly difficult moment; he was set to wear his Captain General of the Royal Marines uniform for the very last time. During a conversation backstage, on arrival, Harry told Major General Matthew Holmes: "I'm devastated that I am having to step down."

"It was so unnecessary," Meghan later told a friend of the decision to strip Harry of his military honors. "And it's not just taking something away from him; it's also that entire military veteran community. You can see how much he means to them, too. So why? The powers [of the institution] are unfortunately greater than me."

Though the evening served as a poignant tribute to Britain's Armed Forces, it also became a moment to thank the much-loved prince for his contributions to the military community. Usually reserved for the end of the performance, guests at the Royal Albert Hall rose to a standing ovation as Harry and Meghan entered the royal box. As they stood, listening to the rapturous farewell and obvious affection, the couple both did their best to hold back tears as they gripped each other's hands.

Over the days ahead, the couple continued with a mix of private meetings and public appearances. Meghan's surprise appearance delighted the children at an East London school, where she showed up at assembly to talk about the role men play in female empowerment to mark International Women's Day. And Harry's time at the Abbey Road Studios to watch Jon Bon Jovi rerecord his song "Unbroken" with the Invictus Games Choir, as a fundraiser for the Invictus Foundation, was fun and meaningful.

Of course there were also more traditional royal engagements, such as Harry opening an immersive British motorsport museum alongside Formula One champion Lewis Hamilton ("There's nothing better than officially opening a building that is very much open," the duke joked, since the doors had officially opened in October 2019).

On March 8, Harry wanted to attend a tribute service to a royal marine who had died in Afghanistan thirteen years earlier. Also attending was the Queen, who hadn't seen Meghan since the couple's bombshell statement. Harry drove them from Frogmore Cottage to the Royal Chapel of All Saints in Windsor Great Park. The Queen was warm and friendly to Meghan, treating her like a granddaughter and not as a defector. The service was for Ben Reddy, who had been killed at twenty-two when K Company of 42 Commando came under fire from militants in the volatile Helmand province on March 6, 2007. A plaque was unveiled in his memory at the event, where Harry wore his navy Royal Marines Corps tie. Ben hadn't just been a fellow member of the armed services. His father had also worked as a gardener for the Queen for many years.

For Meghan, her emotions were most raw at her final private engagement the following day: a meeting with the twenty-two students who received scholarships from the Association of Commonwealth Universities. Meghan had taken over from the Queen as royal patron of the ACU in 2019. And she vowed to continue to prioritize the organization even after officially stepping away, especially given her position as the vice president of the Queen's Commonwealth Trust and a former scholarship student herself.

The meeting took place in Buckingham Palace's 1844 Room, arguably one of the most important spaces from the royal residence's 775 rooms. It's a room rich with history, where the Queen and royal family often receive their most distinguished visitors, from the Obamas, to President Xi Jinping of China, to Angelina Jolie. The Queen's annual Christmas speech has been filmed there, too.

Although it was a difficult day, Meghan made sure to be present with every student she met. Standing at the side of the room, Secretary General of the ACU Joanna Newman looked on proudly. Having come to know the duchess well from their numerous ACU engagements and meetings together, she was excited about their relationship continuing into the future because she understood Meghan's power. "The headlines haven't been about what our patron is wearing or the official engagement started at this time and ended at that time and there was a cup of tea in the middle," Joanna said. "It's about why we are doing what we do and why ACU exists. She's been a real champion of the work that universities do."

After the meeting it was time to move on to the Commonwealth Service at Westminster Abbey. That was when Harry quietly slipped through the door of the 1844 Room to say hello, and the reality—and the emotions—finally set in. Meghan turned around to hug goodbye the last remaining people in the room, including an author of this book.

With the state room almost empty except for a few familiar faces, the tears the duchess had been holding back were free to flow. She embraced some of the dedicated team members whose tireless efforts—to promote the couple's work, launch landmark projects, and deal with the near-daily crises brought on by the tabloids—had come to an abrupt end. "I can't believe this is it," she said, hugging one of the young female aides she had become close with. Though Team Sussex was a much smaller operation than the more sophisticated offices at Clarence House and Kensington Palace, in the short space of a year since setting up, they had become like family.

At the end of the engagement, Harry joined Meghan and gave her a hug before she quickly changed into her clothes for the Commonwealth Service. "The last hat for a while, guys!" Meghan said with a smile, her tears now wiped away.

The short car ride to Westminster Abbey brought Harry and Meghan to their final engagement together as senior working royals. But if they ever needed confirmation that stepping away from the institution was the right move, the machinations that had preceded the Commonwealth Service served as a useful reminder. Although they had been part of the procession of senior royals who entered the church alongside the Queen in previous years, this year they discovered they had been removed from the lineup. The decision had been made without their consultation, and they were informed long after the two thousand orders of service had been printed for guests, with their names notably absent. This year it would just be the Duke and Duchess of Cambridge, the Prince of Wales, and the Duchess of Cornwall walking through the Abbey with the monarch. It felt intentional. "Harry was more than disappointed," a friend said. "He spoke up, but the damage had already been done."

In an effort to smooth things over, a the Cambridges agreed to take their seats at the same time as the Sussexes, Prince Edward and Sophie, Countess of Wessex. But if looks were anything to go by, the Cambridges appeared unhappy with the decision. While Harry and Meghan both greeted William and Kate with smiles, the Cambridges showed little response. It was the first time the two couples had seen each other since January. "Harry," William nodded, ignoring Meghan. For the minutes that followed before the Queen's arrival, William and Kate continued to sit with their backs to the couple, only turning around to chat with Edward and Sophie, who sat behind them, next to the Sussexes. Although Meghan tried to make eye contact with Kate, the duchess barely acknowledged her.

While the couples had been in a slightly better place after Archie's birth, relations fell apart again in January as the family negotiated Meghan and Harry's new roles. William, a Kensington Palace source explained, remained upset that private family matters were made public by the couple. "It's not anger," the source explained. "It's hurt."

"It should have been the one public moment where the royal family put their arms around the couple for a show of support," a source close to Harry and Meghan said. "They purposefully chose not to put them in the procession and not to be welcoming. It was most unpleasant." A Buckingham Palace spokesperson shrugged off the Queen's procession change, saying there was "no set format" for the event.

After the service, Meghan flew back to Canada—she had booked the first flight after the engagement to return to Archie. "Meg just wanted to get home," said a friend, noting that the duchess was emotionally bruised and exhausted. "At that point she couldn't imagine wanting to set a foot back into anything royal again."

Harry stayed in the UK for three more days, in order to attend final meetings about their departure from royal duties and discussions with his new team, which included James and Heather. But he had no further contact with his brother or sister-in-law. "To repair that relationship will take time," a friend of Harry's said.

"They see things differently. They feel that the experience that they've gone through over the last couple of years, they come at it from different points of view. William will need to get over his brother leaving the institution. They've both been frustrated with each other, but as Harry said himself, at the end of the day the bond of a brotherhood is much bigger than anything else."

Back in Vancouver Island, the couple felt they could finally take a breath. Initially they had put pressure on themselves to prepare announcements for the day after they officially stepped back as senior royals on March 31, "but they realized that slowing down was what they needed," a friend said. "They gave themselves space and instantly felt happier and more relaxed." At that moment, spending time with Archie was more important than rushing to carve out a new life for themselves. Though Harry admitted to friends that the weight of the past few months was not off his shoulders quite yet, being back in Canada, away from the noise back home, felt good.

As they re-immersed themselves into the lush surroundings of Mille Fleurs—the fresh spring air being the perfect respite after the frenetic pace of their final days in London—Harry and Meghan both came to the realization that they needed to take each day one at a time. But as much as they wanted to continue their time at their idyllic rental, pressure from the coronavirus epidemic that had now gripped the world with talk of closing the borders for up to several months, was forcing them to consider accelerating their summer plans to move to California. The couple had been talking about a US move since they began planning their lives away from the UK, which was why they used the careful wording of "North America" in their statements about the future, giving them the option to move when the time was right.

With the borders soon to close, Harry and Meghan made the decision to bring forward their move to California. If they were to be unable to travel for the foreseeable future, being in their eventual base—and close to Doria—was what felt right to them.

With so much to plan, the couple ran a tight ship at home. After spending the mornings together and with Archie, the couple started their days checking in with staff back in the UK, including James and Heather. Morning briefings at 10:00 a.m. over video calls (they liked to see who they were talking to) were de rigueur. People were often delighted when a curious Archie occasionally made a cameo on the calls, popping his head into the frame of the webcam. The newest member of the team was Catherine St-Laurent, their chief of staff and the executive director of their nonprofit. The Montreal native, who had worked in Brussels and London, led the communications for the Bill & Melinda Gates Foundation for several years before laying groundwork for Melinda's own investment and incubation company, Pivotal Ventures. "I am delighted and honored to be able to play a role in realizing their vision as they embark on this journey of learning, listening, and inspiring all of us to act," she said.

Another firm fixture in their new working world was Meghan's close friend and Sunshine Sachs partner Keleigh Thomas Morgan, who represented the former actress for two years until she married into the Royal Family. Highly regarded in the PR world, the publicist was better known for the work she did launching the Times Up movement in 2018 and her representation of Jennifer Lopez, but she had also quietly helped with promotional work for Meghan's issue of British *Vogue* and Harry's eco-travel initiative Travalyst.

British tabloids had attempted to discredit the PR agency, claiming it had previously represented Michael Jackson and Harvey Weinstein, but the accusations weren't true. Instead, the New York–based firm is mostly comprised of publicists with political and advocacy backgrounds. "It's what attracted the couple to them," a source close to the Sussexes said.

As the coronavirus pandemic continued to escalate globally, Harry and Meghan, who had sent most of their belongings ahead of them, traveled privately to Los Angeles on March 14. They set up home in a large Mediterranean-style villa in a gated community popular with a number of high-profile entertainers and industry people. It wasn't permanent (both loved the idea of finding somewhere smaller, perhaps closer to the sea), but that was perfect for now. Settling into their new life, including Archie getting familiar with the house's pool, the couple had time to reflect on where they had been and where they might go.

As exciting as this new chapter was, Harry and Meghan were under no illusions that challenges lay ahead—both personal and global. The two realms merged on the afternoon of March 24 when they received a call from the palace: Charles had tested positive for coronavirus and was headed into isolation. It was news Harry had been dreading. His father, who was 71 years old at the time and so more at risk for complications from the virus, had been out at public engagements until a couple of weeks earlier. Though doctors described the Prince of Wales as in "good spirits" and his symptoms as mild, it was still enough to fill Harry with worry. He immediately called Charles at Birkhall, his Scottish home where he was now quarantined. Harry regularly checked in on his father until he was out of quarantine and recovered—as well as Camilla, who had isolated herself as a precaution. Before the Queen made her televised address regarding the virus, Harry rang her up, too, in order to wish his grandmother good luck.

Despite a pandemic raging throughout the globe, the tabloids didn't give up their pursuit of Harry and Meghan. They were still dealing with their ongoing court cases against three British tabloids—a process that continues to reveal dramatic developments—when *The Sun* revealed on March 10 that Harry was the victim to Russian phone hoaxers posing as Greta Thunberg and her father. Two calls taped in December and January featured Harry speaking openly about the tensions between him and his family. "We are completely separate from the majority of my family," he said. When asked about Prince Andrew's friendship with

Jeffrey Epstein, he replied, "I have very little to say on that." (The couple have always avoided talking about the matter, preferring to keep their thoughts to themselves.) However, he didn't hold back when it came to airing his views on President Donald Trump. "The mere fact that [he] is pushing the coal industry is so big in America [*sic*], he has blood on his hands." Although the contents of the call were nothing he wouldn't openly share given half the chance, being made the center of a joke was humiliating for the prince, who was furious when he discovered that the tabloid had paid handsomely for exclusive access to the tapes.

Perhaps the leaked call was why Trump, who was famously thin-skinned, did little to hold back his feelings toward the couple when he waded into the debate about their security costs as non-working royals. The subject had been at the center of numerous newspaper opinion pieces in the UK, with much of the British public angered at the notion that the couple might continue being funded by taxpayers, even to protect their personal safety. "I am a great friend and admirer of the Queen," Trump tweeted on March 29. "Now they have left Canada for the US however, the US will not pay for their security protection. They must pay!"

Meghan's response to the president's tweet was to roll her eyes. The Sussexes had never asked the US government for support and had always planned to cover their own security costs after March 30. They quickly fired back through a statement of their own. "Privately funded security arrangements have been made," a spokesperson said. The freedom to shut down inaccurate reports was liberating, and a feeling both were excited to exercise.

Freedom. That was a word that could be applied to so much about the couple's new life, both personally and professionally. As a couple who hoped to change the world, they planned to engage in projects that brought together their strengths to solve problems. For as long as they had spoken about setting up a charitable organization, they knew that America would be at the center of it.

It was an even bigger charitable landscape and also meant they wouldn't be accused of competing with members of the royal family in the UK. Initially it was the couple's idea to set up the Sussex Royal Foundation, a near–carbon copy of the Royal Foundation, after they split from Kensington Palace in April 2019. "They felt pressure to immediately set up their own," a source familiar with the plans said. "But over the months that followed, the more people they spoke to, including aides from the Obama and Gates foundations, the more they realized what motivated them—and the more they realized they didn't want to be spending all their time raising money for grants when there are already other organizations doing it so successfully." By late November 2019, they started to wind up their work on the foundation, and by the beginning of the year they were already starting afresh with a nonprofit organization that would drive them for years to come.

The name for their nonprofit was one that had been in their minds since they got married—Archewell. "Before SussexRoyal, came the idea of 'Arhche'—the Greek word meaning 'source of action,'" the couple explained. "We connected this concept for the charitable organization we hoped to build one day." It also served as inspiration for something else—their son's name.

Although they might not be working royals anymore, Harry and Meghan will never give up on their original principles and ideals. Harry will always be interested in preserving the environment and supporting those with HIV, mental health issues, and veterans. For Meghan, her focus remains on empowering women and girls all over the globe. "They want their legacy to be modern and relevant to a new generation," the source said. "Work that doesn't repeat what other people are already doing and stands the test of time." And they are willing to wait for it. Though they both admit to being impulsive sometimes, the couple are entering a listening period, only launching Archewell "when the time is right."

Curious and open to new ideas, Harry and Meghan want to

explore technological innovation. It's the reason they paid a private visit to Palo Alto in January, quietly stepping into a brainstorming session with professors from the Graduate School of Business and Center for Social Innovation at Stanford University. They have been advised by leaders in all arenas, including the Obamas, who have helped their team network and recommended new people for them to collaborate with. Above all, the couple want to continue with what they have always set out to do: empowering others. "To accentuate, celebrate, and get people to recognize their place in both the world and in the communities around them," a source close to Meghan said.

On March 30, Buckingham Palace shared with the press the final details of the couple's future beyond their household transition. It was the last task for Sara Latham, who had helped shut down the Sussex office and took a new job advising the Queen's private office on special projects, as well as a chance to send new media contact details. From April 1, Harry and Meghan would officially be independent.

Moments later, Harry and Meghan had the final word, posting on their @SussexRoyal account for the last time. Though they had wanted to continue using the account, courtiers made it clear to them that it served as royal record and they should start afresh. Conscious of the current global crisis, the couple said, "As we all find the part we are to play in this global shift and changing of habits, we are focusing this new chapter to understand how we can best contribute. While you may not see us here, the work continues. Thank you to this community—for the support, the inspiration, and the shared commitment to the good in the world. We look forward to reconnecting with you soon. You've been great!"

AUTHORS' NOTE

This book takes place between 2016 and 2020 and is based on more than two years of reporting. The events described in these pages draw on hundreds of hours of conversations and interviews with more than one hundred sources, as well as our own time accompanying, observing, and interacting with the Duke and Duchess of Sussex on all of their formal and informal royal engagements. We have joined them on a wide variety of domestic trips and foreign travels. The reporting process has taken us around the world, including trips to Australia, New Zealand, Fiji, Tonga, several countries in Africa, France, Canada, New York, and Los Angeles. We have spoken with close friends of Harry and Meghan, royal aides and palace staff (past and present), the charities and organizations they have built long-lasting relationships with and, when appropriate, the couple themselves.

In many instances, we have granted sources anonymity to allow freedom to candidly provide direct quotes without their names being attributed (either due to the sensitivity of roles or to protect careers). Many individuals have also spoken to us on what is known as "on-background," meaning the information from conversations can be used as guidance but no quotes repeated. In a few cases, conversations have been strictly off-the-record.

Some of the scenes in this book have been witnessed personally while for others we have relied on the consistency of accounts provided by sources we have been given access to and come to trust. Conversational dialogue in scenes featured in the book has been drawn directly from accounts shared by multiple sources, who have corroborated the same information. These are versions of events both of us believe to be true.

As two fact-driven, objective journalists working in an era of fast news and clickbait reporting, we have continued to follow a strict standard of fact-checking and all information featured in this book has at least two sources. In cases where sources from opposing parties have disagreed on versions of events, we have put forward both.

The aim of this book was to portray the real Harry and Meghan, a couple who have often been innacurately portrayed and victims of those with personal agendas. Our mission has been motivated by the desire to present the truth of misreported stories that have become gospel simply because of the amount of times they have been repeated. It is thanks to the cooperation of the sources featured in this book that we have been able to share what we feel is the definitive story of the Duke and Duchess of Sussex. To everyone that has helped bring this book, and their story, to life, we are eternally grateful.

ACKNOWLEDGMENTS

(from Omid)

How could I even begin without thanking the incredible team at Dey Street and HarperCollins who have made this special book a reality, especially during such a challenging time in our world. Peter Kispert, Ben Steinberg, Heidi Richter, Kendra Newton, Kelly Rudolph, Ploy Siripant (I love our cover!), Andrea Molitor, Pam Barricklow, Carolyn Bodkin, Andy LeCount, Christine Edwards—I'm a lucky man to have such an talented team led by the strong editorial hand of Carrie Thornton. Carrie, it's been a pleasure learning from you. Of course, none of this would be possible without Liate Stehlik.

Albert Lee, after all these years I'm so glad we still get to work together. Thank you for always being there with just the right advice and guiding me through every challenge. Those specials were just the start! Zander Kim and David Weiner at UTA—I appreciate all your help. Rebecca Paley, thank you for helping me find my voice. I've learned so much from you and can't wait to take you out for tea and crumpets! And Reena Ratan, thank you for the support and the incredible photo research.

Carolyn, we actually finished it! So happy we were able to create *Finding Freedom* together.

To all the people who have contributed to this book, whether generously taking time out of your schedule to meet up or dealing with my fiftieth "sorry, just one more question" email, what a journey it has been! I wish I could thank you by name, but in order to preserve anonymity I'll just have to say that it is only with your help that these stories came to life. I only hope I can be as helpful in return some day.

To all my colleagues who have been so, so supportive as I've juggled this project with the others I am lucky enough to have. To the awesome teams at ABC News, *Good Morning America,* and ABC Audio thank you for making going to work so much fun—I promise to always bring Yoshi on location. To my *Harper's Bazaar* family, so proud to work with you all—thanks for keeping me sane with the memes. And to anyone who clicks, reads, watches, or listens to any of my work—thank you for always being supportive. You make the long hours worth it.

I have to, of course, thank my amazing friends for their patience and understanding as I went through every range of emotions putting these pages together. You'll be pleased to hear you won't have to listen to me talking about "the book" anymore!

And lastly to my beautiful family—thank you for always supporting me and believing in me. Love you to the moon and back.

ACKNOWLEDGMENTS

(from Carolyn)

A huge debt of gratitude to Liate Stehlik at HarperCollins and to Carrie Thornton at Dey Street books for believing in this project, for your vision, your guidance, and your leadership assembling such a fabulous team. Carrie, we were so lucky to find such a talented editor with such vast experience.

Albert Lee, from the very beginning until the very end your unwavering support, your enthusiasm, and knowledge of the book world has been invaluable. Thank you also to Rebecca Paley for your creativity and passion bringing this book to life. None of this would have been possible without the incredible editorial team at HarperCollins and Dey Street Books including Andrea Molitor, Peter Kispert, Heidi Richter, Kendra Newton, Kelly Rudolph, Ploy Siripant, Pam Barricklow, Andy LeCount, Christine Edwards, Beth Silfin, Arthur Heard, and Carolyn Bodkin. David Wiener, Steve Sadicario, and Zander Kim at UTA, I am very grateful. A special thanks to the many individuals who agreed to speak on background who generously gave of their time, sometimes repeatedly as I returned with more questions, more requests for clarity so I could tell an authentic portrait of Harry and Meghan's life.

Brenda Rodriguez thank you for your faith in me. Peter Hunt, Laura Day, Michael Hager, Mark Miller, Miguel Marquez, Michelle Dodd, Julie Bick, John Green, Santina Leuci, Alexa Miranda, Marc Eisenberg, I am so lucky to have you in my life.

Omid, I'm so grateful we were able to create something so meaningful that meant so much to both of us.

Phyllis McGrady, I can't imagine any of this would have happened had you not sent me on this incredible journey to London 18 years ago. You have been an incredible mentor and I appreciate your ongoing friendship. Mark Robertson, you never cease to amaze me. Thank you for your kindness and support.

Anne Morris Salinas, no matter how high the hurdle, you have been there with encouragement. I wouldn't have had the confidence to embark on this path without you. David and Victoria Wright thank you for always being there and bringing your three little girls into my life. Moomer, Phinna, and Deanna you make it all worthwhile. Karen Trosset, I can't thank you enough for your unwavering support and friendship through thick and thin. Anne Ferguson Foster I'll never be able to truly express my gratitude for the overwhelming generosity you and Dave have given me the last year.